HONKY IN THE HOUSE

Writing & Producing *The Jeffersons*

D0838654

By Jay Moriarty

Honky in the House
Writing & Producing The Jeffersons

Copyright ©2020 by Jay Moriarty

ISBN 978-1-7330795-8-7 (print)

ISBN 978-1-7330795-9-4 (eBook)

Cover artwork & design by Leo Posillico
www.leoposillico.com

Book design by Nan Barnes
www.StoriesToTellBooks.com

Antler Publishing
antlerpublishing@gmail.com

Antler
PUBLISHING

HONKY IN THE HOUSE

Writing & Producing *The Jeffersons*

ABOUT THE AUTHOR

Jay Moriarty has written and produced half-hour comedies including *The Jeffersons, All in the Family, Good Times, Maude, What's Happening Now!!, Dear John, The Royal Family, Here and Now, Cosby, Los Beltran*; developed and written pilots for networks and studios including CBS, NBC, ABC, Warner Bros., Columbia, Paramount; and served as an Adjunct Professor in the Writing Division of the University of Southern California School of Cinematic Arts (film school) for eleven years.

DEDICATION

This book is dedicated to those who inspired it, including: my muse, Nancy Allen; my daughters, Colleen & Heather; my grandchildren, Lucas, Maddie, Maya Jayne & Lacey; my sons-in-law, Marcus & Jeff; Mike Milligan, Norman Lear, Don Nicholl, Mickey Ross, Bernie West, Lew Weitzman, Sister Mary Pius (Frances Hogan), Jack Hanrahan, Tom Santley, Steve Gavin, Leo Posillico, Muhammad Ali, all three Kennedys, Animal Brotherhood of America (ABA), Laurence & Irene Peter and especially to that young black man who in 1963 spoke to my all-white high school classmates, illuminating us regarding the dearth of black faces on TV. Our speaker mentioned that as a kid watching Tarzan being chased by natives in the jungle, he'd be yelling "Look out, Tarzan, they're right behind you!" When he should've been yelling, "Get that honky!"

SPECIAL THANKS TO

Mike Brody, Joe Bove,
Adrienne Armstrong,
Joel Parker, Jerry Gels

My life has been the poem
I would have writ,
But I could not both live
And utter it.

~Henry David Thoreau

CONTENTS

GLOSSARY OF ABBREVIATIONS

AITF	All in the Family
B&B	Bendetson & Bendetson
B&W	Baser & Weiskopf
K3	Ku Klux Klan
K&B	Koenig & Balmagia
MJ	Mother Jefferson
MH2	Mary Hartman, Mary Hartman
M&M	Murphy & Malloy
MTM	Mary Tyler Moore
NRW	Nicholl Ross West
S&B	Shulman & Baskin
T&M	Tanner & Miller
TAT	Norman Lear & Bud Yorkin's Company
WGA	Writers Guild of America

Illustration by Glen Hanson

AUTHOR'S FOREWORD

Let's get one thing straight. I'm no dummy. I went to college. I read *The Iliad* and the *Odyssey*. At least, I've read excerpts. I know what they're about. At least, I know what the *Odyssey* is about. It's about a guy who goes on a journey and learns about life on the way—isn't it? Well, let's put it this way: If I wanted to know what *The Iliad* and the *Odyssey* were about, I could read Cliffs Notes and I could quote from those works and I could impress the hell out of you with how smart and literate I am. But the idea of this book isn't to impress you. Well, maybe just a little. I mean, if you're easily impressed, who am I to say that's wrong? The idea of this book is to tell you what happened to me when I took off for Hollywood to write comedy for TV. Come to think of it, I guess it's sort of like the Odyssey, huh? Anyway, I tell the story through the third person of Murph. Some names have been changed; but all the people are real. Murph is me, of course. Everything that happens to Murph in here happened to me. It takes place a while ago, in the acclaimed "Golden Age of Sitcoms." A lot has changed since then, but a lot is the same. You may find it curious, or even puzzling, that it's written in the third person instead of in the first person where you'd be reading a lot of words like I, me, my, we and myself. My dislike of those egocentric words dates back to my 7th grade English teacher, Sister Mary Pius. Besides, I feel I'm a different person now from who (or is it whom?) I was even five, ten, especially twenty, thirty, forty years ago. I don't know if I'd have the nuts (and I mean that as a triple entendre) to do now what I—or Michael Francis Murphy—did back then, like get married right out of college and head to Hollywood with no job. I know who Murph was then and what he was thinking while he was chasing and living his dream, and that's the story I want to tell. The book begins with Murph leaving Ohio and takes us through his years working for Norman Lear, mainly writing and producing *The Jeffersons*, thus the title of this book, *Honky in the House*. I hope it makes for good reading. And if it doesn't, well, hey, how exciting do you expect the life of one guy who spent twenty-two years growing up in the Midwest to be, anyway?

Chapter 1

LEAVING OHIO

('68)

Murph never suffered from an inferiority complex. If anything, he had a superiority complex. Which, when you think about it, is the other side of the same coin, isn't it? I mean, Murph had an attitude. It wasn't an attitude he wore on his sleeve. At least, he wouldn't like to think it was. It was an inner attitude. And his inner attitude said, "Hey, I'm as smart as the next guy. Nobody's been on this planet for more than an average of sixty years or so, and the planet's billions of years old, so we're all just guessing when it comes to knowing what's really going on here. And I'm as good a guesser as anybody."

This attitude served Murph well. In fact, it may be the single most important attribute he had, as far as explaining why Murph was able to survive in Hollywood where so many others with equal or similar amounts of talent have been chewed up, spit out, and stuck under the theater seat. (Great metaphor, huh?)

This attitude—a quality Emerson might characterize as "self-reliance"—may explain why Murph always felt out of place in the Midwest. To the salt-of-the-earth people around him, the object of life was to fit in, not stand out. As Murph's Uncle Ned used to say, "Self praise stinks." But Murph came to believe that modesty is the opiate of the mediocre.

Not that Murph went around bragging. He could practice the art of self-deprecation (and in the Midwest, it has definitely been developed to the level of an art form) as well as the next Ohio native. But deep down Murph bought into the American dream. He believed he could become anything he wanted.

And what Murph always wanted to be was a writer. Even when he wanted to be a priest, he wanted to be a writing priest. And what he liked to write most was comedy.

It was a revelation for Murph when he first learned that Lucy had writers. Before that, he thought Lucy and Ethel were just naturally funny and said whatever came into their heads.

As far back as he can remember, Michael Francis Murphy enjoyed making people laugh. His mother always accused him of wanting to be the center of attention. And she was right on the money. As the oldest of four, Murph learned that the best way to get his parents' attention—at least without breaking anything or doing something that would end up with him getting creamed—was to make his parents laugh.

At an early age—ten, eleven, twelve—he wrote plays and staged them on his driveway and invited people from the neighborhood. The folding chairs were usually full; but then there's not a lot to do in Finneytown, Ohio during the summer. Or during the rest of the year, for that matter.

In grade school or in high school, Murph's teachers would read his papers out loud. Sheesh! He was embarrassed at first. But when he heard laughter in the room, he felt powerful. He was beginning to learn that the only thing better than laughing is the power to make someone else laugh.

As a high school freshman, Murph submitted an audition piece to write for the school paper (enticing assignment: write an article about the recent Mothers' Club card party), which resulted in Murph being offered his own column (For Freshmen Only), the first-ever freshman to have his own column in the St. Xavier Prep.

Murph got the idea early on that writing was something he could do better than most; and this, coupled with the fact that there wasn't really much else at which he seemed to excel, helped Murph to focus on a career in letters.

But even though he knew what he wanted to do, Murph didn't go around telling everybody. If you told people in the Midwest you wanted to write comedy for a living, they'd think you were nuts or worse. You might as well say you want to be an astronaut.

One time Murph mentioned his aspiration to a family friend and she said in all seriousness, "I didn't know you had a sense of humor." Murph thought that was an odd comment. Doesn't everybody have a sense of humor? Granted, different people laugh at different things. But can there actually be someone somewhere who has never laughed at anything and has absolutely no sense of humor? (If people come to mind, don't send me names. My hunch is these are people I'd rather not know.)

Murph realized that if he wanted to make a living writing comedy for television, he'd have to leave Ohio. He didn't know much about the business, but he did know that. Most television production was centered in either New York or Los Angeles.

In a worst case scenario, Murph figured that he could move to New York, where he might starve and freeze; or to L.A., where he'd just starve. So being a person who wouldn't care if he never shoveled another driveway, and not caring much for tall buildings—either looking at 'em, working in 'em, or living in 'em—Murph decided he'd move to California.

Murph had been to California once, when the Murphy family of seven—Mom, Dad, Grandma and four kids— travelled west in their Chevy Station Wagon. Murph was seventeen at the time, old enough to share driving duties with Dad. The family spent three weeks touring the Midwest and Western states, heading to the Pacific through the northern route and returning along historic southern Route 66.

Murph loved the time they spent in LA. The sun was shining every day and he found inspiration and adrenaline in the blue sky and palm trees. Not to mention the tactile rush of sand between his toes on the beach and the cleansing feel of saltwater waves engulfing his body. Honestly, Murph couldn't understand why everybody, no matter what you wanted to do or be, didn't live in Southern California.

Murph graduated from college on June 6, 1968, the day after Robert Kennedy was shot. Murph was sitting in the huge auditorium with his graduating class, listening to some aging Jesuit talk about how this was Murph's true commencement in life, while Bobby Kennedy, who symbolized the hopes of an entire generation, lay dying.

That's a heady description: "symbolized the hopes of an entire generation." There aren't too many people you

can say that about. In fact, in Murph's lifetime, probably the only other Americans you could say that about were John Kennedy and Martin Luther King. Both of them were gunned down in their prime too. And both of them died before Bobby, which made Bobby's death feel all the more tragic.

Racial tension, war, and generational misunderstanding were tearing the country apart. America was asking for whom the bell tolls, and Midwest Murphy was heading west to write comedy.

Murph married his high school sweetheart, Marianne, on July 6. At the wedding reception, Murph's mother's brother and his Godfather, Uncle Art, observed that Murph getting married before having a job was a mindblower. "Takes more balls than I had at your age," said Uncle Art. Uncle Art, like a lot of people in the Midwest, even though he was right-handed, was innately skilled at tossing left-handed compliments.

Murph had heard these concerns before, mostly from his parents. After his second year in college, Murph packed his car—at the time a 1958 black and yellow Plymouth convertible with huge fins and push-button gears—planning to abort college and head to California to pursue his dream of writing for television. But his mom, who, throughout Murph's upbringing had begged him to "act like you've got some sense," now pleaded with him to complete college so he'd have "something to fall back on."

Murph finally acquiesced to his mom's wishes, partially because he thought completing college was probably a good idea; but largely because he knew that his ratty old Plymouth would never make it all the way to the west coast.

But even now, Murph's dad thought his son the college graduate was pretty naïve. "How do you expect to get a job out there? You don't know anybody. If you stay here in town I can help you. I know a lot of people."

Murph wasn't worried. He figured as a college graduate with an English degree, he could get a job in LA. Preferably a job doing some sort of writing, whether it was journalism, advertising or public relations.

He wasn't naïve enough to expect he could walk onto the set of a TV show or movie set and get a job as a writer. At that time, Xavier University, like most colleges, had no screenwriting courses or programs. There was virtually nowhere to study film or TV writing, or to learn any of the other related cinematic or television arts. But Murph's plan was to settle in the heart of the entertainment world and gradually learn what a TV writer, producer and director do. At 22, he felt that, like the Rolling Stones, he had time on his side.

Two days after they tied the knot, Murph and his new bride crammed all the wedding presents they could fit into Marianne's '66 Mustang and headed across the prairies and through the Grand Tetons and the Rockies, where they honeymooned for two weeks, before arriving at the Promised Land, the City of Angels.

Not knowing any better, the newlywed Murphys first looked at apartments in the city center of Hollywood, which was then, as it is now, pretty cheesy. We're talking old, run-down, bathroom at the end of the hall—places you wouldn't feel safe spending an hour, let alone a night.

Murph and Marianne then headed to Burbank, influenced by *Laugh-In*, the number one comedy show on TV at the time, which proudly filmed in "Beautiful Downtown Burbank." They discovered the El Capitan Apartments, located on Olive Avenue, just down the street from NBC Studios. Location, Location, Location. Not to mention Palm Trees and Pool. At $32 a week, the price was right for the duo, who, thanks mostly to cash wedding presents, were sporting a bankroll of 900 smackers.

The first few weeks in California, Murph spent mornings looking for a job and afternoons body surfing at the beach. Marianne, on the other hand, who had spent her post high school years working as a florist while taking a few night classes in college, landed a job pretty much right away at a Burbank flower shop.

Murph combed through the trades—*Variety*, *Hollywood Reporter*, *Advertising Age*—looking for writer-related job opportunities. He wore his only suit, light brown and nicely tailored, and carried his limited resume' to interviews.

At one point, Murph visited an employment agency and was offered a job at the agency. The young guy at the desk, just a few years older than Murph, said Murph could work there until another job came in that interested Murph. "That's what I'm doing," the dude explained.

While Murph was pleased to receive an actual job offer, he didn't even ask about the pay. He was determined to land a writing job and didn't want to get sidetracked taking a job helping other people find jobs.

An interview at NBC resulted in a job offer as a page working on one or more of NBC's shows for $75 a week. Murph was also offered a job writing for a Burbank newspaper which paid $550 a month. But Murph had seen the charts which said a recent college graduate at the time should expect to earn $600 a month. So neither of those jobs met his salary requirements.

Murph had experience writing high school sports for the

Cincinnati Post and Times Star, and he was aware that newspaper jobs didn't pay much. Working as a copywriter at a successful advertising agency, however, could be rewarding. But Murph soon learned that his lack of experience in that area—no portfolio at all—would make it all but impossible to land a good copywriting job.

In another interview, Murph met with a genial goateed gentleman named Buster something who was looking for help with some public relations writing. They had a nice chat, and Murph enthusiastically explained that he had come to California with the goal of writing for television. Buster flattened his goatee with the palm of his hand, then tossed a doleful glance at Murph and said, "Kid, they're gonna break your heart."

Chapter 2

WORKING FOR THE MAN

('68)

A week or so later Murph noticed a small classified ad in the *LA Times* that said COMMUNICATIONS WRITER. The employer was Pacific Mutual Life, located on Sixth Street in downtown Los Angeles. Murph wasn't sure what a Communications Writer was; but he did minor in Communications and he wanted to be a writer, so he responded to the ad.

Murph reported to the Personnel Department (a forerunner of what's become known as Human Resources) in the Pacific Mutual Life Building, home office of the West's Largest Mutual Life Insurance Company (later known simply as Pacific Life).

The Personnel Director, a woman named Janice, interviewed Murph and explained that the job was for a writer in the company's Communications Department. Responsibilities included writing articles for the company's monthly magazine, which was distributed to all PML agencies throughout the country; creating promotional and advertising materials, brochures, news releases and occasionally writing speeches for company executives. Starting monthly salary: $600. Bingo!

Janice gave Murph an information card to fill out and a test to take. The test was an IQ test of sorts with, as Murph later remembered it, pretty much common sense answers.

Murph completed the test and waited outside Janice's office while she graded it. Then Janice emerged, told Murph he scored "way high" and said she wanted him to meet with the department head. Murph took the elevator to the sixth floor where he met Tom Santley, Assistant Vice President of Communications.

Tom was over thirty, but he had a distinctly youthful vibe about him. He mentioned that Janice was very impressed with Murph's test score and they chatted briefly in a conference room. Then Tom handed Murph a yellow pad and a pencil and asked for a writing sample. "Write something about the freeways," then walked out, leaving Murph alone.

Here, in its entirety, including that line drawn after the second paragraph, is what Murph wrote:

The San Diego Freeway stretches like a tightrope between the Santa Monica and Ventura Freeways in the greater Los Angeles area. It is composed of eight lanes—four heading north and four south—which are divided by a five-foot high hurricane fence in the center. Automobile streams flow up and down this freeway throughout the day, especially during the after-work rush hours.

I have driven this route to and from my office in Santa Monica for almost five years now. One becomes used to the heavy freeway traffic after a while, and

*soon the driving experience becomes a small pleasure.
The daily movement of vehicles is organized and
reflects an efficient, operating society. Taking part in
this ordered system each morning and evening gives
me a satisfied feeling of belonging.*

*It is late. I am heading north on the San Diego
Freeway after ten and one half hours at the office. A
boy with guitar in hand is standing on the roadside
up ahead, thumb extended. For some reason I feel
sorry for him and stop. He scrambles up to my car
and hops into the front seat alongside of me.*

"How far you going," I ask.

"You going all the way to the valley?"

"Where in the valley?" I ask.

*"Well, I'm headed to Topanga Canyon Road
eventually."*

*"I'm not going that far, but I'll take you as far as I
can," I tell him.*

*We ride for about three minutes without uttering a
word. I glance quickly at my new rider and I notice
only that his hair is dark, thick and long; and his nose
is small, but somewhat pointed.*

He says "Aren't you going to give me a lecture?"

"What?"

*"Or at least ask me why I live like I do?" he asks.
"Most guys who pick me up want to know why I'm a
'hippie,' how I manage to survive—you know—where
I get my bread and all that. Then they give me a
lecture—you know—how I can change if I want to,
how I can become respectable, get a job, all that—like*

*all it takes is one little swat from the fairy godmoth-
er's wand. These guys, you know, they don't realize
how insignificant it all is. Salinger said that a mature
man is willing to live humbly for a cause. That's
the whole answer. Until a guy realizes that he—and
everybody else—is insignificant, he hasn't grown up.
Know what I mean? We're all heading down a dark
alley towards a bottomless pit."*

*His speech is becoming more excited. "Like Dylan
says, you guys know something's happening here,
but none of you can say what it is. Nothingness,
man—you know—insignificance, that's the answer.
If all the—"*

*"You better get out here," I say pulling to a stop near
the Marshall Road exit.*

*My rider becomes boisterous and indignant. "What's
the matter, man, did I shake you up? You yellow—"*

*He jerks his guitar from the back seat where he had
placed it and, mumbling to himself, climbs out of my
car. I reach over and close the door, then I step on the
accelerator, driving away as swiftly as I can.*

'Probably on some kind of dope,' I think.

And I drive on quietly into the darkness ahead.

When Murph read this many years later, he was surprised at what he wrote and even more surprised he was
hired. 'Maybe they hired me so I wouldn't kill myself,' he
thought, smiling.

Apparently the guys from PML were impressed—or desperate. "We should make this a movie," said Tom Santley.

This was September 1, 1968. *TIME* magazine's Man of

the Year was Youth. Persons twenty-five and under. Baby Boomers. Born in 1946, Murph was a classic Boomer. Soldiers returned from WW II in 1945 and were having babies in 1946 like nobody's business. Now these babies were young adults.

This was the Sixties, an era hard to describe and impossible to comprehend unless you were there. If Dickens were to write about the Sixties in America, his tome might start with the sentence: It was a time unlike any other.

A time of sit-ins and protest marches. Challenging authority. Polarization—young vs. old. Blacks vs. Whites. Hippies vs. Squares. Silent majority vs. vocal minority. A battle of bumper stickers: AMERICA – LOVE IT OR LEAVE IT vs. AMERICA – CHANGE IT OR LOSE IT. Seemed like all of American culture was being influenced and often controlled by Youth—music, politics, sexual boundaries.

Their movie was *The Graduate*. Their bible was *The Catcher in the Rye*. Their anthems were *You Can't Always Get What You Want* by the Rolling Stones and *Louie, Louie*, a song to which nobody knew the words. Their soundtrack was Dylan, the Beatles and the Stones. And the Boomer Battle Cry was "Don't trust anyone over thirty."

Drugs became a big part of that culture. Everything from smoking weed (marijuana) to dropping acid (LSD). That's where Murph drew the line. He never saw much sense in taking smoke into your lungs, regular smoke or the funny-smelling kind. And dropping strange pills into his body or putting powder up his nose–well, that just scared the shit out of Murph! He was too much of a control freak for that!

Not to mention that drugs were illegal, and Murph loved his freedom too much to risk even a minute of his limited time on this planet locked up behind bars. There's a reason they call it dope, he thought.

Boomer that he was, Murph wasn't crazy about working for an insurance company. Especially a life insurance company. Murph figured the only way you could get a good deal with a life insurance policy was to die.

But short of writing for television, it was a pretty good gig. Murph usually arrived a little late in the morning and stayed a little late at night, attempting to beat freeway traffic both ways. He was usually home around 6:00-6:30, which left him plenty of time to write and explore in the evening.

During his first few months at PML, Murph spent most of his time taking photos and writing articles for the company magazine. He was pleased to see his name on the magazine masthead under Editorial Staff. Sure it was just an in-house publication, but he was a writer.

If you asked Murph back then to name his favorite writer, he'd tell you without taking a beat, "John Updike. That man's prose is poetry." Murph even made a point once, returning from a college trip to NYC, to drive through Shillington, Pennsylvania, John Updike's hometown.

Murph's favorite modern novel was *Rabbit, Run*. In that book, Updike makes the point that when you're running away from something, you're also running toward something. Since leaving Ohio, Murph could identify more every day with Rabbit. 'He runs, ah runs.'

Chapter 3

CHASING THE DREAM

('69-70)

Two TV shows that appealed to Murph were *Rowan & Martin's Laugh-In* and *The Smothers Brothers Comedy Hour*. Both were variety shows and both were shows that had a very *now* feel and featured relevant comedy.

For example, on *Laugh-In*, character actor Arte Johnson might say, stuttering: "I-I th-think we sh-should g-get out of V-Vi-Viet N-Nam." And Dan Rowan would remark, "That's easy for you to say."

The Smothers Brothers, Tommy and Dick, successful and well-known for their cleverly funny musical routines and albums, favorites of Murph's since his high school days, concocted a TV show which featured satirical and often subversive sketches poignantly performed and written by the likes of David Steinberg, Pat Paulsen, Steve Martin, Rob Reiner, Bob Einstein and sometimes Mason Williams.

Murph studied both of these shows religiously and attempted to write jokes for *Laugh-In* and sketches for the Smothers Brothers show. Like most aspiring writers in those days, Murph had no access to actual scripts which might provide a written format to follow.

Eventually, Murph began writing entire scripts for Smothers Brothers episodes, even naming the appropriate musical acts—Pete Seeger, Joan Baez, Jefferson Airplane—that would appear. The hardest part, Murph learned, was not writing a script, but getting someone to read it.

Most shows and producers in Hollywood will not read material unless it's submitted by an agent. And most agents will not read unsolicited material. Makes breaking into TV a little tricky for an aspiring writer.

In truth, Murph had not made any all-out efforts to contact agents because, at this point, he didn't feel he had anything that would greatly impress an agent. And he didn't want an agent to read something that was just so-so, fearing that might keep an agent from reading future material. But now, after a couple years at PML, he figured it may be time to get some sort of feedback or advice from a real live agent.

The Writers Guild published a list of agents registered with the WGA and would mail a copy of the list to anyone who requested the list, which Murph did. The list noted certain agents—just a few—who would read unsolicited material. Murph decided to meet with two of them, Polly Connell and Jim Carlson, each of whom had their own agency. Polly was maybe fiftyish and Jim was at least ten years younger.

Murph had written a piece titled *Back Home* which was longer than a short story, but shorter than a novel. Maybe a 'shovel.' It was fiction, but written in the first person. He showed it to both Polly and Jim as a writing sample.

Jim read it and said if Murph could write it as a screenplay, he thought he could sell it. But Murph figured it

wasn't really long enough or involved enough for a feature and couldn't figure where else Jim might sell it. Murph asked Polly to send it to a book publisher, which she did. But the publisher returned it saying it was too short for a book.

Murph told Jim and Polly that what he really wanted to focus on was writing comedy for television. And both Jim and Polly told Murph they'd be willing to read whatever he wrote in the future.

Chapter 4

GAME CHANGER

('71)

L ike most Boomers, Murph's entertainment of choice
growing up was TV. Television, aka the "Tube," and
situation comedies, affectionately labeled "sitcoms," blos-
somed in the 1950s and 60s.

Murph grew up laughing at Lucy & Ricky; Ralph &
Norton; Bud & Lou (Murph still thinks Bud Abbott is
the best straight man ever!); Dave & Ricky Nelson; the
Anderson Family (*Father Knows Best* wins best Tongue-In-
Cheek title); and, of course, Wally & The Beav in the 50s.

In the 60s he watched Rob & Laura Petrie; Sgt. Bilko (Phil
Silvers was Murph's dad's favorite); Dobie & Maynard
G.; Clem Kadiddlehopper & Freddie the Freeloader (Red
Skelton's laugh-out-loud sketches); Andy, Barney & Opie
along with some *Our Miss Brooks, My Three Sons, Mr.
Peepers, Mr. Ed, The Real McCoys, The Beverly Hillbillies, Julia*
and Toody and Muldoon.

So Murph was watching TV early in 1971 or thereabouts
and a new sitcom came on with a disclaimer on the screen

that said something like 'Get your kids out of the room and be sure you're sitting down when you watch this show. If you're offended by words that you or people you know say or hear all the time, you better change the channel quick!'

Murph couldn't believe the things he was hearing on his TV. Things your father, your uncle, or your idiot neighbor might say. Words like spic, kike, jigaboo, jungle bunny, Chink.

So this blue collar buffoon named Archie calls somebody a "Chink," and his son-in-law, whom he calls "Meathead," chides Archie for using a racial slur and says the guy Archie's talking about is not even Chinese, he's Japanese.

And Archie says something like, "Oh, so if there was a Chinese guy and a Japanese guy standing next to each other, you could tell the difference, you dumb Polack, you?" And Meathead says, "Yes." And Archie says, "Yeah, you'd say, 'Which one of you is the Chink and which one's the Jap?'"

It was shocking! It was funny! It was poignant! It was satire. The kind of thing that's supposed to close on Saturday night. At least on Broadway. But here it was on Murph's TV!

Lenny Bruce, a comedian whom Murph had studied and read a lot about, used to go onstage and say "nigger nigger nigger nigger nigger" and also repeat the words kike, spic, Polack, wop—making the point that: "The more you say a word, the more you take away its power. Then you could never make some six-year-old black kid cry by calling him the N word at school."

As George Carlin said, 'No dirty words. Just dirty minds.'

The first thing Murph thought after watching *All in the Family* was, 'I'd give anything to write for that show!' Well,

not anything—not his soul, of course. Maybe his Willie
Mays baseball card…if he had one.

Within months, *All in the Family* became the number
one most watched show on television. The show tackled
real-life topics never before touched in American sitcoms.
Things like homophobia, race relations, politics, religion.

For Murph, AITF was an epiphany, a game changer. He
never thought you could mix funny and serious and make
it work. *All in the Family* proved that you could. You'd be
laughing one minute and moved to tears the next. In almost
every episode there would be at least one moment where
your brain would get chills. At the end of a number of episodes, and this is no lie, Murph would find himself saying
out loud, softly, "Wow…" AITF, Murph thought, was
medicine for the soul. It showed the power of comedy—
how comedy could entertain and educate at the same time.
It wasn't meaningless jokes or slapstick comedy; although
those elements were sometimes brilliantly worked into the
show (the first toilet flush ever heard on American TV was
on *All in the Family*).

When Murph's parents came to visit that summer,
Murph decided to take them to see a taping of AITF. It was
the first sitcom taping Murph ever attended.

Norman Lear—who developed and produced AITF,
based on a British series titled *Till Death Us Do Part*—did
the warm-up before the taping. The whole experience was
magical to Murph, especially when Mr. Lear announced
the names of the writers for the evening's episode. Murph
felt more than ever that this is what he was meant to do.

When the taping was over, Murph had an almost uncon-
trollable urge—and he'll tell you truthfully he's never had
an all encompassing moment like this anytime before or
since in his life, which should show you how seminal and

almost spiritual this urge was—to jump over the rail that separated the audience from the stage and run to Norman Lear and tell Mr. Lear that one day Murph would be working for him.

The only thing that stopped Murph—and as he looks back now, he's glad it did—was a fear that he might break an arm or a leg in the fall which would put him in a cast and maybe in the hospital for months and hinder his ability to sit at his typewriter and write something that would get Mr. Lear to hire him.

So Murph wrote a treatment for a story titled "The Draft Dodger" where a friend of Meathead's who's been living in Canada comes back at Christmas to visit his sick mother and ends up at the Bunker's house. This was a time when a sizeable number of young people, subject to being drafted into the Army, were moving to Canada rather than go to Vietnam. These "draft dodgers" agreed with Muhammad Ali, who refused to fight in Viet Nam. "No Viet Cong ever called me nigger," said the Champ.

Murph thought this would make an interesting Christmas episode of AITF, with Archie and Meathead discussing, among other things, what Jesus would do if He were drafted.

With high hopes, something aspiring writers live on, Murph took the treatment to Polly Connell and she sent it to Tandem, Lear's production company. It seemed like a year—but was probably no more than a month—when Murph got a response, and it wasn't the one he hoped for. It consisted of two simple words from Polly, two words he would have to get used to in years to come: "They passed."

WHAT MADE SHERWOOD Oaks Experimental College one of the most important sources of knowledge for Murph and for many aspiring writers, directors, producers and the like was its founder and CEB (Chief Energizer Bunny) Gary Shusett.

Gary was able to convince major names in the entertainment industry to appear and speak in an intimate classroom setting. Names like Paul Newman, Robert Towne, Paul Schrader, Tony Bill, David Ward, George Carlin, Richard Pryor, *Godfather* producer Al Ruddy, Stephen Cannell, Rod Serling, Martin Scorsese, all of whom Murph was able to see in person.

From Oscar-winning writer (*The Sting*) David Ward, Murph learned how much input the screenwriter has in most movies. When asked what his first film *Steelyard Blues*, starring Jane Fonda, Donald Sutherland and Peter Boyle, was about, Ward said he had no idea.

It was a revelation to Murph that the movie screen could say "Written by David Ward" and because of changes by the director and actors—not to mention the studio—filmgoers could be watching something that was completely foreign to the credited writer.

Another screenwriter guest at Sherwood Oaks related the apocryphal but revealing joke about the Polish starlet—She slept with the writer!

When screenwriter Robert Towne was asked about the role of the writer in the filmmaking process, he shared that for him "the rush comes when the last page leaves the typewriter." What happens to the script after that, Towne added, is "somebody else's problem."

When asked if he ever considered acting, Towne responded that he had enough trouble playing the lead in his own life.

When the subject of drama vs. comedy came up, screenwriter Paul Schrader opined that "the best comedy writing at the time is being done on television."

If you want to write comedy, he offered, TV is your medium.

Comedian George Carlin, attempting to analyze comedy, suggested that basic comedy evolves from combining two unrelated elements. For example, the Army and an Indian tribe. Or a weather report and drug culture, a la the Hippy Dippy Weatherman. Carlin also posed an intriguing question about Murph's favorite baseball team: If the Cincinnati Reds were really the first major league baseball team, who did they play?

When Paul Newman was asked what advice he would give a young actor, Newman replied, "Don't get your break too soon."

Murph thought this was also good advice for young writers. Expanding the analogy, Murph wrote in his notebook: **Before you write a check, make sure you have enough money in the bank.**

Chapter 5

SEVERANCE

('72)

Scheduled for the summer of 1972 was the move of PML's home office from Los Angeles to Newport Beach, California, about an hour south of LA, two hours in traffic.

Murph and Marianne drove down to Newport Beach to look at places to live; but rents there were much more expensive than in North Hollywood. Besides, Murph fully expected to be going to meetings at networks, studios and agents sooner rather than later, and he wanted to remain close to LA and the center of the entertainment industry.

The company was offering six months' severance pay to employees who were not going to move; and six months' severance to Murph sounded like a bronze parachute. The way Murph saw it, both opportunity and destiny were knocking. Murph had a thought and he wrote it down: **Life, like comedy, is about timing.**

He had been at PML going on four years now. And four-year periods at this point in his life seemed to mark significant maturation segments. Four years in high school, four years college, and now four years post college. During these last four, the Murphy family had doubled in size. Murph and Marianne now had two adorable daughters, sixteen months apart—"Irish twins."

You might think that Murph, at the age of 25, would feel pressure having children to feed and clothe. The truth is it inspired him. He felt that his bald-at-birth but eventually curly haired—Colleen, blonde; Heather, with a wisp of strawberry—blue-eyed daughters were rooting for his happiness and success; and he was determined to prove himself worthy of their love and respect.

Now, with the company's move just months away, Murph remembered a Bob Dylan song lyric, typed it on paper, and taped it on the inside of his cubicle at work. The note read: "I just don't fit. I believe it's time for us to quit."

Murph decided to use some of his severance pay and time off to see Europe. He and college friend Joe Bove made plans to take their wives, Marianne and Janie, to Europe for a month. This would be the first time overseas for all four.

Murph and Joe managed to join a charter flight of teachers leaving from Cincinnati. The cost was reasonable, $500 round trip per person. Murph and Marianne were able to leave Colleen and Heather in Cincy with the grandparents.

Joe decided he would purchase a Volvo from the factory in Sweden, pick it up in London, use it to drive around Europe, then drop it off at the factory in Sweden and have it shipped to the U.S. for pickup. Joe planned the basic itinerary, 13 countries in 28 days. Nightly lodging was to be determined on a daily basis, depending on where they happened to be.

Murph found the whole experience to be informative and engaging, except for a brief interlude in Austria which Murph, in an attempt to downplay the impact, later referred to simply as the Innsbruck Incident. Murph found himself in a minor spat with his wife and Marianne instructed Joe to stop the car, which he did. Marianne then climbed out and started walking toward the Alps.

Murph just sat there, thrown. "Aren't you going after her?" asked Janie.

She'll be back, thought Murph. Where's she gonna go?

"She misses the kids," offered Janie. Joe and Janie had no kids as yet.

Murph managed to gather his senses and some sensitivity and went after Marianne. He apologized, even though he wasn't sure what he did, and talked his wife back into the car.

When Murph and Marianne returned to Cincinnati, they were thrilled to see their daughters! The girls, both under three years old, were now potty-trained, thanks to Grandma Charlotte, Murph's mom.

Murph soon learned that his wife's unease in Austria, when she started heading for the Alps, was about more than just missing the kids. She was worried about the future. Her husband was now out of work. No steady job, no steady income.

Maybe Murph's dream of writing for TV was just a pipe dream. If her husband's dream was his destiny, wouldn't he at least have sold a script by now?

Marianne liked being home in Ohio. She missed having her extended family around—parents, grandparents, siblings, cousins, not to mention friends she grew up with. Maybe, she suggested, they would be better off living in Cincinnati. Wouldn't this be a better place to raise their kids than in California?

Murph had been expecting Marianne and his daughters to share his dream and be as committed and excited about it as he was. But was that really fair? Was he being selfish?

Murph thought about it. Could he be happy living in Cincinnati? What would he do for a living? Sell shoes? Sell furniture? Work for Procter & Gamble?

P&G's headquarters was in Cincinnati. Murph worked there in college. Part-time job on Saturdays, operating the elevator, checking employee ID's. There was one Vice President who came to work every weekend. Never took a vacation in 26 years. Peter Farmer. Friendly guy. Figured the company couldn't get along without him.

One Friday night there was a plane crash at the airport. Peter Farmer died in that crash. Saturday morning, less than 12 hours later, maintenance workers at P&G were removing the furniture from Mr. Farmer's office and moving someone else in. Murph never forgot that lesson. In corporate life, no one is irreplaceable.

Murph couldn't see himself in corporate life. When Murph announced to his co-workers at PML that he was leaving, Fred Kummerle, head of the Printing Department, asked with sincere parental concern, "What are you gonna do when you're forty-five?"

Murph knew one thing he didn't want to be doing when he was forty-five—if he lived that long. He didn't want to be thinking 'What if...?' What if he stuck with his dream? What if he didn't give up? What if he tried harder?

He recalled the words of activist/scholar Benjamin Mays: "The tragedy in life doesn't lie in not reaching your goal. The tragedy lies in having no goal to reach," wrote Mays.

"**No goal, no soul**," wrote Murph.

If he gave up on his dream at the age of twenty-six, how could he encourage his daughters to follow their dreams? How could he tell them they could grow up to be or do anything they wanted without feeling like a hypocrite? And if there was one thing Murph definitely did not want to be, it was a hypocrite.

Murph planned to visit for a few days before heading back to LA. He stayed with his in-laws, sleeping in Marianne's old bedroom. He slept in the first morning, coming down for breakfast about 10:00 a.m. The kitchen was empty, but a place was set for him.

Next to his plate was a business card. On the card was the name of a local barber. Marianne entered and explained that her mom had given her that card to give to Murph. "Mom thought you'd want to get a haircut."

Admittedly, Murph's hair was probably longer than it had ever been. When his friend Lou, aka "Iceman," stopped by to say hi, Ice reacted by greeting Murph with, "Hey, it's Bob Dylan!"

Murph glanced at the barbershop card and placed it in his wallet. This was the same kitchen where Murph's mother-in-law once insisted that Martin Luther King was a Communist. To which Murph responded by quietly walking out and driving away. Murph's mother-in-law was not a bad person. Bad is not the same as ill-informed.

Marianne decided to spend another week with the girls visiting in Ohio while Murph headed back to LA. Murph stopped in the airport to buy a pretzel and as he searched his wallet for cash, he spotted the barbershop card and dropped it in the trash.

BACK IN LA, Marianne learned from a friend that a house nearby was for rent and she decided it was time the Murphys move from their two-bedroom apartment to a small three-bedroom house with a yard. The increase in monthly rent would be about $50, a significant but not insurmountable bump.

Murph didn't have a regular job now; but he had received six months' severance. And he'd managed to keep things afloat by scaring up enough freelance gigs writing promotional copy, plus developing some board games—including a spoof on planned obsolescence in the auto industry called *Beat Detroit, The Game That Will Crack You Up*; a Sherlock Holmes mystery game called *221 B Baker Street*; and *THE PETER PRINCIPLE GAME*, based on the bestselling book by Dr Laurence J. Peter (who became a lifelong friend)—to keep things afloat while he pursued his TV writing goals. Marianne was a full-time Mom now, but she managed to earn money babysitting for some other mothers. All things considered, the opportunity felt like destiny. So they moved.

With a third bedroom, Murph now had an office where he could put his desk. (At the apartment, his desk was in his bedroom.) The Murphys had a yard now, front and back, but Murph had to mow the grass. With a push mower. Just like the old days in Ohio. Until his dad got a power mower. And later a sit-down tractor.

Cutting grass was Murph's first job. As a teenager, he would cut neighbors' lawns for four bucks a yard. As the oldest, it was also Murph's responsibility to mow his own lawn. Murph's brother Tim, three years younger, had the job of trimming the walks, driveway and around the bushes with a hand trimmer. In the spring when their grass was covered with bright yellow dandelions—which looked like flowers but were really weeds—their mother would pay Murph and his brother a dime-a-bucket to remove the dandelions with a weed digger.

When Murph was a little boy, he would take a bouquet of dandelions to his mother. When he later learned dandelions were weeds, he was puzzled. How could such a pretty flower be a weed?

Dandelions Are Weeds. Murph thought that might be a good title for something. Maybe a short story. Or a book. Or not. Maybe a title like *A Bouquet of Dandelions* would be more subtle.

Murph wasn't crazy about cutting grass again, but at least his kids had a yard to play in. It was a small yard, of course, like most California yards. Murph found it ironic that people with big yards in Ohio cut their grass themselves, while people in California, with very small yards, all had gardeners. Except for Murph. At least for now.

Murph's wish for the future was that someday he'd be able to hire a gardener. Right now, an extra $35 a month for a gardener seemed unnecessary, if not extravagant.

Murph and his girls also missed the pool at their old place. But the kids made do running through the sprinklers in the yard. Murph found himself thinking that as far as material luxury was concerned, if he could one day afford to 1) pay somebody else to cut his grass, and 2) have access to a pool, he'd be a happy man.

Chapter 6

PAYIN' DUES

('73)

After four years of research and observation, Murph had concluded that the three things required or desired for a career in writing comedy for television were 1) a spec (written entirely on speculation) script, 2) an agent, and 3) a partner—not necessarily in that order.

Murph figured it was time to find an agent who specialized in TV comedy. So he called Jack Hanrahan, a writer he had met, for references and Jack gave him two names: Lew Weitzman and Larry Grossman.

Larry Grossman never returned Murph's call. Lew Weitzman at William Morris said, "Call me back next week."

When Murph called Lew the following week, Lew explained he was just leaving William Morris and starting his own literary agency. 'This could be excellent timing,' thought Murph.

Murph arranged to meet Lew at the Radford Gate of the MTM lot, where Lew had a meeting. This was the lot where the Mary Tyler Moore and Bob Newhart sitcoms were shot.

Murph gave Lew nine pages of stand-up material he had written about growing up Catholic, titled *The Baltimore Catechism and Other Memories*. There were riffs about Guardian Angels; mortal and venial sin; plenary indulgences; End of the World; and Judgment Day where, before the sentencing, God explains all the great mysteries, including the Blessed Trinity and how *My Mother the Car* ever made it to the screen.

The material begins with talk about Catholic school. Curious? Here's an excerpt:

We'd be sitting at our desks and Sister'd say: "Okay boys and girls, put your catechisms away. Let's see who studied last night. Henry, 'Who made us?'"

Henry'd stand up real quick, leaning on his desk: "Godmadeus."

"Very good, Henry. Thomas, 'Why did God make us?'"

"GodmadeustoshowforthHisgoodnessandtosharewithusHis everlastinghappinessinheaven."

"Very good, Thomas. Sally, 'What is the one true Church?'"

"TheCatholicChurchistheonetrueChurch."

"Very good, Sally. Patrick, 'Why did God make us?'"

"Godmadeus to…uh, Godmadeusto…toshowforthHisgoodnes-sandtoshareHis… GodmadeustoshowforthHisgoodnessandto… Uh, would you repeat the question, Sister?"

(SISTER, CURTLY) "'Why did God make us?' God made us to show forth His goodness and to share with us His everlasting happiness in heaven. Write that twenty-five times for tomorrow's class, Patrick."

Then after Catechism class Sister would tell us all about Russia and how the Communists brainwashed their children.

Lew liked Murph's material and offered to represent him.

SINCE MOVING TO LA, Murph spent a lot of time hanging out at comedy clubs like the Improv, The Comedy Store, The Ice House and others. He watched comedians like Jimmie Walker, Freddie Prinze, Jay Leno, David Letterman, Jimmy Brogan, Richard Pryor, Ritch Shydner, Andy Kaufman, Sam Kinison, Steve Landesberg, Kevin Nealon, Garry Shandling, Richard Lewis and many others develop their comedy and personas.

At one point, Murph thought he'd like to do stand-up. But there were reasons why he decided it wouldn't fit his lifestyle—the big one being that you didn't get paid. It wasn't until around 1979 or so that comedians finally went on strike forcing Comedy Store owner Mitzi Shore to pay them around fifteen bucks a set.

TO MURPH, THE words "writing workshop" always seemed like an oxymoron. Writing, he thought, should be a personal expression that flows from the soul of the individual. And the word "workshop" implies a group effort with the goal of tackling some project like the construction of a house, or a sailboat or some complex Rube Goldberg contraption.

So Murph never attended nor was ever interested in anything called a "writing workshop." But when he noticed a "comedy writing workshop" on the list of courses featured in the latest Sherwood Oaks Experimental College catalogue, it caught his eye. Murph had learned that producers, shows, networks, studios like to hire teams. For one reason, they get more bang for their buck—two for the price of one. Plus, in the particular art of writing comedy, where laughter is the goal, it makes sense to have a partner so you can bounce lines and ideas off each other in hopes of determining what's funny. (If you tell a joke in the forest and no one's around, is it funny?)

So Murph decided to sign up for the Sherwood Oaks comedy writing workshop in hopes of finding a partner. The workshop instructor was Harvey Miller, who was a writer and about to become producer for the TV series *The Odd Couple*. The series was based on a play by Neil Simon, who began as a writer on Sid Caesar's *Your Show of Shows* in the 1950s.

At the first gathering of the workshop, in a small upstairs theater in North Hollywood, members of the class introduced themselves. One guy about Murph's age named Sean mentioned that he had just had an article rejected by the *National Lampoon*. That attracted Murph's attention for three reasons:

1. Murph figured if this guy reads and likes the *National Lampoon*, it's likely they share the same sense of humor;

2. the mention of rejection displayed the proper amount of self-deprecation found among intelligent and secure persons (particularly comedy writers);

3. the fact that Sean actually wrote and submitted an article showed a writing ambition.

National Lampoon was a humor magazine staffed by former *Harvard Lampoon* writers, the motto of which was 'Nothing is sacred.' Magazine covers included a photo of a cute dog with a gun to its head with the warning "If You Don't Buy This Magazine, We'll Kill This Dog."

After class, Murph approached his classmate and said he was looking for a writing partner. Murph suggested they exchange some writing samples at the next class. The following week Murph brought his stand-up material and Sean brought the rejected *National Lampoon* article. The next time they got together, both were encouraged.

It didn't hurt that both had Irish surnames and Irish-American fathers with German-American mothers. Or that each was raised Catholic. Or that each had married his high school sweetheart and each had two young kids—one with two girls, the other with two boys. Sean could say his father was currently a sportswriter for a local paper, a pedigree Murph could only attempt to match if he mentioned that in college his father wrote for the school newspaper and took first place in an essay contest by writing about the health benefits of walking. As an added coincidence, Sean's father grew up in Cincinnati, Murph's hometown.

But to Murph, the most encouraging thing was when he learned how Sean had come to sign up for this workshop: As a birthday present, Sean's wife gave him tickets to the Super Bowl, which was in LA this year, and he sold the tickets to pay for this workshop. Now that was commitment! The kind of commitment Murph figured was needed to make it in this business!

Murph made it clear to Sean that he wasn't looking for a friend. Murph thought that was important. He had plenty of friends back in Ohio. He was looking for a business partner. Sean was on board and they agreed to try writing an *Odd Couple* script together.

Over the next few weeks in class, students worked on various writing projects while Murph and Sean, somewhat appropriately, sat in the back and fooled around. One thing both remember is a dude they called "Six Box," who intimidated the whole class when he told the instructor he had six boxes of jokes at home.

"Six boxes?!" reacted Murph.

"Are these like shoe boxes or grocery boxes?" wondered Sean.

"I don't even have one box," said Murph.

"I only have six jokes," offered Sean.

When the duo finished their *Odd Couple* script, they were pleased. Especially with the cover page which read "Written by Mick Murphy and Sean Malloy."

They showed their script to Harvey Miller who read it and said he liked it. Murph and Sean, of course, would have loved to hear that Harvey thought their script should become the next episode of *The Odd Couple*. But, as Murph and Sean were to learn, later rather than sooner, the chances of a show buying a script from an outside writer were slim and none, and Slim just left town on the nun's horse.

Murph took Sean to meet Lew Weitzman, whose first office after leaving William Morris was a closet-sized space adjoining Lew's accountant's office. The three had a nice chat, after which Sean and Murph agreed that, although they didn't know many agents, Lew was probably the nicest agent in Hollywood. And they branded him "Sweet Lew."

Sweet Lew read their *Odd Couple* script and sent it to Tom Patchett & Jay Tarses, writer/producers of *The Bob Newhart Show*, with a note that said something like "Am I crazy or is this funny?" And Tom Patchett responded with a note that said, "You're not crazy."

So, full of youthful confidence—or naivete, however you want to pronounce it—the two Irishmen, Mick Murphy & Sean Malloy, became official writing partners on St. Patrick's Day, March 17, 1973, over lunch and a pint (or two) of beer at Casey's Bar on Grand Avenue in downtown

Los Angeles, less than a block from Murph's former PML office.

MURPH AND SEAN launched their writing career agreeing to abide by two simple but immutable rules:

1. Never show dissension in front of others. The 'strength in unity' pledge, also known as the Godfather rule. They could argue like Irishmen when alone, but always remain united, not divided, around others. Especially in pitch meetings.

2. When discussing a joke or a line, if either of them would say "I hate it," they would drop the joke and immediately move on.

One of the first meetings Lew arranged for his new un-credited writing team was with Sid and Marty Krofft, creators of, among other children's programming, *H.R. Pufnstuf,* a show about...sheesh, really now, who the heck knows what that show is about?

So our heroes are sitting across from Sid Krofft and Sid says something like: "So, I was thinking the other day when I was in my backyard and looking at the sky, where do witches go when they retire." Then he looks at Sean & Murph.

"Do you know where they go?" Murph shakes his head and Sean says "Nope."

"They go to Witch Mountain." Sean and Murph react and wait.

"Witch Mountain," Sid continues, "is a big mountain that's on an abandoned studio lot. Three witches live there. And one of them is Witchiepoo." (Witchie hoo?)

"Witchiepoo is the witch on H.R. Pufnstuf," explains Sid.

"Have you seen H.R. Pufnstuf?" (They haven't.) "We'll screen it for you."

Sid directs Murph and Sean to a small room with a screen and a standing projector, turns the projector on and the light off and leaves.

Murph & Sean watch the screen for a few minutes as talking flutes and sneezing trees and God knows what else start colliding through a wacky landscape...when suddenly Murph looks over and sees that the film is off the reel and continuing to pile up on the floor.

Not knowing how to turn off the projector and not wanting to damage the film, Murph scoots to the door and opens it to an empty hall. He calls down the hall, "Excuse me...Hello...Anybody here?"

No answer. The place appears empty. Feels like the guys are in a Marx Brothers movie and can't get out. Sean has a sudden brainstorm and pulls the projector cord from the wall and the film stops unwinding. They look down the empty hall and Murph says, "Let's blow this joint."

On the drive back home, Murph started calling Sean "Marty" and Sean called Murph "Sid"—nicknames that lasted much longer than they should have.

Murph called Sweet Lew and said, "No more kids' shows. We want to write prime time comedy."

Lew said, "You guys belong at MTM." MTM was the studio that produced *The Mary Tyler Moore Show* and *The Bob Newhart Show*. Murph thought those shows were well written, with good characters and some clever jokes. But aside from the fact that Mary was a single woman with ambition (the writers initially intended for Mary to be divorced, but the network objected) and Bob was a psychiatrist, there was nothing really groundbreaking about those shows. "Mayonnaise comedy," as one producer put it. (Or, in the words of *Maude* writer Bob Schiller, "When Maude had an abortion, Mary had a pimple.")

As a Boomer, Murph liked relevant comedy. "We want to write for *All in the Family*," he told Lew.

IT WAS A call Murph will never forget. In the spring of 1973, Lew managed to arrange a lunch meeting for Sean and Murph with Don Nicholl, Mickey Ross and Bernie West who, along with Norman Lear, were responsible for the lion's share of the writing for the number one show on television.

More than a year before, Murph had ordered an audio tape cassette interview of Mickey Ross and Bernie West from *Writer's Digest*. In this interview, which apparently took place at a dinner table in either Mickey's or Bernie's house, the two former college friends (Baruch College, NYC) who—amid clinking glasses and noisy silverware— talked about their previous experience as a comedy duo in the Catskills and how they sent a spec script to Norman Lear after seeing the pilot of *All in the Family*.

Murph was fascinated with this taped interview and found himself listening to it over and over, searching for possible career clues. These guys, thought Murph, are doing exactly what I want to do.

Murph and Sean went to the *All in the Family* offices at CBS Television City where they met the legendary trio and the five moved together through the bowels of CBS, down a freight elevator and through a back exit which led to LA's historic Farmers Market, where they had a casual lunch in the sunny outdoors.

As far as Murph could tell, their lunch meeting could not have gone better. There were laughs, smiles and solid vibes all around. Murph and Sean told their idols how they thought *All in the Family* was by far the best show on television and the only show they really wanted to write for.

Later in the afternoon they heard from Lew who said 'The guys like you and they'll probably have you come in when they get back from hiatus in a month or so and give you an assignment or two.'

Well, Murph and Sean were pleased; but they thought, 'Hey, why settle for an assignment or two, we want them to hire us on staff. Let's wow 'em, bowl 'em over, knock their socks off, as they say in the Midwest. Let's write a script and get it to them when they get back.'

So M&M, as Sweet Lew called them, spent most of the next month in Sean's kitchen (where he was babysitting for his two boys while his wife Judi went to work at City National Bank) writing an *All in the Family* script. This was the first entire script they penned together since their *Odd Couple* endeavor.

When the script was finished, they got it to Don, Mickey and Bernie. What they got back was not what they expected: a polite letter from Don that basically said: 'Thank you for thinking of our show. You guys have talent. But *All in the Family* is not the only pebble on the beach.'

Sean and Murph were at Sean's place mulling over their Dear Sean and Murph letter when Sean's friend Steve Harper stopped by. Steve looked at the letter and expressed his condolences, saying something like: "Well, I guess you guys are going to be looking into other career paths."

M&M reacted, making it clear to Steve that they were disappointed but undeterred by Don's pebble on the beach letter. Then Steve made a metaphoric proclamation that Murph never forgot and hoped would define the writing team's destiny: "You guys are nails!"

Murph thought of a quote he had seen: "Adversity

introduces a man to himself."

He also recalled something Harvey Miller had said in class when asked by a student what advice he would give to a young, aspiring writer. Harvey said that in his experience, both in the entertainment business and in life, **"Persistence is the only thing that always pays off."** Murph wrote that down.

And he also scribbled an insight of his own, the profundity of which had meaning to both his personal and work life at the time: **Maturity can be measured by how we react to change.**

M&M RECKONED THEY should have a second spec script, and Sean suggested a *M*A*S*H* script. *M*A*S*H* was a good choice because, unlike *The Odd Couple*, which was a multi-camera show, filmed in front of a live audience, *M*A*S*H* was a single camera show with no audience. From a portfolio perspective, it was a good balance.

Even more important, *M*A*S*H* was an industry darling—a show that was considered smart and witty by persons in the entertainment business and by a multitude of devoted fans.

But if you want to know the truth—and it's a truth Murph figured he'd never reveal in any sort of memoir, unless maybe if he were a really, really old dude, like 70 or so, and didn't give a crap whether potential readers, all two or three of them, might stop reading his book—Murph wasn't crazy about *M*A*S*H*.

He loved the movie, a biting satire on war. But the TV series had none of the bite and was way too soft to be labeled satire. Murph's biggest problem with *M*A*S*H*, besides the little asterisks between the title letters, was that it wasn't funny. The two main characters, spewing mostly sarcasm and putdowns, were at best a couple chauvinistic wise guy frat boys.

Granted, there were occasional thought-provoking episodes of *M*A*S*H*. But in Murph's mind, if this series, centered around a military medical unit in the Korean War, was an attempt at either comedy or serious social commentary, it failed on both counts.

Sean, however, volunteered to write a *M*A*S*H* script. He said he had a friend who was an avid *M*A*S*H* fan and he'd have her read it.

FOR THE REMAINDER of 1973, meetings for M&M were few and far between. In those days, there were three networks—ABC, CBS and NBC. Pickups for new shows were usually in May, shows began production in July and August, and the new fall season would begin airing in September. Most scripts were staff written. Story pitches from freelance writers were usually limited to credited writers. And Murph & Sean had no TV writing credits.

With Christmas 1973 approaching, Murph and writing partner Sean, still with no TV credits, employed the Squeaky Wheel theory, sending agent Sweet Lew a season's greeting card accompanied by a black & white photo of their four kids—Colleen, Heather, John and Kevin—foraging through a garbage can.

The photo produced the expected chuckles from Sweet Lew, and may have had a hand in generating activity for M&M soon to come in the New Year.

Chapter 7

PAYIN' OFF

('74)

In the spring of 1974, M&M got a call from Sweet Lew saying *Good Times* is looking for stories. *Good Times* was a brand new sitcom developed by Norman Lear and aired on CBS as a mid-season replacement. The show was a spinoff of *Maude*, which was a spinoff of *All in the Family*. It was a groundbreaking series, the first-ever sitcom built around a black family.

In the new show, Esther Rolle, who played the maid on *Maude*, was married and the mother of three. The family lived in a housing project in a poor area of Chicago. The children were teenage JJ (Jimmie Walker), an aspiring artist; his younger sister Thelma, who wants to go to college and study in the medical field; and eleven-year-old Michael, referred to by his father (John Amos) as a "militant midget" because of his vocal stance on issues of race discrimination.

Lew said Allan Manings, exec producer of *Good Times*, was willing to look at story ideas and suggested Mick &

Sean write a small paragraph on any ideas they had. Murph & Sean wrote three ideas, which were sent to Manings.

A few days later Lew heard from Manings, who said Norman Lear liked one of the stories and Manings would like to meet with M&M. Driving to their meeting, Sean & Murph discussed which of the three stories might be the one Lear and Manings liked.

Sean thought it might be the one about Thelma getting pregnant. Murph figured it was the one about Michael failing or refusing to take an IQ test.

Murph had read an article in *Psychology Today* magazine that dealt with scientist William Shockley's theory that Blacks had innately lower intelligence than Whites, based on lower scores by Blacks on standard IQ tests. A black professor at Washington University in St. Louis developed an IQ test known as the BITCH (Black Intelligence Test of Cultural Homogeneity) test on which Whites scored much lower than Blacks. Standard IQ tests, claimed professor Robert Williams, were culturally biased.

So one of M&M's story ideas centered on young Michael refusing to take an IQ test at school because he feels those tests are racially biased. "They don't tell you how smart you are, just how white you are." Michael tells his parents about the BITCH test and his parents show the test to a White school official who fails to answer multiple questions like 'What is an alley apple?' The correct answer is neither a fruit, nor a bowling pin, nor a tire...but a brick.

Turns out it was the IQ test Murph and Sean were meeting about. They met in Allan Manings' office with Allan, Norman Paul and Jackie Elinson, each distinguished writers in their own right. Allan sat behind his desk while Norman Paul lay stretched out on the sofa as the five writers discussed and fleshed out the story. During the meeting, Norman Paul, who seemed only half-awake, would toss out mumbled lines from the couch. Both Murph and Sean hoped the other was comprehending Norman's thoughts and writing them down. But they realized later both had been too intimidated to ask the veteran writer, "What the f*** are you saying?"

Then Allan said, "Okay, guys, you have an assignment. Go write the story."

When Murph & Sean walked out of Allan Manings' office and down the hall, Murph could not feel his feet touch the ground. No joke. He was walking on air. It's truly a feeling he's never experienced before or since. When they high-fived, both Murph & Sean swear their feet were not touching the ground. This was a formative moment in M&M history—their first TV assignment.

For any perspiring writers out there who'd like to know how this assignment thing works, or at least how it worked back then, listen up. Writers are sent to first write a Story Outline, which can be an 8-10 page narrative, hopefully broken into scenes. This is submitted to the exec producer or to whomever gave you the assignment.

The production entity then has the option to either 1) pay you for writing the story and send you to script, or 2) pay you for the story and "cut you off."

Two common reasons for cutting off the original writer:

1. They (EP or Producer) decide the story doesn't work.

2. They decide to give it to another writer (usually a writer on staff) to write the teleplay. In this case, the original writer will receive "Story by" credit, and whoever writes the teleplay will receive "Teleplay by" credit.

Script payments are made in three installments:

1. Story

2. 1st Daft

3. 2nd Draft

If you are sent to script, you are guaranteed to be paid for both 1st and 2nd drafts.

These payment stipulations are determined by the Writers Guild. As for timeline in delivering script assignments, the WGA suggests:

1. 1 week for Story Outline;

2. 2 weeks for 1st draft;

3. 1 week for 2nd draft.

In most cases, the production company can request a "polish" (short rewrite or punch-up of 2nd draft) if they wish. But on most TV series, rewrites beyond 2nd draft are done by staff writers.

M&M turned in their Story Outline within a week, and reported a few days later for notes with Allan, Norman Paul and Jackie. (An important note for aspiring TV writers: Script notes from the executive producer are like orders in the Army from your commanding officer—they are not casual suggestions.)

This time Murph & Sean paid close attention to the body on the sofa (Norman Paul) who contributed both good notes for the script and big laughs for the room. Norman, Murph later learned, was a key writer for George Burns, famous not only for his humor but for taking a swing at Frank Sinatra in a Vegas bar. Frank's boys pulled Norman aside and asked Frank if they should take him to the desert. Frank nixed that, saying, "Let him go, he's one of

Georgie's writers." Which may prove if you can write good jokes, you can get away with anything.

Two weeks later, M&M delivered their first draft of "The IQ Test"; met for more notes with the *Good Times* trio; then a week later handed in their second draft.

When "The IQ Test" was taped in front of a live audience, M&M were invited to the taping and brought their wives. In the opening minutes, Murph thought this might be the wrong night. Sure, in the warm-up, Allan Manings did introduce them: "Tonight's show was written by Mick Murphy & Sean Malloy." But Murph didn't recognize any...wait a minute, there's a sign on stage that says, "Happy Birthday, Michael" and it is Michael's birthday in their script and the kid can't have more than one birthday but...wait a minute, there's a line they wrote! This has to be their show. But what happened to other...lines, good lines that...were changed.

The structure remained the same...the story and the scenes...but the dialogue...Murph recognized about three of their jokes in the whole show. As they were leaving after the show, audience members approached and congratulated the stunned team, who didn't know whether to say "Thank you" or "What the f*** just happened?"

Then after the show aired, players at Murph & Marianne's weekly volleyball game told Murph how much they enjoyed the show, some repeating lines and saying "I could tell that line was yours!" Murph could only produce a sheepish smile and accept the unwarranted kudos. Really, what else could he do? Say, "Not only was that line neither mine nor my partner's, I thought it sucked!"?

Actually, Murph thought the show was fine, except for the culminating scene where Florida and James confront the school official. In this way over-the-top scene, the official is played by noted actor Austin Pendleton as a goofy, nerdy white guy whose calculator literally explodes! Even though it got a big laugh from the audience, Murph felt this sketch approach was untypical of a Norman Lear show and hurt the reality of the episode's message.

For Murph, it was a learning experience. His takeaway: he wanted to write on staff.

IN SEPTEMBER OF 1974 a new sitcom aired on ABC called *That's My Mama*. Theresa Merritt played Mama and Clifton Davis played her thirtyish son (also named Clifton) who inherited his father's barbershop, set in a middle class black neighborhood in Washington, DC.

M&M met with the show's story editor, Larry Stigler, and pitched a story idea where there have been some break-ins in the neighborhood, so Clifton, against Mama's wishes, brings a gun into the house for protection.

Mama tells Clifton in no uncertain terms that she does not want a weapon in the house. Clifton reminds Mama that a knife is a weapon too.

Mama: "Yeah, but you can't spread peanut butter with a gun."

At the act break, Clifton accidentally shoots his brother-in-law, Leonard, who is headed for a Halloween party dressed as the Lone Ranger. At the end, Clifton concedes that Mama's concern about the gun was justified and gets rid of it.

The story was pretty well worked out and the producers, Walter Bien and Gene Plummer, sent M&M to write the story and script. Murph & Sean wrote the first draft in a motel room, in order to help focus away from their kids. When Walter found out they were writing in a motel room, he arranged for them to have a temporary office at the show.

They weren't officially on staff, but it was the next best thing. They were driving to the ABC offices on Prospect Avenue every day and mingling with the show's staff. They even became official competitors in the office pinball competition organized by associate producers Alan Baumrucker and George Crosby.

They were getting paid to write their script, which was well received by the producers and the audience. In fact, the night "The Gun" episode aired, LA Mayor Tom Bradley declared "That's My Mama Day" in honor of the show's portrayal of gun safety.

WITH THE WRITING of their second script, Murph & Sean were required to join the Writers Guild. An aspiring writer could write his or her first assignment under the Taft-Hartley Act, but recognized Writers Guild of America rules required anyone writing more than one script for a WGA signatory to become a WGA member. (All major networks, studios and production entities were WGA, DGA, SAG and AFTRA signatories.)

The good news about joining the Guild was that it sounded cool and you got a neat wallet-friendly card showing proof of membership. The bad news was you had to pay an initiation fee and dues. At that time, Murph and Sean were too young to realize the future value of health and pension benefits.

So Murph and Sean were now registered as an official writing team, employing an ampersand in their credit to indicate the writing partnership of Mick Murphy & Sean Malloy. A writing credit where two or more names are separated with the word 'and' indicates the writers are writing separately and not as a "bona fide" team.

Murph & Sean pitched another *Mama* story idea to the producers where Clifton is dating a woman who has a kid; but when they split up, the kid wants to stay with Clifton. At the act break, the kid says, "But Clifton, I love you." A single man dating a woman with a kid was a fresh idea for television at the time. The producers liked the story and assigned M&M to write the story outline and the script. Even though they still weren't technically on staff, Murph & Sean were able to continue using their ABC office while writing their second *Mama* script, "Clifton and the Kid."

Everything about their *Mama* writing experience was nice. With few notes from the producers, Murph & Sean felt trusted and respected as writers. And with the *General Hospital* offices down the hall, and active stages throughout the complex, Murph was beginning to feel like a comfortable cog in the entertainment wheel.

One day upon arrival at work, while walking past the *General Hospital* offices, Murph noticed stacks of wrapped birthday presents flowing from the entrance of the GH offices. "Whose birthday?" Murph couldn't resist asking a young woman who worked on the show.

"Oh, it's nobody here," she said. "Those presents are for a character on the show."

"Huh? You're kidding me. You mean all these presents are for some fictional character on *General Hospital*?"

The young woman told Murph this happens all the time. A couple weeks ago, she said, the LA police showed up here responding to a call about a kidnapping. The kidnapping was on the show. And on another episode, a character was attempting to adopt a child, but a judge ruled she didn't have the $5,000 necessary to close the adoption. The show received a check from a viewer made out to that character for $5,000.

Murph's Midwest mind was blown! "You mean there's somebody out there who's smart enough to have $5,000, but dumb enough to send it to a soap opera character?"

Could there really be that many people out there who think characters on TV are real? Murph was...how do you spell flabbergasted!? But then, Murph recalled reading in *TIME* magazine that 73% of people in the US believe in angels. So maybe he shouldn't be so surprised.

At Christmas time, Murph & Sean were invited to *That's My Mama's* Holiday Party, where they brought their wives and had a blast. Murph distinctly remembers he and Sean walking outside in the cool December air, standing in line at the Andy Gump port-o-potty. With 1974 coming to an end, Murph had a good feeling about the approaching year. M&M looked at each other, locked in confident smiles. "We're doing it," said Sean, reading Murph's mind. And the two writing partners high-fived.

Chapter 8

CREDITS

('75)

Momentum is a curious thing. You can't see it...but you can feel it. It doesn't just happen, it has to build. You have to start with a strong foundation, and then you build—one brick at a time. According to author Malcolm Gladwell, it takes 10,000 hours to be really good at something. That's a lot of hours, or bricks.

Murph and Sean had been working together for two years now—piling up bricks. Building self-confidence. Jelling as a writing team. They were still far from the required 10,000 hours, but they were getting closer. They could feel the momentum.

In the spring of 1975, *Maude* had completed its second season and was looking for stories. The character of Maude (Bea Arthur) was Edith Bunker's cousin and the political polar opposite of Archie. Maude was married to her fourth husband, Walter (Bill Macy); and her best friend, Vivian (Rue McClanahan) lived next door.

Even though M&M had no *Maude* ideas yet, they asked

Sweet Lew to arrange a pitch meeting ASAP. Murph and Sean knew that when shows were hearing story pitches, there were a limited number of slots to fill, and plenty of competition from freelance writers

Murph looked through his current magazines, often a good source for topical story ideas, especially for Norman Lear shows like *Maude*. M&M's approach to story pitches now was to try to flesh out three "story ideas," each with a brief beginning, middle and end. And then list as many one or two line "notions" they could think of in the event that after pitching their three ideas, the producers/story editors were willing to keep listening.

When M&M met with *Maude* story editors, the legendary writing team of Bob Schiller & Bob Weiskopf, the Bobs, facing each other across double desks—the standard writing team arrangement—had just moved into new offices on Sunset Boulevard and were still learning how to use their multi-line push-button phones.

Following introductions, Weiskopf's phone began ringing and he started pushing buttons, confused, and asked his partner something like "How do you work this thing?" And Schiller said something like "It's a new invention. You pick it up and talk into it." And Sean & Murph started laughing. And Weiskopf picked up the entire phone and threw it at Schiller.

Later Murph said something to Sean like "At least he didn't throw it at us."

Needless to say, the four comedy writers were instant pals.

The current *TIME* magazine had a picture of a dog on the cover, and inside was an article about expensive pet funerals. One of the stories M&M pitched to the Bobs was Vivian's dog dies and she's planning an elaborate pet funeral, which Maude thinks is absurd.

One of the Bobs said something like "There could be something funny there..." which, to a hopeful writer, to offer a sports analogy, sounds like the wonderfully promising crack of a bat to a hitter. Now he/she just has to see if the ball stays fair and makes it over the fence.

The Bobs and M&M kick around a bunch of "What ifs." What if, at Maude's insistence, Vivian entrusts her cherished pet to Maude while Viv and Arthur go away and the dog dies? Maude is beside herself. How is she going to break this to Viv, her best friend? Viv misses her dog and calls to check on him. Walter tries to help out by barking near the phone. Viv says the bark doesn't sound like Chuckie, her dog. Maude makes some lame excuse. When they hang up, Walter suggests they get another dog that looks just like Chuckie. All four writers are laughing.

By now it was becoming more than clear to Murph and Sean that the way to land a script assignment for a series is to find a story they (the series producers or story editors) want to do. And the way to find a story they want to do is to meet with them, talk with them, listen to them, hear them and take copious notes (always have a pen and pad at hand). Never blindly write a script and take it...to...well, let's not go there, no need for M&M to beat themselves up anymore about that. But shouldn't their agent have known to...hey, didn't we just say, "No dwelling." Look ahead, not back. Murph had a consoling insight and later wrote it down: **A mistake is only a mistake if you make it twice.**

So M&M were sent off to write the story outline for "Viv's Dog." When they finished, Murph thought it was maybe the most solid story outline they had written to date. So when the Bobs called and informed M&M that Rod Parker, *Maude*'s producer, wanted to cut them off at story and have a staff writer write the teleplay, Murph &

Sean were…well, they weren't thrilled.

The Bobs seemed sincerely apologetic and almost embarrassed, telling Sean & Murph that it was a good, solid story and they did a fine job on the outline. "Viv's Dog" was produced; and later, when the Bobs went to Israel to appear at a comedy seminar, they made a point of telling Murph & Sean that the episode they took with them to screen was "Viv's Dog." Hey, no dwelling.

Murph was learning **there's more to writing than writing.** Note to perspiring writers: Thick skin. If you're planning to work in TV, develop it.

SOON AFTER, *CHICO and the Man,* a sitcom starring Freddie Prinze (who claimed in his stand-up act to be half Hungarian and half Puerto Rican, making him "Hungarican") as Chico and actor Jack Albertson as "the Man," had been picked up for a second season and was looking for stories.

M&M went to NBC to meet with the show's producer, Michael Morris, to pitch. They wrote three short synopses of potential stories and took them to the meeting. They sat opposite producer Morris, who sat behind his desk in his small office. Morris reached over to his inbox and picked up a copy of M&M's *Good Times* script, which Sweet Lew had sent as a writing sample.

"I read your script," said Morris. "Do you think this is funny?"

Murph & Sean looked at the producer, not sure where he was going with this.

Morris tossed the script back into his inbox. Then he leaned back in his chair, put his feet up on his desk, and slid his glasses onto his forehead as he said: "Let me tell you about comedy."

And he proceeded to quote some lines apparently from a *Chico* script and said, "Now that's funny." Neither Murph nor Sean was laughing. In fact, Sean stood up and stepped toward Morris, stopped only by the producer's desk. Murph was glad to see his partner's aggressive action, because it allowed Murph to play peacemaker, distracting Michael Morris by handing him the page with their story synopses and starting to pitch their three stories, none of which seemed to interest Morris.

After departing NBC, they called Lew and relayed their experience. Lew confirmed their suspicions that Michael Morris was neither a comedy professor nor the winner of a Mr. Congeniality Award.

A CBS PILOT titled *Joe and Sons* was picked up for the fall season of 1975 and M&M were invited to view the pilot and pitch stories. Richard Castellano played Joe Vitale, a blue collar widower raising two teenage sons. Joe's best friend, scatterbrained Gus, was played by Jerry Stiller.

Murph & Sean felt the show had promise and met with *Joe*'s congenial creator/producers, Bernie Kukoff and Jeff Harris. After a couple story ideas fell flat, Murph decided to pitch an idea based on a story he wrote for the school literary quarterly in college.

Murph's pitch went something like this: Richard Castellano plays Joe Vitale, so he and his boys are Italian, right? And if they're Italian, they're probably Catholic. And if they're Catholic, they go to Mass on Sunday. But what if Joe finds out his oldest son, Mark, isn't going to Mass on Sunday. Instead, he's hanging out playing pool with some friends. So Joe confronts him and Mark admits it, and at act break Joe says to Mark, "Well, you do believe in God, don't you?" And Mark thinks and says, "I don't know."

And in the second act Gus comes by and Gus is Catholic too and they're having this discussion about whether God exists. And we learn that even though Joe and Gus are the same religion, they have very different ideas about who God is. And Estelle, the neighbor across the hall stops in and she's Protestant and she says, among other things, "How do you know God's not a woman?" And Joe and Gus both laugh at this—"Everybody knows God's not a woman!"

Gus says he's seen pictures, and God is obviously a man with a long flowing beard. Joe says those are drawings, not photographs. Estelle asks Gus how old God is. Gus shrugs and says He looks like He's in his early sixties. Joe's younger son Nick asks Gus how tall God is. "Six four," says Gus.

Gus tells Estelle it says in the Bible that the Blessed Trinity is the Father, the Son and the Holy Ghost—not the Mother, Son and Holy Ghost. Nick says Sister Margaret told his class it's not the Holy Ghost anymore, it's the Holy Spirit. And it's not really a dove.

Joe says he knew there'd be trouble when they started letting guitars in church. Gus agrees, saying since they changed the Mass to English, he doesn't understand what's going on anymore.

Joe says, "Look, we should just let everybody decide for themselves what they think God is." Then Mark catches his father's eye.

Frankly, Murph was surprised when Bernie and Jeff said "Let's do it." He thought they might shy away from the God stuff.

So Sean and Murph wrote the story outline, then met for notes at either Bernie or Jeff's house. Sean thinks it was Bernie's house, but Murph seems to recall it was

Jeff's—although neither is dead certain.

But, whoever's house it was, one thing they're both sure of is that the meeting was in the master bedroom and the wife—either Bernie's or Jeff's—was seated at the vanity brushing her hair while the guys were gathered around the king-size bed for notes. Don't ask. Although Murph seems to recall there were kids in the kitchen eating breakfast with a nanny, which may provide some sort of an explanation.

WHILE MURPH & Sean were in the middle of the first draft of "Mark's Doubt" for *Joe and Sons*, Sweet Lew received a form letter addressed to M&M announcing that *The Jeffersons* was looking for story ideas and inviting them to pitch. The letter was signed by the show's story editors, Lloyd Tanner and Gordon Miller.

The Jeffersons, another spinoff of *All in the Family*, had aired mid-season with thirteen episodes and was now being picked up for a full season of twenty-four in the fall. The show was developed by Norman Lear and created by Don Nicholl, Mickey Ross and Bernie West, now a recognized writing-producing entity known as NRW Productions.

Knowing that Don, Mickey and Bernie were exec producing *The Jeffersons*, Murph and Sean were a little leery about pitching; since they figured that NRW would have to approve any writing assignments, and Don's "pebble on the beach" letter had seemed pretty definitive about whether NRW thought M&M would be right for their shows.

But then, they figured 'What have they got to lose?' Besides, they'd been watching NRW's shows, both *All in the Family* and the recently released spinoff starring George,

Weezy & Lionel, and they were more than curious to see if they could come close to solving the mystery of what NRW wanted.

So they scheduled a meeting with Tanner & Miller. Murph had noticed an article in *TIME* magazine about grown adoptees attempting to discover the identity of their real parents. This was a novel concept at the time.

What if a young woman appeared at the door saying she was Louise's daughter, and her birth certificate showed that she was born while George was away in the Navy? M&M fleshed this idea out a little and pitched it, along with two others, to Tanner & Miller. The story editors explained they would run the ideas by their bosses (NRW) and get back in a couple days.

In a couple days, Murph & Sean had a welcome problem. They'd be working on two assignments at the same time. Apparently, NRW approved the "Louise's Daughter" story and M&M headed to CBS to meet on story notes with Tanner & Miller. (It was a Writers Guild rule, and a good one, that if a show meets with a writer a second time on the same story, it's an automatic assignment.)

Both *Joe and Sons* and *The Jeffersons* were CBS shows, and coincidentally offices for both shows were across the hall from each other at CBS Television City. So M&M dropped off their first draft of "Mark's Doubt" at *Joe and Sons*, then crossed the hall to meet with Tanner & Miller on "Louise's Daughter."

Sean & Murph heard that a select list of established, more credited writers had received *Jeffersons* assignments and were in effect competing for a staff position for the coming season. And in fact, on a story board in *The Jeffersons* office, they noticed a few impressive names who were working on assignments.

So Sean & Murph were now busy writing two scripts, "Mark's Doubt" and "Louise's Daughter." And then a totally unexpected, if not crazy, thing happened. Michael Morris called. Yes, Michael Morris from *Chico and the Man*.

Apparently, the show's creator/exec producer, Jimmy Komack, came to Morris asking why they don't have more stories in the works. Morris explained he'd been meeting with writers, but hadn't come up with much yet. Komack asked to see any written story submissions and Morris gave Jimmy what they had, which included M&M's stories.

Bottom line, Komack sparked to one of M&M's stories and told Michael to put it in the works. So Michael called and wanted to meet again with M&M.

Neither Sean nor Murph were keen on seeing Michael Morris again; but Sweet Lew reminded them that they weren't exactly at the stage of their careers where they should be turning down work. "You hit the trifecta," said Lew. "You'll be writing three scripts at the same time."

The M&M story Komack liked was titled "The Invention," inspired by some ads that were running on television offering to assist inventors in marketing their inventions. Some of these companies were less than legitimate. The basic story was that Chico comes up with an invention which he hopes will help him strike it rich.

In their second meeting with Michael Morris, the producer told M&M to make Chico's invention "training wheels for a motorcycle." If your brow just furrowed or your entire face winced, you can imagine how Sean and Murph reacted. But they kept their thoughts to themselves. They didn't want to debate Michael Morris on what's funny or even what's believable. And they weren't sure whether the "training wheels for a motorcycle" was Jimmy Komack's idea or not.

Speaking of Komack, creator of *Chico* and other notable shows such as *The Courtship of Eddie's Father*, stuck his head in while M&M were there and said hi. Jimmy informed Michael that *Chico* was being brought in (delivered to the network) at 22:40 this season and then left.

Michael turned to M&M and said, "We're delivering at 22:40 this season." Now M&M were green, but they weren't too green to know there was no way they could be expected to write a second draft that would time out at exactly twenty-two minutes and forty seconds. But they continued to listen to whatever Michael Morris had to say, hoping to get out of there soon so they could get back to writing their other two scripts.

Cutting to the chase, as they say in Hollywood, M&M focused on writing and re-writing *The Jeffersons* and *Joe and Sons* scripts, and put the *Chico* thing on the back burner.

After delivering the second draft of "Mark's Doubt," Bernie & Jeff asked M&M if they had other ideas and Sean & Murph pitched a story about Joe's crazy Uncle Charlie coming to visit. Charlie's dementia is getting worse and Joe and the boys have to decide whether or not to put him in a home. Bernie & Jeff liked the idea and sent M&M off to write the story.

Two days after handing in the first draft of their *Jeffersons* script to Tanner & Miller, Sweet Lew got a call from Don Nicholl saying they wanted to meet with M&M for notes on the script. When Murph & Sean arrived, they were summoned to NRW's office where they met with Don, Mickey & Bernie for the first time since their lunch two years ago.

The guys (NRW) had their focus faces on, and they got right to work giving notes on the script. Murph was a little surprised Tanner and Miller weren't in the meeting, unsure whether that was good or bad.

Having completed the first season of thirteen episodes, *The Jeffersons* was preparing to shoot the first episode of the second season next week. Don mentioned that "Louise's Daughter" was "close," and they wanted to "move it up" to third in shooting order.

Murph wasn't sure if that meant their script was good, or that the other scripts were bad. But the notes were few, good and detailed; and Don asked M&M if they could deliver the second draft in a few days. Murph and Sean, of course, said something like "Sure."

So Murph and Sean rented a room at Sportsman's Lodge (hotel). They wanted to make sure they gave this rewrite their best shot—figuring if they could give NRW what they wanted, they could maybe get another assignment in the future.

Coincidentally, on their final night in the hotel room, as they were typing a second draft for delivery to NRW the next day, a rerun of *The Jeffersons* was on TV. Sean & Murph listened to George and Weezy as Murph sat typing at his typewriter.

At one point on TV, George yells "Aha!" to Weezy. So Murph, inspired by the TV, types a line where George says "Aha!" And then Murph has Weezy respond, "Don't you Aha me!" And George says, "I'll Aha you if I want—"Aha! Aha! Aha!" The writing theory here being that if one Aha is good, three Ahas are three times as good! It's a rhythm thing. And comedy is a lot like music. The Beatles didn't just sing, "She loves you, yeah." They sang, "She loves you, yeah, yeah, yeah…"

When Murph finished typing the last line of their script, he remembers saying to his partner, after two days of hard re-writing, "This is good. If they don't like this, they can kiss my a-double-s."

After their *Jeffersons* script was handed in, M&M realized their first draft of *Chico* was already two days overdue. They thought momentarily about just settling for story money and bowing out of the *Chico* script assignment. Then one or both remembered their rent payments, not to mention food for the kids.

So Murph & Sean decided to pull an all-nighter. They met at Murph's house with both typewriters, taped a page to the wall that said in large, bold numbers **$3,500** and went to work.

Ordinarily, they would talk out scenes in the first act, and complete a first act, which would propel them into the second act. But this night, they talked out scenes for both acts and then each of them wrote an act. Sean wrote in Murph's office and Murph typed in the kitchen, while Murph's wife and daughters slept.

When dawn broke, they had two twenty-page acts, and neither had read the other's act. They decided to have a copy made and then, because both were too tired to even walk, and, of course, because neither wanted to face Michael Morris with a script they've barely read, they asked Murph's friend Joe Bove who was visiting from out of town, to deliver the script to *Chico's* NBC office. Joe, a writer in his own right, was happy to be involved in show business.

After sleeping for what seemed like at least two days in their respective beds, M&M got a call from their agent. They'd been offered staff jobs by both *Joe and Sons* and *The Jeffersons*.

Well, you might think that Murph & Sean would be thinking, "Wow! This is our big break!" But frankly, Murph's first thought was simply, "It's about time!" Murph had an illuminating thought about the universe and he wrote it down: **Nothing happens overnight.**

M&M had a choice to make, but it wasn't really a Solomon's choice. *Joe and Sons* was a new show. It could get cancelled anytime. *The Jeffersons* was picked up for an entire season, twenty-four episodes. Bernie and Jeff were certainly talented, fun guys. But *The Jeffersons* was a Norman Lear show.

Not that Murph wouldn't mind taking notes in Bernie's (or Jeff's) bedroom again, especially if the hot wife were there in her robe…oops, now it's starting to sound creepy.

If you've ever tried writing or performing comedy, and condolences if you have, you may already be aware there's a thin line between creepy and funny. Defining that line is the secret to comedy. Murph had a thought and wrote it down: **Comedy is risk.**

As you've probably already guessed, M&M jumped at the chance to work on staff with NRW, their idols. Who better to work with and learn from?

They called Sweet Lew and asked if they could just deliver their "Uncle Charlie" story to *Joe and Sons*, and let someone else write the teleplay. Lew thought Bernie & Jeff would understand.

Then M&M realized they hadn't yet heard from *Chico* and they still owed them a second draft. They considered stopping in nearby St. Charles Church, lighting a candle and praying that they never heard from *Chico and the Man* again. But Murph imagined that if God decided to talk to them, He'd say something like, "Sure, I could do that. But it would be wrong. Besides, I already got you the staff gig with NRW. What more do you want?"

Murph called *Chico* and asked for Michael Morris, but instead was connected to another producer on the show, Ed Scharlach. Murph introduced himself and said he was calling about their first draft of "The Invention." Ed said no worries; they were going to take the script from here. Murph wanted to say something like "Great!" then hang up, look skyward and say "Thank you, God!" But Murph found himself insisting that Ed let them write a second draft, explaining they had to rush a first draft and felt bad about it. Ed said something like, "Okay, if that's what you want to do."

M&M attacked the second draft of *Chico* with newfound energy and purpose; and after they handed it in, Ed called and said "This script reads like it was written by two different writers!" Murph and Sean were relieved. But they vowed to never again write anything just for money.

Chapter 9

DESTINY

('75)

Funny how destiny works. Or doesn't work. Maybe destiny is bullshit. Maybe human beings, in spite of what we might like to think, control their own destiny. Or is there really such a thing as pure luck?

Two years ago, Murph's dream of working with Don Nicholl, Mickey Ross and Bernie West was dead. Finito. Kaput.

So what could explain this almost miraculous result? Murph remembers his mother telling him on more than one occasion: "The trouble with you is—you don't know when to quit." Was that true? Maybe, for Murph, that was both a blessing and a curse. And Murph remembered that word used by Harvey Miller—persistence.

Attempting to uncover a formula for success, Murph composed the following theory: **"The degree of success is directly proportionate to the consistence of the persistence."** Or, as Mark Twain wrote, "It's funny, but it seems the harder I work, the luckier I get."

And speaking of destiny, Murph couldn't help reflecting on the fact that M&M's first assigned script was for *Good Times*; their second and third for *That's My Mama*; and now, after "Louise's Daughter" was leapfrogged to the head of the show's production list, their first official staff job would be on *The Jeffersons*—all so-called "black shows."

If Murph's goal were to write relevant comedy for TV, this opportunity seemed relevant even beyond what *Laugh-In* and *The Smothers Brothers* could offer. It felt right. Like a perfectly-sized fur-lined glove in the winter. Like destiny or kismet at play.

In any case, here they were. Murph and Sean, reporting for work at their new office at Beverly & Fairfax, CBS Television City, working for their new bosses, Don, Mickey and Bernie. The job offer with *The Jeffersons* had a six-week option, meaning Norman Lear's production company, TAT, would have the option after six weeks to either release M&M, or keep them on staff for the rest of the season.

First day at work, they were greeted by Story Editors Lloyd Tanner & Gordon Miller. Lloyd and Gordon were older and more experienced. Before working together on the sitcom *Get Smart*, Lloyd was a writer for Jay Ward Productions, famous for the *Rocky and Bullwinkle* cartoon series, hands down Murph's favorite animated TV series; and Gordon had a distinguished career as a jazz musician.

One of Lloyd's unique features was that he had only one arm and, on occasion, he was not above asking if you would lend him a hand. In the jazz world, towheaded Gordon was known as "Whitey," probably a handle he avoided as a writer, especially while writing for *The Jeffersons*. Some friends who knew them referred to them as "Whitey and Lefty"—although Murph and Sean never pushed it that far.

Lloyd and Gordon took M&M under their wing. Gordon explained that every morning at 7:00 a.m. he and Lloyd met for breakfast at a local coffee shop; and they arrived for work at 8:00 a.m. Then they would work till noon and take an hour lunch break during which they would not work. "Eating and writing are two different activities," declared Gordon.

So for the next two days, Sean and Murph met for breakfast at 7:00 a.m. sharp and arrived at their new office at 8. After the second day, Murph and Sean agreed that 7:00 a.m. was too early to be meeting for breakfast and for them, writing and regimentation didn't mix.

'If this is what we have to do every day to be writing for television,' thought Murph, 'I'd rather sell furniture for a living.'

WHAT MURPH & Sean were about to learn is that staff writing is about re-writing. At least at TAT/Tandem. Norman Lear (whom everyone in the company affectionately called by his first name) was quoted as saying, "Around here a second draft is like a memo."

Staff writers rewrite other writers and rewrite themselves. 'The WGA should be called the Rewriters Guild,' thought Murph. NRW had given four scripts to M&M with the simple direction, "Read these and let us know what you think." Don also instructed Sean & Murph to listen only to them, not to Gordon or Lloyd.

Don was the alpha dog, albeit a few years younger than Mickey or Bernie. He was a long, thin Doberman Pinscher, who spoke with a British accent and used words like lovely and brilliant, except when talking about a script. Mickey was a cuddly Maltese Shih Tzu, a talented writer with an excellent story mind who had a flair for directing and loved working with actors. And Bernie, the joke-meister... well, perhaps Bernie could be a bug-eyed pug with specs and a hearing aid who embraced the role of foil and jester.

All, of course, were 'best in show' and had the distinctive pedigree of working with Norman from the very early days of *All in the Family*.

Upon reading the scripts in question, Murph felt, as he imagined NRW must feel, these drafts were, to be nice, far from ready to shoot. Murph was confident he and Sean could strengthen the stories, add humor and make the characters more consistent.

The first script they attacked was titled "George Won't Talk." The story line suggested an interesting premise where George, as a successful black businessman, was being invited to speak in Harlem but didn't want to go. But the script slogged along in obvious need of laughs and a more focused second act.

Murph & Sean kicked it around, then pitched the following to NRW: George is invited to speak to some students about his success as an entrepreneur. At first he thinks he'll be speaking at a college; but then he finds out the venue will be a basement in Harlem, near where the Jeffersons used to live.

A nicely attired black gentleman, the head instructor in this program, stops by and tries to convince George to come talk to some young people in Harlem about how to start their own businesses. George says he doesn't mind *talking* in Harlem, he just minds *walking* in Harlem!

The instructor says, "Ah, so that's it. You're afraid to go to Harlem."

George says, "Nowadays, even the Globetrotters are afraid to go to Harlem!"

The instructor, Mr. Thompson, tells George it will be

good promotion for Jefferson Cleaners, especially George's store in Harlem, and convinces George to give it a try for one night.

So in a couple nights George goes to speak in Harlem; but when he arrives home later, bursting through the door, he's furious. His cleaning truck has been vandalized!

In Act 2, Mr. Thompson shows up with a young black man returning the cleaning that was stolen from George's van. Thompson introduces the young man as "Train," the leader of the bunch who ripped off George's van. George reacts, taking off his coat, saying "Okay, Train, I'm gonna kick in your caboose!"

Mr. Thompson has to restrain George as Lionel enters and recognizes Train as his childhood friend from their old neighborhood. Turns out Lionel and Train used to steal apples from fruit stands, among other petty disturbances, when they were young. At this point in the pitch, Mickey says exactly what Murph & Sean hoped he would say: "There but for the grace of God goes Lionel."

So NRW sent M&M off to write the first draft of their first rewrite. When rewriting another writer's script, Murph & Sean felt an obligation of sorts to keep anything from the original writer's script—stage direction; a character name; dialogue, especially a joke—that would work in the new draft.

When Murph & Sean turned in their rewrite and met with NRW, the Trio reacted positively to the rewrite, with one notable exception. Don felt the Act Break line was too soft. When George returns from Harlem and tells Louise how they stripped his car clean—tires, wheels, carburetor, even his Willie Mays bobblehead—and swears they'll never get away with it, George says something like "See what happens when you try doing something nice for somebody, Weezy? No good deed goes unpunished!"

Don asked M&M to try to come up with a harder exit line. Now this hit M&M right between the eyes. Because Murph & Sean remembered well how Don reacted to their spec *All in the Family* script a couple years before. At that time, following Don's "Pebble on the Beach" letter, Murph sought additional info from Lew as to what exactly the Trio didn't like about their spec script and the only ambiguous hint Murph received was the word *soft*.

Now Murph was hearing that word again. Soft. He hated that word. M&M did not want their comedy writing to be branded as soft by anyone, especially NRW. If Don had said, "I don't like using clichés" (*No good deed goes unpunished.*), it would have made more sense, thought Murph. But what exactly does he mean by a *harder* line?

So for their next draft, Murph & Sean kicked around alternate act break exit lines and finally settled on one word—a word they felt no one, not even a staunch Brit like Don Nicholl, could call soft. So, for an act break line, M&M had George use one word referring to the criminals who ripped him off: *Niggers!*

After reading the recent rewrite, NRW met with M&M and Don said "Nice fixes...except for the Act Break line." And then Don said two words Murph was beginning to fear he'd never hear from Don Nicholl: "Too hard."

So the actual Act Break line became George saying something like, "Let that be a lesson to you, Louise. Don't ever ask me to do anything nice again!"

When "George Won't Talk" was taped, the role of Mr. Thompson was played by Robert Guillaume and "Train" was played by Ernest Thomas, both of whom went on to star in their own sitcom series—Guillaume in *Benson*, and Ernie as Raj in *What's Happening!*

ANOTHER SCRIPT M&M were asked to tackle was titled "George and the Manager." The script as it was had something to do with George having a problem with a manager of one of his stores, but there was no solid story line. In an effort to come up with something title-appropriate, Murph & Sean landed on an issue which, in the 1970's, had just begun creeping its way into the mainstream mindset—sexism.

Hard to believe, but until 1920, a little over 50 years before, women could not vote. Women were considered uneducated and, in the matter of politics, unimportant. Women were expected to be good wives, good mothers and, in the workplace, good secretaries or assistants. Even former male slaves in America were awarded the right to vote in 1870—although there were plenty of barriers imposed to keep blacks from the polls, especially in the South. Simply put, if you were born with a vagina instead of a penis, your vote did not count.

M&M pitched a new story and wrote a script where Emily, the assistant manager of George's downstairs store, enters and informs George that the manager has quit. Louise suggests that George make Emily the new manager. George hems and haws (mostly haws) and tells Emily he'll think about it and get back to her as he ushers Emily out the door, telling her to go back to the store and take care of things "like a good girl."

When Emily leaves, George chastises Louise for putting him on the spot in front of Emily.

"You know I can't make her my manager," he says.

"Why not?" asks Louise.

"Because (searching)...she hasn't been there long enough."

Louise points out that Emily has worked for George for

five years and is well qualified.

Lionel enters from the bedroom and George tries hard to change the subject; but Louise continues, asking George why he won't hire Emily as his new manager. Lionel chimes in with, "Hey, Pop, that's a great idea."

"Who asked you?" snaps George.

"Is it because she's white?" presses Louise.

"That's only half the reason," replies George.

Louise: "What's the other half?"

George: "She ain't black!"

Lionel reminds George that he already has a white manager in his Queens store.

George says that's right, he already has his "token white."

Louise and Lionel start to protest, but George tells them as a black businessman, he should hire black managers. If he doesn't, who will?

Lionel says there's a minority employment agency right next to his school and offers to contact them and let them know George is looking for a new manager. George is cool with that, but Louise still feels bad for Emily.

Sure enough, Lionel is able to get a solid recommendation for a new manager from the employment agency. When George comes home from work, Louise, Lionel and Jenny are there (Jenny is giving Lionel a haircut in the kitchen) and Lionel reads from the stellar resume' of job applicant Dale Parker, whose qualifications seem to be just what George is looking for. Lionel has arranged a 4:30 meeting and Dale Parker should be arriving any minute.

George tells Lionel a man's hair should be cut by a man barber; and Jenny mentions that a lot of men are getting their hair cut by female stylists these days. George thinks it's terrible how women are putting men out of work, wanting to take over men's jobs—like becoming managers.

"You think only men should be managers?" asks Jenny.

"Of course," says George. "That's why they call it manager, not womanager!"

The doorbell rings and George answers it to a well-dressed black woman.

Woman: "Mr. Jefferson?"

George: "What can I do for you?"

Woman: "You can make me your new manager. I'm Dale Parker."

In Act 2, Dale Parker introduces herself to Louise. George asks Dale why she has a man's name. Louise points out that Roy Rogers' partner also had a man's name.

George: "Trigger?"

Dale hands George a copy of her resume' and he proceeds to look it over while he pokes holes in her qualifications. Dale catches on pretty quick, realizing where George is coming from.

Dale: "My husband was one of those 'a woman belongs in the kitchen' men."

Louise: (interested) Really? How did you change his mind?

Dale: I divorced him.

Dale finally takes her resume' back and gives George a piece of her mind, telling him she would never work for a narrow-minded man like him; and as she exits, she advises George to remember that "Some of your brothers are sisters!"

With Dale gone, Lionel, Jenny and Louise try to shame George for his male chauvinism, but he refuses to back down. The doorbell rings and George opens it to Mother Jefferson, who enters. George greets his mother then continues arguing with Louise, Lionel and Jenny.

George: "No man should have to take orders from a woman!"

Mother Jefferson: "George, help me with my coat."

George reacts and helps Mama, to Louise and Jenny's amusement. George explains to Mother Jefferson that he needs a new manager for his store and MJ suggests he give the job to Emily.

George: "Not you too. Mama, women aren't cut out for tough jobs."

Mother Jefferson: "A woman raised you, George."

George tells his mother that running a cleaning business is a tough job and he can't be worried about watching what he says to a manager. Louise says there's nothing he can say to a man that he can't say to a woman.

George: "I can't swear at a woman."

Mother Jefferson: "George, you're talking like a damn fool."

Jenny and Lionel leave, and Louise finally convinces George to give Emily a trial as Acting Manager. As George goes to call Emily, Emily arrives at the door. Excited, she tells all present she has accepted a job with Feldway Cleaners as General Manager of all their cleaning stores. George says he was going to offer her the manager job and give her a raise, but Emily says she already promised Feldway. As she leaves, Emily thanks George for teaching her everything he knows about the cleaning business. "Yeah," grumbles George, "and now Feldway's gonna know it too."

"Now what am I gonna do?" George asks Louise and Mother Jefferson.

"We have no idea," says Louise. "We're just weak little women."

"That's right," says Mother Jefferson, as the two women

head for the kitchen. "We're just going into the kitchen where we women belong." And they exit as George reacts, foiled.

STILL ANOTHER SCRIPT M&M were asked to "save" was titled "George vs. Wall Street." The title suggests a story where George decides to explore investing in the stock market, which, on its face, seems to have good comic potential. The actual script, however, was very confusing with no clear story line and very little comedy.

You might wonder, as Murph did, how a script like this gets assigned in the first place. Who assigned it? Why? And how did a second draft end up so muddled and devoid of jokes?

But, if there was one thing Murph learned during his tenure in the corporate structure of Pacific Mutual, it was that there's no positive percentage in asking questions like that. Finger pointing is pointless. When your boss asks you to fix something, the only 'Who?' is you. The only 'Why?' is because you're asked. And the only 'How?' is how you're gonna fix it.

In this particular case, to throw up (pun intended) an analogy, staff writers are the script janitors of a TV series. If someone barfs in the school hall, the janitor's job is not to ask who barfed or why. The janitor's job is to clean up the mess.

So once again, taking a clue from the title, M&M struggled to find a stock-related story that would be both funny and understandable to the lay audience; and they settled on a simple investment in the futures market—George purchases bean futures, then roots for a flood to wipe out a major crop so bean values will increase.

It was a thin story which needed, as Murph & Sean

would say, "something else going on." You might wonder, when a script needs a total rewrite, including a new story, why not just toss it out and assign a new script? The simple answer is money. If a new script is assigned, a new deal memo must be drawn up with a new title. And the writer of that script must be paid full WGA price, even if the writer(s) is on staff.

So if a show has to "eat" a script and assign a new one, it affects the budget. But if a show can keep the same title and have staff writers "rewrite" the script, all's well that ends well on the bottom line. Thus Murph and Sean concluded that if they were ever to become Story Editors or Producers, a good rule of thumb would be: **Never assign a story or script that you can't rewrite yourself.**

So the 'something else going on' devised by M&M and approved by NRW, was George finds out that Lionel has turned down a $20,000 a year job offer. (Twenty grand was a lot of bread in the mid 1970s.) The offer is from a major company for employment as an electrical engineer, the field in which Lionel has always claimed he wanted to be involved. And employment would begin immediately after graduation.

Louise asks Lionel why he turned down the job.

Lionel says one reason is because he's not sure it's what he really wants to do.

"That's only *one* reason," offers George. "I can give you twenty thousand reasons for taking it!"

Lionel says he needs time to "find out who I am."

George says, "I'll tell you who you are. You're my son! And no son of mine turns down a $20,000 job offer!"

The episode takes place in real time, in the middle of the night, the first act in the Jefferson apartment and the entire second act in the Willises' kitchen, with George in his pajamas the whole time. Excited about a pending flood in Peoria (that will make him even richer), George has been boasting that, as a successful businessman, he's "living like Whitey!"

The interesting thing here is that George finds himself experiencing a mind-numbing situation not uncommon to other successful businessmen, mostly white, who can now afford to provide the first member of their family with a college education, only to discover that, since money is no longer an issue for the family, the child (in this case, Lionel) is less concerned with practical matters like a job or money, and more concerned with embarking on a personal quest to 'find oneself.'

During their first six weeks, Sean & Murph spent every waking moment focused on their work at *The Jeffersons*. This was their big opportunity, their big break, if you will, and they didn't want to blow it. If for some reason their option wasn't going to be picked up, M&M wanted to make sure it wouldn't be for lack of effort.

They arrived early on a Saturday morning to polish their rewrite of "George vs. Wall Street" before Don, Mickey & Bernie arrived to read it and give what Murph hoped would be just a few final notes.

When Don read the script, he came to M&M and said, "You guys have the big thing interrupting the small thing, when it should be the other way around." Don was right, of course. The B story (Lionel's job offer) had become the big story and should be treated as such.

Murph braced for more notes and a long weekend rewrite. However, Don knew M&M had been working hard the past few weeks and had put a lot of time into this particular rewrite. "We'll take it from here," said Don. "You guys take the day off." So M&M left NRW with their talented secretary/assistant Carol Summers, a respected member of Team Troika since the beginning of *The Jeffersons.*

IN THOSE DAYS, a half hour of prime time network television usually consisted of about 8 minutes of commercials and 22 minutes of actual show time. At two double-spaced pages per minute, the average half-hour script came to around 44 pages. (Rule of thumb for single-spaced movie scripts was one page per minute.)

A freelance *Jeffersons* script titled "Jenny's Grandparents" came in at 56 pages and, because the story line was so slow and confusing, it seemed to go on forever. When Murph & Sean met with NRW to discuss this script, Don asked what they thought. "We think it would make a good novel," said Murph. Both Don and Mickey gave welcome smiles.

The premise of this story was that Tom Willis's white father and Helen Willis's black father both objected to Tom & Helen's marriage and both have vowed never to step foot in Tom and Helen's house. It was tricky territory for a sitcom, but eventually the script was honed into a light-hearted farce on the heavy-hearted topic of prejudice.

BEFORE THE PASSING of six weeks, Sweet Lew called to say that M&M had been picked up for the rest of the 24 episode season. M&M were of course thrilled and their dependents were relieved. At least for now, Sean and Murph were doing exactly what they wanted to do and were getting paid for it. Does it get any better than that?

WHEN FREELANCE SCRIPTS are rewritten by staff writers, which happens 100% of the time, you may wonder how the on-screen *Written by* credit is determined. In general, the Writers Guild, which all working writers are required to join, strives to protect the interests of the original writer.

So in most cases, at least at Tandem/TAT, on-screen credit was awarded to the original writer or writers, no matter how much of the shooting script was actually a rewrite.

However, if a staff writer feels that he/she deserves to share on-screen credit for a rewrite, he/she may go to arbitration, a process adjudicated by the WGA. In this case, all written material from original outline to shooting script is provided to the Guild and a panel of writers is selected at random to read the submitted material and determine the appropriate credits. The submitted material is presented to the arbitration panel without the writers' names in an attempt to avoid any personal conflict.

Besides the obvious kudos involved, on-screen writing credit determines residual payments. Only on-screen credited writers receive residuals, which are paid on a sliding scale, but (thanks to striking writers in the 1970s) in perpetuity.

As mentioned before, the Writers Guild, in matters of arbitration, and in fact in all matters, gives benefit to the original writer, whether the work is for hire or speculative. In other words, if the story is even close, the original writer will receive sole Story credit. And only if the script is pretty much a total rewrite with a definite difference in words and intent, will a second or other writer receive or share Teleplay or Screenplay credit.

In their first season on *The Jeffersons* (Season Two), M&M chose not to arbitrate credit for any rewrite they did, except for "George and the Manager," where they arbitrated for shared Teleplay credit with the original writer and were awarded as requested.

After the first few shows of the season, M&M were listed in the on-screen credits as Program Consultants and, after their option pickup, as Assistant Story Editors. These credits appeared at the end of each episode at the top of the crawl, immediately following guest actor credits. These credits were not contractual, but were a nice gesture by NRW and appreciated by Murph & Sean.

Astute readers or viewers, like M&M's parents, might ask why not list Mick's and Sean's credits simply as 'Writers'? Once again, this is a WGA issue. The Writers Guild protects the 'Written by' credit by not permitting any other on-screen credit to include the word *writer*. Which explains (in some crazy way) why members of the writing staff on scripted shows are credited as Producer, Co-Producer, Story Editor, Script Consultant, Creative Consultant, etc. (This restriction is waived for late night talk or variety shows where a large writing staff can be listed simply as "Writers.")

A more accurate title for Executive Producer might be Head Writer or, a term which came into vogue in later years, Showrunner. Why would a writer want to be called a Producer or Executive Producer? Well here's how it happened.

In earlier years, shows like *I Love Lucy* listed credits simply as Producer, Director and Writer. But the writer, who was in charge of delivering a script each week, found his/her script being frequently altered by the Producer. When the writer protested, the Producer's actions were defended by "You're the writer, but I'm the producer."

At the end of the season, the writer, tired of seeing his hard work constantly changed each week, said he wasn't coming back to the show —unless he could be the Producer.

Finally, the Producer gave in and said, "Okay, you can be the Producer."

So next season, when the writer, now the Producer, saw his writing still being changed, he demanded an answer: "Why are you still changing my scripts? I'm now the Producer."

"Yeah," agreed his boss. "But I'm the Executive Producer."

MURPH WAS SURPRISED to learn that Mike Evans, who played Lionel on *All in the Family* and in the first thirteen episodes of *The Jeffersons* (Season One), was leaving the show. Apparently Mike approached Norman at the Season One wrap party and told his boss he was planning to move on in pursuit of other acting opportunities.

Murph remembered reading that Mike's casting was quite serendipitous. Supposedly Mike was hitchhiking and was picked up by Rob Reiner, who was on his way to work. Rob asked Mike what he did, and Mike told Rob he was an aspiring actor. Rob mentioned that a show he was doing was looking for a young black actor and suggested Mike audition. Mike did and the rest is TV history.

Mike Evans as Lionel was a likable, humorous, familiar character to *All in the Family* audiences and Murph could only think of two reasons Norman would let Mike slip away. One, Norman wouldn't want to stand in the way of anyone's career; and two, Norman may not want to set a precedent of offering more money to an actor just because he says he's leaving.

Murph was not fully aware at the time, but Norman Lear had an extensive entertainment background as a writer/ producer of both TV and movies. In TV, *The Carol Burnett Show*, *The Martha Raye Show*, *The Colgate Comedy Hour* and in movies, *Come Blow Your Horn, Cold Turkey, The Night They Raided Minsky's, Divorce American Style,* were just a few on the long list of Norman's credits.

Now the show had to find a new Lionel, which was not an easy thing to do. At that time, black actors in general and particularly young black actors were not readily available, simply because there were not many opportunities available for actors of color to practice and develop their craft.

Chosen as the new Lionel was a young man Norman supposedly saw and liked in a TV commercial named Damon Evans—no relation to Mike. Damon was a handsome, clean cut young man with a preppy appearance and persona; where Mike had a slight street edge which, Murph thought, made him more accessible and believable as someone who had grown up in Harlem and Queens.

But no one could question Norman's proven expertise in casting. *All in the Family* had introduced Bea Arthur as Maude, *Maude* had introduced Esther Rolle as Florida, and Florida begat *Good Times,* the first black family sitcom... and M&M's first TV writing credit.

Chapter 10

WORKING WITH NORMAN

('75)

W hen M&M started on *The Jeffersons*, the show's offices
were at CBS Television City, a large complex in the
Fairfax District of Los Angeles. Not long after Murph and
Sean started, offices and production facilities were moved
to a new site known as Metromedia Square, or Metromedia
Studios, located on Sunset Boulevard in Hollywood.

This was good for M&M because their office was
now closer to home, a straight 10-15 minute shot down
the Hollywood Freeway from their homes in North
Hollywood. With the move, all of Norman's expanding empire would be under one roof, including *All in the
Family*, *Good Times*, *The Jeffersons*, *Hot l Baltimore* and others
in development like *One Day at a Time*. The only exception
was *Sanford and Son*, starring Redd Fox, which was housed
at NBC and overseen by Norman's partner in TAT, noted
film director Bud Yorkin.

At Metromedia Norman's office was located on the

second floor, right above the *Jeffersons* offices. It was a large corner office, overlooking Sunset Boulevard and an entrance to the Hollywood Freeway. The office contained Norman's desk and personal items, plus a sizable conference table. On the wall was a large painting of Norman as a black man, a gift from Rod Parker, Executive Producer of *Maude*.

Writer/Producers from each show would meet with Norman in his office, one show at a time, to discuss stories for upcoming episodes. Writers from *Maude* might be inside, while writers from *Good Times* would be waiting outside for their turn. Each of these meetings was taped on Norman's hand-held cassette recorder and the tape was given to the writers as they left.

There was an obvious difference with NRW, who seemed to have more executive freedom than other series producers. Murph assumed that was because Don, Mickey and Bernie had worked in the trenches with Norman for longer and were key figures in the success and development of *All in the Family* and *The Jeffersons*. It appeared that Norman was more 'hands on' with his other shows than he was with *The Jeffersons*, maybe because he trusted NRW more, or because NRW insisted on it.

NRW took M&M to meet and discuss stories with Norman on a few occasions, and Murph was duly impressed with Norman's unique warmth and intellect. On the day following their initial meeting, Don said to M&M, "Norman likes you guys."

At first, Norman had trouble telling which Paddy was which: calling Sean, Mick and Mick, Sean. So Murph had two plastic nametags made which they wore around Norman. One said NOT MICK and the other said NOT SEAN.

Up to this point, in addition to re-writing scripts, M&M had been attending readings on Wednesday, run-thrus on Friday and Monday, and tapings Tuesday nights, contributing jokes or dialogue changes where needed or requested.

When they finished their latest rewrite, Don asked them to think of stories for an original. Murph had seen an article in *Ebony* magazine stating that the highest suicide rate in the United States was among black women. There seemed to be a variety of reasons, one of the key triggers being a romance gone bad.

In an attempt to figure how *The Jeffersons* might do an episode shedding light on this unsettling issue, Murph and Sean discussed a story where Florence is dumped by her boyfriend and is contemplating suicide.

They pitched this area to NRW and were met with a wall. Don said something like, "Suicide. Are you daft? No way. Forget it! Come up with something else."

Murph was surprised at their reaction. After all, *All in the Family* was known for dealing with serious subjects — that's what sets AITF apart from other sitcoms — and these were the guys who won Emmys writing for *All in the Family!*

But any notion Murph or Sean may have had about *The Jeffersons* doing an episode dealing with suicide among black women had just met a quick death. Back to the drawing board.

So M&M worked up some other story ideas and pitched them to NRW. The guys responded to two of them and Don told M&M to pitch those notions to Norman. So Murph & Sean met with Norman — just the three of them — and pitched those ideas. Norman listened but wasn't intrigued. He asked M&M if they had anything else. They didn't.

So Murph mentioned he saw an article in *Ebony* magazine saying the highest suicide rate in the country was among black women. Norman lit up like a neon sign! And the sign said Y-E-S! Murph said they were trying to see if they could do a story dealing with suicide involving Florence.

Norman jumped on it right away, saying, "Help brings problems into the household." (At this point Florence was just a recurring maid, not a live-in housekeeper.) Norman said something like, "We can open the play with the maid cleaning everything, spic and span. Louise is confused. This isn't like Florence. George is glad she's finally doing her job, acting like a maid. 'If she keeps this up, maybe I'll give her a raise!'"

So when they left Norman's office, Norman was excited about finding a new episode for *The Jeffersons* and M&M were wondering if they were going to be around to write it.

When they met with NRW, Don said, "Well, how'd it go?" When Murph explained what happened, Don's face turned to stone.

Murph tried to assuage Don, telling NRW he thought it could be a good episode. But the newest members of *The Jeffersons* writing staff were met with three cold stares and three words from the boss that were more of a dare than a directive: "Go write it."

"FLORENCE'S PROBLEM," THE title they gave their assignment, became M&M's problem. They were in the doghouse with NRW. In fact, they even wore disguises—plastic moustache nose-and-glasses—to the next run thru. It was an attempt at comedic diversion of sorts, an admission of guilt, with the added purpose of hiding their faces.

Hiding their faces because: if they were smiling, after

going over their bosses heads, they could seem smug, cocky, uncaring. If they appeared afraid, NRW might be afraid too—afraid these two twenty-somethings couldn't deliver what they were promising. And if they appeared mopey, upset, avoiding...let's *face* it (pun intended), there is no good facial expression for a situation like this.

So they had to develop a story and write a script about suicide. First, they did some research. Norman was right on the money—Murph was impressed. Seems it's not uncommon for persons planning suicide to be upbeat, resigned to a belief that they've found a solution to all their problems: they'll move on to a better place. But before they go, they often make an effort to get things in order. Which explains the prevalence of suicide notes; and also Florence wanting to get the Jeffersons' digs looking 'spic & span.'

So thanks to Norman, "Florence's Problem" has a beginning. Now what's needed are the middle and the end. M&M discussed the basic middle being Florence acting strange, Louise being concerned and George pooh-poohing Louise's concern. The end, or turnaround, was going to be tricky. Sure, you could do a misunderstanding story, where we find out that Florence isn't really thinking about suicide, but that would not be a Norman Lear show.

Murph and Sean figured they'd have to use the main characters—George, Louise, and probably Lionel and the Willises—to turn Florence around.

And they could use Tom Willis to lay in information (for the audience) about the prevalence of suicide among young black women. (Tom works for a large publishing company that publishes books on a wide range of subjects.) All this, of course, would come toward the end of Act 2.

When writing a script, Murph and Sean worked in a variety of ways, usually determined by the nature of the story itself. For instance, they might start by splitting scenes. One might say, "I can see the opening." And the other might say, "Okay, you write the opening and I'll take a shot at the turnaround." Or, with a simpler story, they might each take an act, write their act, then switch and rewrite each other's acts, then put the whole thing together and rewrite, cut (or expand), punch up and polish together. Or when a story needs to build beat by beat, like this suicide story, one scene thrusting them into the next, they will focus on writing the first act together, hoping to complete a tight Act 1 before moving on to Act 2.

Act One

ACT 1 STARTS with Florence in the kitchen, cleaning behind the refrigerator. When Louise enters, Florence is upbeat and joking. Florence mentions to Louise that today she's going to do something she's never done before, visit the top of the Empire State Building. She also mentions she saw *Lady Sings the Blues* last night for the third time.

Florence is working hard, cleaning the stove, etc. It's Friday, and Louise offers to give Florence the rest of the afternoon off; but Florence insists she wants to get everything spotless before she leaves.

George enters and calls out and Louise meets him in the living room. Louise tells George Florence has been cleaning everything from top to bottom and hasn't been acting like herself. George says, "Good, she's acting like a maid!"

Florence enters asking Louise where she should put the rags that she washed and ironed. Louise is surprised that she ironed the rags.

Florence mentions she did something today that she's been wanting to do for a long time. Instead of taking the crowded, smelly subway, she took a taxi to work.

When Florence returns to the kitchen, Louise says maybe the reason Florence is acting so strange is because she's in love. Maybe she met somebody. George says something like, "What about that turkey she's been seeing lately?" Louise says, "Wilbur? Florence hasn't seen him in months.' George says, "Yeah? Where'd he go?" Louise says Florence doesn't know, he just called her one day and said he was leaving town.

Florence is wearing her coat and carrying her purse, ready to leave. She attempts to make a long distance call to her favorite uncle in Detroit, but there's no answer. She says she wanted to call him and thank him for taking her to Coney Island when she was a little girl. Mr. Bentley, their British neighbor, stops by to borrow something and Florence asks him if she can do something she's always wanted to do: she gives Bentley a sweet kiss on the cheek. Bentley likes it and says since he's part French, she can kiss his other cheek if she'd like.

George exits to kitchen with Bentley to help him find the wok he came to borrow. Florence tells Louise of all the people she's worked for, Louise is her favorite. Then she hands a gold ribbon to Louise saying it's something special of hers that she wants Louise to have. And she tells Louise to say goodbye to Mr. Jefferson as Florence exits at front door.

Bentley and George enter from kitchen and when Bentley exits, Louise shows George the ribbon Florence gave her. George reads the ribbon which says, THIRD PLACE, 50 YARD BACK STROKE, Harlem Summer Swim Meet and a date. Louise: "I wonder what this means." George: "Simple. It means there were two chicks faster than Florence."

Lionel enters at front door, asking "What's the matter with Florence?" He says he ran into Florence in the lobby and she gave him a kiss on the cheek and sounded like she was going somewhere. Lionel to Louise: "She was giving an envelope to Ralph (the Doorman) for you, but she gave it to me instead." He removes a letter-size envelope from his coat pocket and hands it to his Mom. "Florence said to tell you not to open it till tomorrow."

George grabs the envelope. Louise protests: "Florence said I shouldn't open it until tomorrow." George: "Fine. You open it tomorrow. I'll open it today."

George opens the letter and reads: "Goodbye forever. Love, Florence."

Lionel: "That almost sounds like a suicide note."

George: "Get outta here, everybody knows black folk don't commit suicide!"

Louise is worried, but George says Florence was happier than ever today, laughing and singing and cleaning... "Didn't you hear what she said, she even took a cab to work for the first time ever."

Louise recalls, concerned: "There's something else she was gonna do for the first time today."

Lionel: "What was that?"

Louise: "She was going to the top of the Empire State Building."

Act Break.

Act Two

ACT 2 OPENS in the Jefferson apartment with Louise on the phone. She's trying to reach Florence, but Florence's phone has been disconnected. George says that's no surprise since she goes around blowing her money on cabs.

George tells Weezy to stop worrying, Lionel will find Florence. "But he's been gone for over an hour," says Louise.

The doorbell rings and it's Tom and Helen. Tom says Ralph told them Louise wanted to see them as soon as they got in. Louise tells them Florence has been acting strange and she's worried. She shows them the gold ribbon.

Helen reads it: "THIRD PLACE, 50 YARD BACK STROKE."

George: "Louise thinks Florence is going to kill herself."

Tom: "Just because she came in third?

Louise shows them the note Florence left.

Louise: "She said she was going to the top of the Empire State Building."

George: "Weezy, I told you, you can't jump off the top of the Empire State Building. It's fenced off."

Helen: "He's right about that, Louise."

Tom: "Of course, if you wanted to kill yourself, you could always get out on a lower floor and jump out a window."

George: "Florence ain't gonna kill herself."

Louise: "How can you be so sure, George?"

George: "I told you, she's black."

Tom: "You don't have to be any certain kind of person to commit suicide, George. All you have to be is lonely."

George: "How can Florence be lonely in a big city like this?"

Tom: "A crowd is the loneliest place, George."

George: (To Helen, re Tom) "Oh oh, you better keep your eye on this guy too."

Helen: "Tom did a lot of research for a book they published."

Tom: (To George) "You know the suicide rate among black women is rising higher than any other group?"

George: "That's not surprising, as long as they keep marrying people like you." (Laughs)

Louise: "George, this is serious."

George: "I am serious. Why would Florence want to kill herself?"

Tom: "Maybe she doesn't want to kill herself. Maybe she wants to be saved."

Tom points out that Florence left clues—the note, prized possession... He thinks Florence is crying out for help.

Florence & Lionel enter at front door. To get her here, Lionel told Florence that Louise was missing some cash and thinks Florence took it. Florence is outraged that Louise would think Florence would steal from her.

Helen asks Lionel where he found Florence. Lionel: "Standing on the sidewalk outside the Empire State Building." George: "What was she gonna do, jump off the curb?"

Florence: "Jump?"

They guide Florence to the sofa, sit her down, and tell her the real reason Lionel brought her back. Louise: "We were afraid you were going to jump from the Empire State Building." Florence: "Are you crazy? That would be painful! Splat! I'd be a human pancake!"

Louise shows Florence the note. Florence scolds, "You weren't supposed to open that till tomorrow." Louise: "It says 'Goodbye forever.' Are you going somewhere, Florence?" A beat, then Florence, resigned, says: "Yes, Mrs. Jefferson, I am. I'm going to God's house."

George: "Church?"

Florence: "No, Mr. Jefferson. (Smiling, with Reverie) I'm going to God's house in the sky."

Tom: "But I thought you said you weren't going to jump?"

Florence: "Lord, no. I'm afraid of heights."

Helen: (Concerned) "But you are going to…"

Florence: (Indicates purse) "I've got enough pills saved up to do it peacefully and quietly. I'll just take them when I go to bed tonight."

Tom: "Do you realize what you're saying?"

Florence: "Sure. When I wake up tomorrow, I'll be riding that chariot to the Land of Glory."

Louise: "Florence, we are not going to let you do this."

Florence: "Why not?"

Louise: "Well…because…because it's wrong."

George: "And it's stupid!"

Florence: "What's stupid about wanting to go to heaven? Don't you wanna go to heaven?"

George: "I'm waitin' till He sends for me!"

Florence: "Why wait? I mean, up there, there ain't no food bills, ain't no rent! Yes, Jesus. Ain't no hassling, ain't no dirt, and glory hallelujah, don't nobody never have to clean up up there!"

Helen: "You think God's gonna approve of you killing yourself?"

Lionel: "Florence, what if there isn't any heaven? What if when you die they just put you in the ground and that's it."

George: "Yeah, then you spend the rest of your life covered with dirt."

Florence: "Well, in that case, waitin' ain't gonna change nothin', now is it?"

George and the others react.

Florence: (cont'd) "Look I've been thinking about this for a while now—ever since Wilbur dumped me, in fact."

Helen: "Florence, how many times have you been in love in the last five years?"

Florence: "How many fingers you got?"

Helen: "Ten."

Florence: "Throw in a few toes and you're close."

Helen: "Doesn't that tell you anything?"

Florence: "Aw, it ain't just that. Wilbur was a turkey anyway. It's just...well, look at y'all, you got family, you got nice homes, you got so much money that you can even afford to be sick if you want to. All I got is a sore back."

Helen: "You've got plenty to live for. Money isn't everything."

Florence reacts with a hard stare.

Florence: "Well, ain't that a blip!"

Helen: "Sometimes Tom and I wish we were poor again."

Florence: "You better check your pants, girl, I think they're on fire! Tell the truth. (Looks around)How many of y'all would want to trade places with me? (Others react, sheepish) Well, c'mon, raise your hand. Um, hmm. Carried unanimously. You better check out now, Florence."

Tom: "I think you're being pretty selfish. Don't you care how your friends feel if you do something like this?"

Florence: "What friends? All I got is floors to scrub and windows to clean."

Helen: "We're your friends."

Florence: "You're my employers."

Louise: "We're your friends too, Florence. We care about you."

Florence: "About me? I'm only the maid. And I ain't even a very good one at that."

George: "She's right about that. She's a terrible maid!"

Florence: "Well, in your case, honey, you get as good as you deserve!"

George: "We only hired you 'cause nobody else wanted you!"

Florence: "You mean I only took the job 'cause nobody else would!"

George: "We only let you keep it because we love you!"

All react surprised, looking at George.

Florence: "You what?"

Lionel: "Don't you see, you're more to us than just a maid. You're like one of the family."

Florence: "Lord, I thought black folks only heard that in white homes."

Louise: (crosses to Florence) "If we didn't love you, you think we'd be worried about you like this?"

Florence: "Aw, you're just sayin' that 'cause I said I'm gonna kill myself. You don't really mean it."

George: (crossing to Florence and Louise) "Wait a minute! Are you calling my wife a liar?"

Florence: "No, I..."

George: "You know how many fights Weez and I have had about you? I'm gonna tell you the truth, a couple of times you made me so mad I was gonna fire you. But Weezy told me she wouldn't talk to me if I did. So look, if you wanna kill yourself, go right ahead. But if you do, you damn well better realize you'll be hurting somebody who really cares about you."

Florence takes it in. Florence: "Oh, Mrs. Jefferson, I don't wanna hurt you."

Louise: "Then don't do it, Florence."

Florence: "Oh, Mrs. Jefferson... (starts to cry, searching her purse) I gotta get something to blow my nose..." (exits to bathroom)

Tom: "I think she's gonna be okay now."

George: "Yeah, now maybe. But what about tomorrow?"

Lionel: "Yeah, if she thinks about killing herself once, she could do it again."

Tom: "Not according to the experts. Just because some-body thinks about suicide once doesn't mean they keep on thinking about it. Florence just found out somebody really cares about her. By tomorrow, she'll have forgotten all about those pills."

Helen: (realizes) "The pills!" All react.

Louise: "She's got 'em with her in the bathroom."

George: "Never mind about the pills. What about the razor blades! (rushes to bathroom and yells through door) Florence, you mess up that bathroom, I'll kill you!"

The bathroom door opens and Florence steps out holding empty pill bottle.

Louise: (Worried) "You didn't take them!?

Florence: "No." She reaches into bathroom and flushes toilet. "I just got rid of 'em. I won't be needing 'em now. I'm sorry, I just... Well, you know." Florence crosses to wastebasket and tosses pill bottle. "Well, that's that. I guess I'll be going now..."

Tom stops Florence and asks her to come upstairs for dinner with Tom & Helen. George redirects Florence and says, "She can't. She's having dinner with us." Louise suggests the Willises join them for dinner at the Jeffersons.

George protests: "Why? They weren't gonna kill themselves."

Helen makes Florence promise that if she ever gets to feeling blue again, she will come talk to Helen or Louise. They all agree to dinner at the Jeffersons. End of Act 2.

It took M&M two weeks, one week per act, to finish the script. During that time, they heard nothing from either NRW or Norman about the script. No one, not even Bernie, stopped in to ask how it was going or to pitch a joke. Sean & Murph figured Don must have put Bernie on special notice that M&M's office was quarantined until they either emerged with a completed script or came out with heads down and hands up saying, "You were right. Suicide isn't funny."

So they tightened it up and, at an even 44 pages, they delivered the script to the official NRW wrangler/assistant, the lovely Bea Dallas, for distribution to the supreme troika.

The following day, not a word from NRW. Day two, still nothing. Both Murph & Sean remembered well what happened the last time they submitted a script to Don, Mickey & Bernie without any discussion or notes from the trio. On Day 3, Sean, only half joking, started to clean out his desk and suggested that M&M start writing their own suicide note.

So Murph said something like "Screw it" and started off for Don's office. Bea had stepped away from her guard station, so Murph was able to slip into Don's office where he found Don seated at his desk putting pen to paper, probably writing another 'pebble on the beach' letter.

Don looked up and Murph said, "Have you had a chance to look at our script?" Don nodded.

Murph: "What did you think?"

Don: "Not bad."

'Not bad.' Hallelujah! Murph swore he heard angels. He almost sprinted back to tell Sean what Don said: "Not bad."

Sean sprang up and they high-fived! Those two words from Don were the equivalent of three Gold Stars and a holy card from Murph's 7th & 8th grade teacher, Sr. Mary Pius.

The only major note M&M got from NRW was to rewrite Florence's note at act break. Don just chuckled at Florence's note and said it was "Too too."

Murph & Sean weren't too sure what Don meant by "too too," but they examined the suicide note—"Goodbye forever. Love, Florence."—and decided it was indeed too too—too short and too cartoonish—sounded like something Wile E. Coyote might say immediately before being run over by a steamroller. Maybe it was the word *forever* that was the problem. So they left out that *f word* and fluffed up the note just a touch to say: "Dear Mrs. Jefferson, Thank you for everything. Goodbye. Love, Florence."

When "Florence's Problem" aired, the show received strong positive response from viewers and from Suicide Prevention groups.

Below is one of those letters from a viewer:

January 24, 1976
LETTER TO ISABEL SANFORD
FROM JEFF STEVENETT
LONDON, ONTARIO (CANADA)
I think you are one of the best actresses and I try to watch The Jeffersons every Saturday. Tonight I was watching it and something happened to me that never happened before.

It was the one when Florence, your maid on the show was gonna commit suicide, and this is the truth, I cried. It was the sadest (sic) show that I've ever seen and I couldn't even laugh at the jokes when she was talking to you and the Willises. I guess because I get that way so many times; but when someone I don't know who said "What will the people that love you think" it made me realize that life could be worth living. I'll try to make it short.

I'm only 16 last Jan. 20. ...I hope I will meet you someday and until then "please be my friend."

M&M received an invitation to speak at the American Association of Suicidology. No joke. That was and still is a legitimate organization. Here is an excerpt from that totally unsolicited letter:

> *You will be members of a panel of approximately six to eight media journalists (writers, TV, and radio) and asked to respond to the question "Is there more the media can do to help the prevention of suicide?" We would also like you to talk about the "Jefferson" episode with Florence. Perhaps you would like to show five minutes of the tape, if you feel it would help get your point across. How did you create the idea of the suicidal episode and finally bring it to fruition in such a real, human, sensitive, compassionate and educational way? Needless to say, I think you are both great writers.*

Also needless to say, Murph & Sean were not averse to meeting with anyone who had the good sense to recognize that they were indeed great writers. So they were honored to appear at the AAS event held at the Downtown Los Angeles Hilton on April 30, 1976.

Murph began his short speech with, "Before we wrote the *Jeffersons* episode, I didn't know much at all about suicide. In fact, I hadn't even tried it."

His remark unearthed some scattered chuckles and a few smiles, but not the general guffaw Murph had hoped, reminding Murph of the number one rule of comedy: 'You gotta know your audience.' **Comedy is risk.**

Regarding "Florence's Problem," M&M were duly appreciative of and impressed with the impeccable acting of *The Jeffersons* ensemble and the astute staging/directing by Jack Shea, who had directed *The Jeffersons* pilot and every episode since.

The ability to navigate that razor thin tightrope between comedy and drama in the turnaround scene (thought Murph as he watched the tape two or three times) was classic. Quadruple threat—actor, writer, producer, warm-up specialist—Bernie West, was fond of saying that an actor should bring at least 50 percent to a line; and Murph truly felt that in that climactic scene, the entire cast, even Damon Evans as Lionel (who was now growing on Murph) contributed at least 80 percent.

It was the first episode featuring Florence as a central character, and actress Marla Gibbs expressed her appreciation in a Kwanzaa card note to M&M which read: *Thank you! You helped to make my year! Happiness to you & yours and special thanks for "Florence's Problem." Marla!*

Of course, through all of the accolades M&M and the others were experiencing as a result of this episode, it was fully realized by Murph that none of this would be happening without the courage, passion, vision, persistence and talent of Norman Lear.

In case you're not familiar with Norman Lear shows— and it's quite likely you're not—at least not so familiar as were Murph and Sean, who had been watching and studying shows like *All in the Family, Maude* and *Good Times* for a while now, these shows are two-act plays taped in front of a live audience. Pretty much like the pioneer sitcom *I Love Lucy*.

What Murph liked about shooting a comedy in front of an audience is they'll tell you whether or not it's working. If they're laughing, it's working. If not—show's in trouble.

Each episode is performed twice, once at 5:00 p.m. and once at 8:00, each in front of a different audience. The five o'clock show is known as the "Dress" show (short for Dress Rehearsal) and the eight o'clock show is referred to as the

"Air" show. This mimics a standard theatre production where you might have a dress rehearsal before the play is staged for an audience. The difference here being that both shows are taped and then the best of both are edited into a final cut for airing.

In between the 5:00 and 8:00 shows, catered dinner is provided for the cast, staff and crew. Then the writers, producers, director and cast meet for notes, which include any script changes. For instance, if a joke doesn't work at the 5:00 show, a new line can be provided for the 8:00 show.

In Norman's productions, respect for the audience is paramount. To protect the story line from being revealed too soon, certain upcoming sets are masked from the audience, and guest performers are introduced at the end of the show, not the beginning. The ideal Norman Lear show takes place in real time, with no costume or hair changes. All attempts are made to perform the show straight through, with few or no stops. Following the 8:00 show, the audience is released and any mistakes—lines, camera shots, or others—that need to be corrected are handled in "pick-ups."

These shows are called multi-camera shows because they're shot with more than one camera—usually three. While Norman Lear sitcoms are taped, other multi-camera sitcoms at that time, like *The Mary Tyler Moore Show* and *The Bob Newhart Show* (MTM Enterprises), and *Happy Days* (Paramount), were shot on film. Film provided a grainier appearance than tape, giving a certain distance to the finished product. Producers of filmed sitcoms seemed to like film, thinking they were doing little movies.

Murph, on the other hand, preferred tape, especially for what he thought of as "Living Room" comedies like *All in the Family*, *Maude*, *Good Times* and *The Jeffersons*. These shows were essentially plays as opposed to movies. And tape had a clearer appearance, making viewers at home feel they were watching a live play.

The characters in Living Room comedies were primarily nuclear families (as opposed to workplace ensembles) and the main set in these taped shows was the family living room. So to Murph, watching a show in your own living room at home which took place in another living room felt much more intimate on tape than on film.

Tape also had the advantage that it was more precise and easier to edit than film. What you see on tape monitors in the production booth and on the stage is precisely what's in the camera. Where in a film production, only the camera operator sees exactly what the camera is shooting, which can serve up certain surprises in the editing process.

With tape, thought Murph, there's more 'immediacy.' The laughter and viewing experience feels more personal and inviting. And he figured Norman must feel the same way.

Chapter 11

HANGING WITH
GEORGE & WEEZY

('75)

George Jefferson is an aggressive, boisterous, cocky dude with a black chip on his shoulder holding what he (and others) would consider to be a legitimate grudge against "Whitey." Sherman Hemsley is none of these. Sherman is a quiet, shy, unassuming individual for whom color distinction does not exist and who signs autographs (and never refuses) with the salutation, "Peace & Love." In fact, the name of Sherman's company: "Love Is, inc."

Where George Jefferson appears most comfortable in tailored suit, tie and expensive shoes, Sherman's everyday outfit is white T-shirt, jeans and worn sneakers. Sherman has no car, thus the show provides a driver.

Sherman caught Norman's eye on Broadway in the musical *Purlie* playing the role of Gitlow; and Norman immediately tagged him for a series star.

It didn't take M&M long to learn that Sherman, who

would slip into their office and nap on the sofa between rehearsals, felt most at home hanging with the lowest braves on the tribal totem pole. If script supervisor Sylvia O'Gilvie or Sherman's driver David Hoberman couldn't find him, they'd just look in M&M's office. (Hobie, by the way, went on in later years to become President of Disney Studios and model for the lead character in the movie *The Player*.)

Wife Weezy, played by Broadway actress Isabel Sanford, kept the show grounded, both on and off stage. Best word to describe Isabel is the name on her license plate, TROUPER. Isabel's work ethic was second to none; a pro's pro. Always in good spirits, she studied hard, always knew her lines and never complained.

Isabel was recognized by the rest of the cast, crew and staff as official "Queen" of the show. Curtsies and acknowledgements such as My Queen, Your Majesty and from writers even My Ebony Goddess, My Lovely Liege and My Weezyness abounded.

At pre-show introductions, Isabel was always introduced last as the star of the show, greeted by other cast members, crew and staff on stage with affectionate bows and applause. There was never even a hint of jealousy from Sherman nor from any of the Queen's other co-stars.

Murph didn't realize it at the time, but Isabel was quite a bit older than Sherman, like twenty years. Where were the wrinkles!? As co-star Roxie Roker might explain, "Black don't crack."

Roxie played Helen Willis, the stylish African American wife (by way of the Bahamas) of guileless white husband Tom Willis, played by congenial Broadway actor Franklin Cover.

When Roxie auditioned for the role of Helen Willis,

Norman explained that her character would be married to a white man. Norman told Roxie he would understand if she had any qualms about doing a role like that. Roxie removed a photo from her wallet and showed Norman her husband of fifteen years, a white man named Sy Kravitz. (George to Helen: "Black coffee is stronger than coffee with cream anytime." Helen: "But it ain't as sweet!")

The character of Jenny, Lionel's charming fiancée and the Willises' daughter, was played by Berlinda Tolbert. Although Jenny is passionate, attractive and obviously black, George refers to her as a "zebra" because she's the product of a black-and-white marriage.

Rounding out the regulars was multi-talented New York actor Paul Benedict in the role of Mr. Bentley, the Jeffersons' eccentric British neighbor; and veteran actor Ned Wertimer as Ralph, the building's greedy Doorman. Coincidentally, Ned, in real life, was in an interracial marriage. His wife, Skyne Uku, was a college professor with a PhD in ethnic studies.

The show received lots of letters, both positive and negative, relating to the appearance of an interracial couple in a TV series. Here is an unabridged missive from a viewer in Louisiana who was watching and writing every week:

New Orleans, La.
19 October, 1975
To: Mr. Franklin Cover – C/O Cbs, Burbank, Cal.
(As husband of black wife in tv sketch)
Program: "The Jeffersons"–CBS-TV, 10/18/75)
Just to repeat our previous comments and to reach a few more sponsors:

With about 90% of the people against black and while interracial marriage it's rather nauseating watching you low-grade cockroaches helping those goddam Marxists' producers to sell miscegenation to the American people.... preparing them to accept the Marxists' long standing goal of mass-hybridization.

It is commonly known that mass-hybridization (via miscegenation of course) is the bottom line in the Communistic book – which is now getting special attention in all entertainment areas, mainly on TV.

Mass-hybridization (miscegenation – hooked on with the current glorification of vulgarity, funky jungle culture, gore, sex, perversion, crime, lust, violence, brutality and murder...are the preoccupations of our Marxists' producers –(spiritual comrades of the un-American Hollywood Ten) – in their steady strategy to produce the maximum of chaos, moral decomposition, weakening and final disintegration of American society....to which the moronic Franklin Cover apparently is gladly cooperating.

Very Truly yours,
(Signed)
Sydney Greer,
Gretna, La.

Copies to: Producers, "The Jeffersons" – Pres. CBS
President, Ralston Purina Co. ("Cat Chow)
President, The Pillsbury Co. ("Figuerine)
President, Chesebrough Ponds, inc. ("Q – T")

One day immediately following a run-thru, Isabel suggested they call Mr. Greer and thank him for watching the show. So the cast and others including Murph and Sean went to the offices, put the phones on speaker, located the number, and called Mr. Sydney Greer of Gretna, Louisiana. The phone call went something like this:

Other end of phone: Hello.

Isabel: Hello, is this Mr. Sydney Greer?

Greer: Yes, who's this?

Isabel: This is Louise Jefferson. I'm here with the rest of the cast and we just wanted to call you and tell you we really appreciate you watching our show.

(Silence on Greer's end.)

Isabel: Would you like us to send you a picture of the cast?

(Stifled laughter on this end.)

Franklin: Hi, Mr. Greer. This is Tom Willis. Would you like a picture of Helen and me?

(No response.)

Franklin: We have one of Helen sitting on my lap?

(Restrained laughter on this end. Crickets on other end.)

Sean: We also have one of Tom sitting on Helen's lap.

(Raucous laughter. A click on the other end.)

And neither the Jeffersons nor the show's Marxist producers ever heard from Sydney Greer again.

THE WRITING STAFF of *The Jeffersons* at this point consisted of NRW, M&M and T&M (Tanner & Miller). Either T&M or M&M would write or rewrite a script, then it would be passed up to NRW who would do the final polish/rewrite.

Soon after M&M began on staff, there was a commotion in front of the Metromedia building and Murph and Sean went out to see what was going on. Someone had jumped off the freeway overpass on Sunset Boulevard. As they stood on the overpass near Bob Schiller and Jackie Elinson (writers will embrace any diversion), someone said, "I wonder who it was." Schiller responded, "It was probably a Tandem writer." And Jackie said, "If he left a suicide note, they'll probably rewrite it."

After the final rewrite, a script is sent to mimeo. At that time there were no computers/printers as such, and multiple script copies were made on a mimeograph machine. The paper and ink used in the mimeo process combined to produce a distinct feel and smell; and to writers like Murph or Sean, or cast members, or anyone involved in production, the mimeo smell delivered a uniquely satisfying high, indicating to all that production was imminent.

As a rule, the cast and staff would gather in the rehearsal hall on Wednesday morning at 11:00 for a table reading of the script. *The Jeffersons* rehearsal hall, by the way, had a straight-on view of the Hollywood Sign high on the hill above Sunset Boulevard. If there were cell phones back then, Murph probably would've taken a selfie through the floor-to-ceiling rehearsal hall window with the iconic Hollywood Sign in the background and posted it on social media.

The cover of each script contained the name of the show, the title of the episode and the names of the director and credited writer(s) for that episode. Each week's script cover would be a different random color so it could be distinguished at a glance from the previous week's script. Don had one hard rule about script covers—no green. Apparently, there's a British theatre superstition about green being bad luck.

Producers, writers, director, staff and production crew along with a representative or two from the studio and/or network would be present. For the writers, this reading is important because it allows them to hear the lines in the mouths of the characters. It's also important for timing—it gives the script supervisor an initial idea of how long the show will be.

Following lunch and maybe a few line changes, the director and cast begin rehearsing Wednesday afternoon. Any substantial line changes are printed on colored pages, usually pink (never green), which are delivered to actors and inserted into the script (in place of former pages).

Rehearsal continues all day Thursday and Friday morning. Friday afternoon all re-assemble for a rehearsal of the play known as the "Producer's Run-thru." At this run-thru actors are expected to be "off book" (know their lines). If an actor should "go up" (forget a line), he/she can call out "line" and the script supervisor, who works closely with the cast and director, will read the appropriate line.

Following this run-thru, the cast is released, and the writer/producers meet with the director and script supervisor for performance and line notes. The director will communicate any performance notes to actors on Monday morning on stage, where sets for the episode will be up and cameras will be present.

Monday is blocking day—the day when the director works with the camera crew and actors to "block" the play on camera. Writers and actors like Mondays because this is the first time the camera crew will see and hear the play. A camera operator's laugh helps convince both writers and actors that a joke line still works. This is also the first time the writer/producers will see the camera shots on the stage monitors.

Following a camera run-thru Monday afternoon, the director and writer/producers meet again for performance, line and camera shot notes. These notes will be incorporated in Tuesday's rehearsal.

On Tuesday, a final camera dress rehearsal and note session is usually held before the 5:00 audience is brought in; then following the 5:00 taping, the cast and crew break for dinner and final notes before the 8:00 show, as previously mentioned. Noteworthy here is that before joining the others for dinner, Sherman makes a plate of food and takes it down to the security guard at the main entrance. (Bet Mary Tyler Moore doesn't do that.) How could you not love, and work hard for, a guy like that?

WHEN THE NEW fall series *Joe and Sons* premiered, M&M's episode, "Mark's Doubt," was aired as the first episode instead of the pilot and received stellar reviews. You may recall this was the episode where Joe's son says he's not sure if he believes in God.

CBS took out full page ads in both trades listing excerpts from no fewer than fifteen separate reviews of the episode. Here are some of those excerpts:

"The best writing I've heard on any of the new shows was in JOE AND SONS...even Mark Twain would have been proud to author...it was funny and profound, and for the Family Hour, more adult than a lot of the shows that come later."
~John Barbour NBC TELEVISION

"The show is full of the kind of slightly offbeat, rapid-fire writing that makes a program move...quick, punchy dialogue...the stuff of which hits are made."
~HOLLYWOOD REPORTER

"...at once, touching and hilarious...pace and construction are as good as the gags on this show...more important, anyone—regardless of race, creed or income—can really sympathize with the characters...in short, "JOE AND SONS" features human beings, comically exaggerated, to be sure, but solid and recognizable."
~TIME MAGAZINE

"...fast and funny...the lines crackle...establishes "JOE AND SONS" as a winner."
~NEW YORK POST

"...this week's funniest TV...a few more as good and "JOE AND SONS" could make the survival list."
~NEW YORK TIMES

"JOE AND SONS is a first rate comedy...it is witty, relevant, and it smacks of reality...JOE AND SONS will be a hit."
~CHICAGO SUN TIMES

"...believably and warmly drawn...a haven for those who are weary of glib one liners and phony situations...great dialogue..."
~THE PHILADELPHIA EVENING BULLETIN

"...an eminently viable show...blue collar in tone and broad comedy in format...It has the potential to be one of the best new comedies on television."
~THE CLEVELAND PLAIN DEALER

"...has a spontaneous flow...a rhythmically funny immediacy...in a way that often doesn't evidence itself so early in a series."
~LA HERALD EXAMINER

"...the most welcome family on the sitcom block since the Bunkers."
~Jay Sharbutt – AP

A show that debuted in the same time slot on another network was titled *Welcome Back, Kotter*, starring comedian Gabe Kaplan as a teacher who returns to his high school alma mater to teach an academically-challenged group of teens known as the Sweathogs.

Where *Joe and Sons* was praised by the critics, *Kotter* was universally panned. *'Joe' Deep Comedy; 'Kotter' Lacks Taste,* read one headline. Reviews employed terms like "silly," "repulsive," "unbelievable" and "about as funny as a funeral" to describe Kotter, predicting it would be "a sure flop."

Funny thing is, by the end of the season, *Joe and Sons* was cancelled and *Kotter* was TV's new hit! Guess they didn't see Barbarino coming. The Sweathog character of Italian Stallion Vinnie Barbarino was a breakout role for John Travolta, who went on to become, well, John Travolta!

TV GUIDE WAS a weekly publication listing what was on each TV channel every day. Murph looked through it religiously, usually checking to see what stories other shows, especially sitcoms, were doing.

When he checked the week's episode for *That's My Mama*, he was surprised. It sounded exactly like an episode he and Sean had pitched to *That's My Mama* about a year ago. When he checked further, he learned the credited writer was Larry Stigler, the same person to whom Murph & Sean had pitched.

It was the "ugly girl" story, where Clifton is dating a girl who's easy on the heart but not so easy on the eyes, and he's facing peer pressure and teasing from both Earl and Junior, and even a little shade from Mama.

So Murph called Larry to ask 'What's up?' Larry apologized and immediately fell on his sword, saying something like, "When you're in a pinch, you do desperate things."

The show agreed to pay story money to M&M. Technically, screen credit should also have been changed— from *Written by Larry Stigler* to *Story by Mick Murphy & Sean*

Malloy, Teleplay by Larry Stigler. That way M&M would share in any residuals. Credited writers are guaranteed residual payments—fifty percent of the original fee for first rerun on network series. Not to mention decreasing amounts for future runs.

But Murph & Sean figured *Mama* wasn't going to be around for too many reruns, plus the extra bread was manna from heaven, gravy, found money! They hoped more shows would steal past stories they pitched—except for *Chico*.

MURPH AND SEAN shared the same philosophy about their occupation: they both believed being comedy writers should be fun. Anything that resulted in a laugh was fair game. Especially practical jokes.

When *The Jeffersons* first moved to the new Studio, Murph and Sean noticed that everyone in the parking garage parked *head in* except Tanner & Miller. Lloyd and Gordon both backed in, parking *head out*, ostensibly so at the end of the day they could be the first ones off the lot.

So M&M composed an official-looking parking notice and employed the new state-of-the-art Xerox machine to reduce the notice to a smaller size and placed a copy on both Lloyd's and Gordon's windshields. The notice was signed by "B. Jaslow" (made-up name, signature looked a lot like Sean's), Studio Parking Enforcement.

The next day when Murph and Sean arrived, both Lloyd's and Gordon's cars were parked head in. So both Murph and Sean backed in, parking head out. Later, when Lloyd and Gordon returned from lunch, they came in to M&M's office and told the assistant story editors they were not allowed to park head out. M&M had expected T&M to realize it was just a joke, but the Story Editors fell for it hook, line and sinker—even mentioning B Jaslow, head of parking enforcement! So...neither Murph nor Sean wanted to fess up to what they'd done for fear of either embarrassing or pissing off their fellow writers.

So they thanked T&M for the *heads up* about the *heads in* parking rule and promised not to park heads out again.

WHEN BERNIE WEST told Murph about the new series NRW was developing, Murph thought Bernie was joking. The conversation went something like this: Bernie: It's a show about two fat people who've been blissfully married for fifteen years and never had even one fight. Murph: Where does this take place, Mars? Bernie: They own a small take-out lunch counter in Manhattan. Murph: So the series starts with their first fight, right? What's the fight about? Bernie: No, I told you. They never fight. Murph: Is this a comedy? Bernie: Of course. Murph: What do you do for jokes? Bernie: Fat jokes. They're both obese. Now Murph was sure Bernie was joking. Murph: Bernie, how gullible do you think I am? You shoulda saved this one for April Fools'.

When Murph learned from Don and Mickey that Bernie wasn't joking, Murph went home and prayed. Hard. Prayed that NRW would not ask M&M to write for their new show. No doubt because of all those 5:30 a.m. Masses that Murph trudged through knee high snow to attend and serve when he was an altar boy, Murph's prayers were heard and answered. (Or maybe it was the look on Murph's face while Don was describing their new show.)

M&M were able to continue writing for *The Jeffersons* while NRW hired other writers for *The Dumplings*, including Gary Goldberg, who later went on to produce the *Lou Grant* show and create the series *Family Ties*.

From what Murph understood, *The Dumplings*, NRW's new show, was based on a British cartoon that Don liked. Starring James Coco and Geraldine Brooks as a blissfully happy overweight couple, the series premiered at the end of January, 1976, and was canceled following the tenth episode at the end of March, 1976.

Murph figured that after spending all that time in the trenches writing and producing groundbreaking satire on *All in the Family*, Don, Mickey and Bernie very much needed to clear their psyches by indulging in some nice, gentle, conflict-free entertainment. And he hoped the trio had gotten it out of their system.

SINCE THEY BEGAN work in the summer, Murph & Sean had been working hard and were looking forward to a little time off during the holidays.

On Christmas Eve day, Mickey spotted Murph heading out the door at noon and asked, "Where are you going?"

"Gotta buy some Christmas presents for my kids," said Murph.

"Christmas isn't till tomorrow!" declared Mickey.

Murph was taken aback, but he knew Mickey was serious. Murph stopped for a second—or two—or three—then thought 'Screw it! If he fires me, he fires me.' and kept walking out the door.

On the way to his car, Murph thought he recalled Bernie mentioning once that Mickey had gone to Hebrew school… which Murph figured could be at the root of Mickey's apparent cultural aggression. But, as he reached his car, in the true spirit of Christmas, Murph forgave Mickey. And as he drove off, he hoped Mickey would forgive him too.

GROWING EXPONENTIALLY WITH no fewer than six shows on the air and more in development, TAT/ Tandem held its 1975 Holiday Party in a large ballroom at an elegant Beverly Hills hotel. Murph & Sean, in their rented tuxedos with wives at their arms, ran into Gordon and his wife, Martha, at the ballroom entrance to the party and began exchanging pleasantries and laughs.

Martha interrupted Gordon with a serious half-whisper, "C'mon, hon, let's go inside and spend time with the important people." And they did.

Murph & Sean, of course, thought that was a pretty funny moment; a moment which proved to be the genesis of more than a few Martha impressions in the future.

At the party, Murph & Sean met Charlie Hauck, a writer for *Maude*, who wrote the teleplay for M&M's "Viv's Dog" story. Charlie complimented the writers, commenting that their "Viv's Dog" story outline was an early Christmas gift.

Charlie made it clear to Murph & Sean that he was both surprised and embarrassed that Exec Producer Rod Parker had assigned him to write the teleplay rather than have M&M write the script. Murph felt a definite affinity with Charlie, who was also from Ohio (Cleveland) and Jesuit educated (John Carroll University).

Martha may be impressed to know that Sean & Murph talked with other important people that night, including Norman and his wife Frances and Tandem/TAT partner Bud Yorkin. As the music and dancing progressed, both Murph and Sean found themselves dancing with Frances Lear and hoping she was having as much fun as they were.

Dancing with the boss's wife seemed to ignite a little bit of company scuttlebutt as one secretary approached M&M and asked, "Aren't you guys worried you might be risking your jobs?"

Sean had the perfect answer, even if it was fueled by champagne: "Hey, we're comedy writers; we can get away with anything."

Yes, agreed Murph. Definitely an occupational perk.

Last year at this time, Murph and Sean were standing in line outside at the Andy Gump, just happy *That's My Mama* thought to invite the two freelance writers to their party. This year here they were, the youngest staff writers in a stable of true professionals, working with already legendary writer/producer Norman Lear and Nicholl/Ross/West, on a show they loved.

In a Karmic coincidence, the show's theme song was their theme song too. Like the Jeffersons, Murph & Sean were definitely 'movin' on up!'

Chapter 12

COGENCY & COMEDY

('76)

If you asked Murph, he'd tell you he wanted to write comedy that made you think and laugh—not necessarily in that order. Thinking and laughing—the two things that separate humans from other animal species. He also liked comedy that informed.

The week that "The IQ Test" episode of *Good Times* aired, a review in *TV Guide* called it "a nice blend of cogency and comedy."

Murph liked those words. Cogency and comedy. That's what Murph hoped could become the M&M brand—"a nice blend of cogency & comedy."

For example, M&M's *Good Times* script makes you think about the probability that IQ tests in schools are culturally biased and informs you that there is a black intelligence test that white people fail, all in the context of humor.

Their first *Mama* script makes you think about the wisdom of having a gun in the house; and their second *Mama* script makes you think about the increasingly common situation of two people dating where one person has a child and how that child may be affected by the relationship.

Their *Joe and Sons* episode explores religion and suggests there may be as many ideas about the identity of a supreme being as there are individuals.

Their *Maude* story titled "Viv's Dog" became a very funny episode about the exalted position in which some pets are held by their owners. And the motivation behind their *Chico and the Man* story was to entertain while informing the audience that many companies who promise to help inventors market their products are less than reliable.

With the suicide story, they wanted to inform the audience that the highest suicide rate in the country is among black women; and they wanted viewers to think about how they might recognize and react to someone they might know who becomes desperate enough to want to kill herself or himself.

Murph considered himself and Sean very fortunate to be able to work on a show where they could aspire to the goal of writing cogent comedy.

In addition to developing the main characters (George & Louise), *The Jeffersons* Season 2 ('75-76) shows focused on developing recurring characters like Mother Jefferson, Harry Bentley, the Willises, Lionel and Jenny.

In episodes with titles like "A Dinner For Harry" and "Harry and Daphne," we learn that Bentley is single, works as an interpreter at the United Nations, and loves to share stories about an assortment of loopy British relatives. He addresses his neighbors as "Mr. J" and "Mrs. J," which Louise thinks is "polite" and George thinks is "weird."

When Bentley's bad back is acting up, it's not unusual to find the besieged Brit lying face down on the floor in the

Jeffersons' apartment, while George walks on his neighbor's back.

Early on, Murph noticed that when George slammed the door in Bentley's face, it got what Murph calls a "free laugh"—a laugh not indicated by a line or note in the script, a good example of how a live audience can help by telling a show's creative team what's funny.

M&M mentioned this to NRW and to director Jack Shea, thus a quick door slam from George, just missing Bentley's protruding proboscis, became standard shtick on the show and never failed to get a big laugh. In fact, when live audiences would see Bentley enter, Murph could often sense them waiting in anticipation for the eventual door slam.

Mother Jefferson is featured throughout a good number of episodes, especially "Mother Jefferson's Fall," "Lunch With Mama" and "Mother Jefferson's Birthday."

We learn that Mother Jefferson admires and defends everything her son does, and can't resist taking shots at Louise, whom she considers an interloper. Louise tolerates her nettlesome mother-in-law, but, when necessary, Weezy can give as good as she gets.

Besides jabbing at Louise, MJ likes to do crossword puzzles, enjoys a little sip of the bubbly, and, although she lives elsewhere, takes frequent naps at the Jefferson residence (a good device for moving MJ on and off the living room stage as needed).

Lionel and Jenny are featured in a two-parter where they split up. In an attempt to help his son ease pressures at school, George buys Lionel a term paper; and when Lionel decides to use it, a kerfuffle turns into a brouhaha which causes a break-up of not only the engaged couple, but both families—the Willises versus the Jeffersons.

A run from "The Break-up, Part 1," probably one of the

most-used clips in specials and documentaries about *The Jeffersons*, goes something like this:

Tom: "Now calm down. It's not worth breaking up over crazy George."

George: "Who you calling crazy, 'honky?"

Tom: "Don't call me "honky."

George: "Why're you so sensitive all of a sudden?"

Tom: "How would you like it if I called you 'nigger'"?

George: (stunned, looks to Louise) "He called me 'nigger'."

Helen: "That's no worse than 'honky.'"

George: "You're right. Nothing's worse than honky (pointedly) except being married to one."

Helen: "That tears it! C'mon, Tom. I'm getting out of here!"

Jenny to Lionel: "And while you're buying term papers, buy yourself another girlfriend too!" (Removes ring and throws it at Lionel. And the Willis family exits!)

In case you're wondering, according to Murph's research at the time, the derogatory term "honky" entered black culture in the 1940s when it was common for a white dude dating a black girl to drive into a black neighborhood and, afraid to get out of the car, just honk the horn for his date to come out.

In the episode titled "Jenny's Grandparents," Jenny plays a key role in helping Tom's white father and Helen's black father to understand the scourge of pointless prejudice.

In the very funny episode "George's Best Friend," actor Lou Gossett Jr. plays George's old navy buddy Wendall, an inveterate player. When George finds out Wendall is hitting on Louise, George confronts his former friend with: "Nigger, you got to be crazy! I know you done back-doored a lotta people, but I never thought you'd be stupid enough to back-door me! You better get outta my house before I erase your future!"

Sherman ad-libbed the word "Nigger" here. It was rare for Sherman or any member of the cast to ad lib a word or line, especially on tape night. NRW made sure that any script that went to the table on Wednesday was tight. Very few line changes were made during the week. When there were changes, some resulted from cast questions or concerns, but most were from writers following Friday run-thru.

One nice thing about reading on Wednesday and taping the following Tuesday was that if a script should happen to have any major problems, those problems could be addressed over the weekend. But this rarely happened. Usually weekends were spent re-writing the script for the next show which would be going to the table on Wednesday.

Sherman once discussed his acting process with Murph, telling Murph that when Sherman gets a script, he reads through it quickly, just to get the "feel" of the story and let the scenes "roll around in his head," not worrying about his lines until they start rehearsing.

By Friday run-thru, as mentioned previously, cast members were expected to be off book. Changes after run-thru on Monday were frowned on by NRW. They wanted the cast to know if they locked in their lines over the weekend, they could be confident not a lot of changes would be thrown at them before the taping. This, thought Murph, made perfect producing sense. Murph was quite surprised later on to learn this producing philosophy was not always employed on other live-audience multi-camera shows. Quite a few other shows would habitually toss new pages at the actors (and director and camera crew) right up until show time. And on shows like *Barney Miller*, even *during* taping!

WHEN M&M'S *GOOD Times* episode was shot, only a couple of their original jokes were used. Now that Murph & Sean were rewriting *Jeffersons* scripts every day, Murph, determined to prove the deleted *Good Times* jokes were funny, eventually employed every one of those jokes in various Jefferson rewrites. One of those jokes got the biggest laugh of the season to date: It was Lionel's graduation day and, as Florence passes through the living room, everyone is celebrating and embracing, and Florence says: "Lord, I ain't seen so much hugging since Sammy Davis stopped hanging out at the White House." A political joke, it referred to the fact that entertainer Sammy Davis had been famously photographed hugging Richard Nixon before Watergate, but after the scandal hit, Sammy just as famously disappeared.

This was in the episode titled "Lionel's Problem," where Lionel has been drinking to cover his fears that he won't be able to live up to his Pop's impressive entrepreneurial success. The second act is mainly a farce where Louise, Jenny and Mother Jefferson struggle to keep the plastered graduate away from his Pop until Lionel sobers up. This, plus an episode titled "George Meets Whittendale," where George is trying desperately to meet the wealthy man who owns the building, but instead ends up trapped in the guest bathroom with the Willises, provides an early peek at NRW's penchant for farce, which in time became a subtle but welcome ingredient in *The Jeffersons'* blend of comedy.

YOUNG, ATHLETIC, ENERGETIC Sandy Veith started in Norman's company as Norman's driver. It was Sandy who helped M&M move furniture into their new office at Metromedia. And it was Sandy, an aspiring writer, who pitched M&M a story idea which became the second to last episode of *The Jeffersons'* second season.

Sandy's pitch involved George being invited to join a prestigious tennis club only to learn he would be a "token" member. Titled "Tennis Anyone?," the episode featured Tony Award-winning actor Keene Curtis (who played Daddy Warbucks in *Annie*) as a distinguished white businessman who invites George to join his tennis club.

George figures it will be good for business to become a member of this exclusive club and decides to take up tennis and join. Upon his first appearance at the club, however, George learns from a black locker room attendant that George is about to become the first and only black member of the club. At first, George doesn't believe it.

George: "You're joking, right?"

Attendant: "I ain't jokin', token."

Keene Curtis arrives and announces to George that a newspaper photographer will be there to take a photo of the two of them. When the photographer enters, Curtis guides George next to him and, as the photographer snaps the camera, George grabs a pitcher of water and pours it over his stunned sponsor's head!

This was Sandy's first TV assignment and one of M&M's favorite episodes. Sandy went on to become a noted writer/producer, winning a court judgment for over $7 million against Universal for his creation of the popular hour-long series *Northern Exposure*.

In the 24th and final episode of Season 2 ("The Wedding"), the Jeffersons' plans to renew their marriage vows hit a snag when Louise refuses to say "I do" until George agrees to lower the prices in his Harlem store. George the successful businessman is again forced to make a decision between good business and happiness at home; and, to his credit, George chose the second, although it may have been another case of George making the right choice for the wrong reason.

While *The Jeffersons* writing staff in the '75-76 season consisted simply of NRW, T&M and M&M, a number of freelance writers contributed to the 24 episodes produced, including veteran comedy writing teams Robert Fisher & Arthur Marx and Fred S. Fox & Seaman Jacobs; individuals Frank Tarloff, George Burditt, Jim Ritz and hyphenate housewife-writer Dixie Brown Grossman.

Novice writing team Ken Levine & David Isaacs scored their first sale in an episode titled "Movin' On Down" — where George fears he's losing his Midas touch — launching a distinguished TV career as writer/producers on *M*A*S*H*, *Cheers* and many more. At Norman's urging, *The Jeffersons* also made a special effort to hear pitches from aspiring black aka "minority" writers, resulting in credited contributions from scribes John Ashby and Calvin Kelly.

In time, M&M came to think that if a series could claim 3 or 4 really good shows in a field of 24, it was a good season. Murph's Top Four for *The Jeffersons'* '75-76 season would be "Tennis Anyone?," "Florence's Problem," "George and the Manager" and "Louise's Daughter," not necessarily in that order.

If Murph had to pick a fifth favorite, he would probably choose "The Break-up, Part I, which included the classic Nigger-Honky break-up scene. Whenever a story can be developed where the show's very premise is in jeopardy, you have a strong story. For instance, a story where George and Louise's marriage may be threatened ("Louise's Daughter," "The Wedding," "Jefferson vs. Jefferson"– where Louise refuses to lie for George in a court-related matter); or a story where the currently successful Jeffersons may be losing money ("Movin' On Down"); or a story like "The Break-up" in which, if dissension between the Jeffersons and the Willises is not resolved, half the regular cast could disappear.

One thing Murph loved about writing for *The Jeffersons* was the energy and passion with which George and Louise could argue. Never before or since has a sitcom couple been able to go toe-to-toe with such forcefulness, yet at the same time display unconditional love for each other. In a comic sense, they are worthy opponents.

When George and Weezy argue, the stage comes alive. The conflict ignites with cogency and comedy. When George Jefferson argues, he argues from his roots. His passion erupts not just from his gut, but from his entire being, all the way down to his toes.

He has a legitimate gripe, to put it mildly, against Whitey and a system that has not only discriminated against but enslaved people of his race. Throughout his life, George has found himself in a continuous battle with prejudice in a society which, ironically, claims the belief that all men are created equal.

Louise, of course, understands this. And she's accepted her role in helping the man she loves navigate the pitfalls of his rage. George may disagree with his wife, but he trusts her. He respects and secretly appreciates his wife's tug-o'-war efforts to keep him on a path of decency and integrity—despite his firm belief that in order to succeed in Whitey's World, you have to be able to scheme and scam like Whitey.

Chapter 13

STORY EDITORS
('76)

As Season 2 came to an end in late February, *The Jeffersons* was picked up for a third season and so were M&M. Murph & Sean were promoted to Story Editors and Tanner & Miller were promoted to Executive Story Editors. Not that those title changes meant much. NRW were still the main dudes, and the other four were still writers.

But M&M did have a year of staff experience under their belt and NRW did seem to have a growing confidence in their young Story Editors. Whenever M&M would finish a rewrite or an original, they would attempt to read over their draft objectively, as if seeing it for the first time, making additional notes. Then when they met with NRW, they would often indicate to the trio that they also had their own notes; in effect acknowledging that they didn't consider their current draft to be carved in stone, an approach NRW seemed to appreciate.

As Story Editors, M&M were anointed or appointed by the Trio at the Top to handle the lion's share of the pitch meetings with outside writers in the coming season. M&M were not unfamiliar with hearing freelance pitches, but Season 3 of *The Jeffersons* would become a valuable experience as they read spec scripts, spoke with agents, scheduled meetings and worked tirelessly with writers to break stories.

If you were to ask Murph or any staff writer what the hardest part of writing for a TV series is, he or she would tell you "breaking stories." That means breaking a story (or episode) into scenes and knowing the basics of what happens in each scene. This can take days, months or even years. Once you know what the scenes are, one leading to the next (also known as "structure"), you can write the script. And when you have the script, you can read it, make notes, rewrite it, time it out, make cuts, punch it up and shoot it.

The process of "breaking" could be called simply "figuring out" the story—but the word figure is too soft to be accurate. "Working out" implies that the process is work, therefore not easy; but "breaking" the story is more descriptive of the mind-bending struggle writers and writing staffs go through on a daily basis. You have to break a story before it breaks you.

One story-breaking tool which Murph and Sean found extremely helpful is what NRW called a "house number." Murph translated "house number" to mean "something like." Or more specifically, "not this, but something like this."

Murph assumed this device was used by Don, Mickey, Bernie and other writers working with Norman on *All in the Family*. When Murph first heard NRW use the term "house number," he thought the "house" might refer to "in house"—like something that's just meant for us, and not for anyone outside. Just a placeholder for the writers, until they find something better.

Murph never got around to asking about the actual origin or translation of the term; there wasn't time and that kind of micro-analysis didn't matter. Just like there wasn't time for questions like: When did Don leave England for America? Why do we tape on Tuesdays instead of Fridays? How did Lloyd lose his arm? Will we be working on Thanksgiving? Because that stuff didn't really relate to the mission at hand, which was coming up with an act break, or a resolution, or a joke.

If you're still curious about how this house number thing works, here's an example using "Florence's Problem," the suicide story. Say you have the first act worked out, and you even have a pretty good idea how you can get the Jeffersons and the Willises to turn Florence around toward the end; but you're not sure, if Lionel finds Florence at the Empire State Building, how he gets her to come back to the Jeffersons' apartment.

If he tells her the truth, she can just deny that she's intending to harm herself and send Lionel home. So a writer might offer this house number: Lionel tells Florence that Louise is sick and is asking to see her. Now that's a good house number because it could work. However, Louise being sick is a downer and we already have someone thinking about killing herself, and we're trying to do a comedy here. Plus Florence would ask a lot of questions about Louise: How sick is she? Has she seen a doctor? Is she at the hospital? Why is she asking to see Florence?

So telling Florence Louise is sick is just a house number. A placeholder. The writers, in this case M&M, know they need something **like that, but not that**. But the good thing about having a house number is that if they have the rest of the story, they can start writing, confident they'll eventually be able to replace that house number with something better.

What replaced it in the finished script, you may recall, was Lionel telling Florence there was some money missing and Louise thinks Florence took it. Well, Florence wouldn't want to kill herself with Louise thinking she is a thief. And Florence would want to confront her boss right away and declare her innocence: "Mrs. Jefferson, how could you even think I would steal from you? I'm a God-fearing woman!" Which is a funny attitude for Florence to play when she enters the Jeffersons' apartment.

ON FEBRUARY 9, 1976, M&M received a note on Norman Lear's stationery that read:

> Dear Mick and Sean,
> I was so pleased and proud to learn of the
> JEFFERSONS landslide at the Image Awards.
> Congratulations.
> Norman (signed)
> P.S.–Ran out of books. I owe you one.

The books to which Norman was referring were coffee table books featuring photos of silent comedy film stars which he gifted to the cast and others on the show following the annual NAACP Image Awards.

It could hardly be a surprise that the only series on TV featuring an upwardly mobile black family would kick ass in any TV image category. The Image Awards, honoring black performers in film, and now in television, came to be in the late 1960s because before that, there were no black people on television.

When Murph was a junior in high school, the Jesuits, to their credit, invited a young black man to speak to Murph's all white classmates. It was a mind-opening moment for Murph when he heard their speaker say that as a kid, the only time he saw people on TV who looked like him was watching Tarzan. He said the black natives would be chasing Tarzan through the jungle and he'd be yelling "Look out, Tarzan, they're right behind you!" When he should've been yelling, "Get that honky!"

NAACP stood for National Association for the Advancement of Colored People. Colored? That's what Murph was told to call black people when he was a kid. "Colored" was the polite term for "black."

Murph's mother, if asked, would tell you, as most white people would, she doesn't have a bigoted bone in her body. And in many ways, that was true. Like the nuns who taught Murph in elementary school and both his parents, Murph was instructed as a young child that all human beings are created equal in the eyes of God and should be treated as such.

On the other hand, when Murph was a little kid, little enough to be putting coins in his mouth or sucking on the top of an empty coke bottle, seeing how far he could fit his tongue inside the bottle, Murph's mom would say "Don't be sucking on that pop bottle, some colored man might've had that last." Or "Don't put that nickel in your mouth! Some colored man might've had that." Colored Man? Little Murph wondered what color the man might be. Red, green, purple? Was the Colored Man from another planet? And if so, how would that affect Murph? Would Murph change color? If he turned green, Murph thought that would be neat! Green was his favorite color.

At the age of five, and then again at 13, Murph went

with his family on vacation to Florida. They drove through Kentucky, Tennessee, Georgia, Florida. They stopped at gas stations with three restrooms labeled Men, Women and Colored. They saw drinking fountains labeled "Whites Only." Murph's mom explained that's the way it is in the South. Murph felt two things. One, he felt lucky. Lucky he was born white. He didn't recall being offered a choice or doing anything to earn a certain skin color; so luck, pure chance, is the only thing that could explain it. The second thing he felt was empathy. He felt bad for kids who weren't so lucky. Colored kids, both boys and girls, who had to share one bathroom in public and couldn't drink at water fountains. It didn't seem right.

You can imagine how Murph felt when he learned that white people used to *own* colored people. Lucky as hell! Lucky he was born white, lucky he didn't live in the South, and lucky he was alive now and not before or during the Civil War.

He also felt shame. Shame he was born white. Shame that people with the same color skin as his would think it was okay to "own" other people. Shame that even today, just because of the color of his skin, he had an unfair advantage over people who were "colored."

And he could imagine how colored people, both kids and adults, must feel. He knew how he would feel. He would be pissed. Super pissed! Angry! Furious! Livid! Mad as hell at all white people! In fact, as a kid, Murph didn't understand why colored people weren't out in the streets every day beating the crap out of white people, demanding retribution, justice. Maybe that's how Huey Newton, Bobby Seale and Eldridge Cleaver felt when they formed the militant-minded Black Panthers in the late 1960s.

Eldridge Cleaver's book *Soul On Ice* and MLK's *Stride*

Toward Freedom, both of which Murph read during college, played key roles from opposite ends of the spectrum in the movement for racial awareness in the United States.

Shortly after the release of *Good Times* on CBS, members of the Black Panthers showed up at Norman Lear's office, demanding to see the "Garbage Man." They called Norman the Garbage Man because they felt *Good Times* was unfairly portraying blacks as all poor, barely employed people living in the projects. Norman had been thinking about spinning off the Jeffersons from *All in the Family*, and he credits the Black Panthers with sparking him to make the Jeffersons an upwardly mobile black family with George the head of a chain of cleaning stores.

Eldridge Cleaver summed up the need for racial awareness in America, declaring "If you're not part of the solution, you're part of the problem." Murph hoped *The Jeffersons* Image Awards "landslide," as Norman put it, was proof that he and Sean were part of the solution.

YOU MAY RECALL that five years ago Murph wrote a treatment for *All in the Family* about a friend of Meathead's who was a draft dodger living in Canada. Murph's agent at the time supposedly sent it to Tandem but they passed. Now, in 1976, President Carter was considering the possibility of amnesty for draft dodgers and it was causing quite a bit of controversy throughout the country.

Murph thought this might be the perfect time for *All in the Family* to do this story. He always wanted to write a script for *All in the Family*. Now that he was on the inside, Murph realized three things: 1) Nobody pays any attention to treatments and Norman probably never saw it. 2) *All in the Family* just wrapped and probably needs stories for next season. And 3) Now that he and Sean are working here, maybe Norman will listen to an *All in the Family* pitch.

So Murph called Jadi Jo, Norman's assistant, and set up a pitch meeting with Norman. The meeting date was March 17, St. Patrick's Day, M&M's writing anniversary. Murphy and Malloy, the Irish writers, considered this to be a lucky day for them. When the day came, Sean needed to see a dentist, but they agreed that Murph should take the meeting himself, since Murph knew the story and Norman was either going to like it or not.

So Murph met with Norman and pitched the story: Meathead's friend, a draft dodger living in Canada, slips back into the country at Christmas time to visit his sick mother who's in the hospital. He stops to visit Mike and Gloria on Christmas Eve, and they convince him to stay for dinner. During dinner Archie learns that Mike's friend is living in Canada and Archie, half serious, says "Canada, huh? You a hockey player or a draft dodger?" When it's revealed Mike's friend is the latter, the stuffing hits the fan! It's Christmas, the birthday of Christ, and one subject that arises is whether Jesus would be willing to go to Vietnam and kill if he were drafted.

Norman loved it! As he walked Murph to the outer office, Norman said to his secretary/assistant, "Jadi, Mick just gave us a reason for doing next season." How did Murph feel? Well, if you guessed that Murph wrote down Norman's quote and added it to his will with instructions to put it on his tombstone, you'd be close.

You might think Murph & Sean would want to start writing this *AITF* script right away. But they learned their lesson. They knew how this works. They knew not to start writing until they had at least one more detailed meeting attempting to break the story with Norman. They also knew the Christmas episode probably wouldn't be taping before late fall; and they figured the sooner they turned in a draft, the more time there would be for notes (TV Staff Writing Rule # 1: The Quantity of Notes expands to fill the Time Allotted—QN=TA), which could be voluminous and would probably continue up until tape time, a situation M&M hoped to avoid.

They also knew it was hiatus time for all the shows—a break of at least 4-6 weeks before staff would return to start working on scripts for next season. Murph liked this about writing for TV. It was kind of like a teacher's job, although you didn't get off the whole summer.

Murph figured he'd use the hiatus wisely—sleep for the first week, then spend the next month or more, as the country song goes, "putting in a little overtime at home" with the wife and kids.

SO MURPH, MARIANNE and the girls—now ages 6 and 5—went back to Ohio for a visit. Murph met with Entertainment Editor Steve Hoffman of *The Cincinnati Enquirer* for an interview. The first question Steve asked was, "Do you have a pool?" No joke.

Murph had to confess that he didn't yet have a pool. Water sports in the yard were still limited to racing through sprinklers.

Steve's second question was, "Did you ever think of writing for *Saturday Night Live*?"

Well, Murph thought, let's see: 'Did I ever think of moving to New York where it's cold and damp and trying to get a job in late night television where I could be making a pittance compared to what I'm making now, working with writers who would much rather be writing a TV series like I'm doing, while sleeping an average of five nights a week in my office using illegal substances to both stay awake and go to sleep, where the only advantage show-wise is that I don't have to worry about editing…?'

"No."

Steve wrote a nice article with a photo of Murph and everything.

While visiting, Murph got to hang out with some of his old buddies, one of whom commented cryptically, "Murph, anybody can write for niggers." Which made Murph realize that a job he already thought was important was even more important than he thought.

Murph attended a party with some friends, and one attractive young woman came up to him and said, "I hear you're an excellent writer." To which Murph replied something like, "Always believe what you hear."

Then she asked, "Have you ever written a *Waltons*?"

"No," Murph said, for some reason feeling shamed. "It's a good show though. I like *The Waltons*."

"Maybe someday," she said.

At breakfast next morning, Murph's mom asked, "Can't you write something your children can watch?"

"I'll see if they need anybody at *Sesame Street*," Murph answered. His mom looked hopeful.

That night Murph's dad mentioned he had seen an episode of the new sitcom *Phyllis* (an MTM spinoff starring Cloris Leachman) where they had a "gay guy" on the show. "Do they have to do that kind of thing?" he wondered. "Can you let them know your mother and I don't want to watch stuff like that?"

Murph tried telling his father that *Phyllis* was done by another production company and nobody in that company would listen to anything Murph had to say. But Murph wasn't sure his father believed him.

On the plane back to LA, Murph borrowed a pen from a

flight attendant and wrote something down so he'd remember it. When he looked at it the next day, it read: "It's your dream. Live it for yourself, not for anybody else."

ON JUNE 27, 1976, Murph turned thirty. He remembered reading a book by Dan Greenburg where the author says by the time you're thirty, you are who you are. If you told Murph when he was 20 that when he turned 30 he'd be living in California, writing for television, have two adorable daughters and be going to work in jeans, he'd say those three glorious words rarely heard in the Midwest: "Somebody pinch me!"

They celebrated in the office with a cake and a card signed by Murph's co-workers, all arranged by Jody Jill Greenwood, from Tulsa, Oklahoma, M&M's super efficient secretary/assistant/partner. Jody was ground zero for M&M product, typing each draft of their scripts. There were no computers in those days. M&M each typed on a manual typewriter and funneled pages to Jody, who would re-type them on an electric typewriter.

When Jody was typing their material outside their office and they would hear her laugh, M&M would jump up, race to Jody and ask, "What're you laughing at?" Jody Jill was their human joke tester; and her instincts were rarely wrong.

Sean, whom Murph still affectionately called "Marty," would have to wait another six months before turning 30. As rookie comedy writers, Murph figured M&M could hardly be in a better working environment, surrounded by All Star veterans like Milt Josefsberg, Mel Tolkin, Larry Rhine, Ben Starr, Mort Lachman, Lou Derman, Bill Davenport, Woody Kling, Irma & Rocky Kalish, Rod Parker—a group whose credits included material for such classic performers as Bob Hope, George Burns, Danny Thomas, Lucille Ball, Jack Benny, Jackie Gleason, Carol Burnett, Red Skelton, Dean Martin & Jerry Lewis.

Mort Lachman travelled the globe with Bob Hope as Hope's key writer, and Mel Tolkin was the legendary head writer for Sid Caesar's *Your Show of Shows* in the 1950s. Norman hired proven gag writers and guided them in developing topical storylines for shows like *All in the Family*, *Maude* and *Good Times*, a formula which resulted in a record number of Emmy nominations and wins.

AITF writer-producer Milt Josefsberg, while writing a book about his years with Jack Benny, made regular visits to M&M's office to share Jack Benny stories. Murph & Sean loved Milt and loved hearing his stories, but they also loved their jobs; and trying to escape Milt's stories so they could work on their script became a continuing sitcom scene in itself.

Once Milt made it into their office, easing him back out became an Olympic event. If, for example, after listening to one of Milt's stories, Murph or Sean would say something like, "Hey, great story, Milt. We need to finish this script now, so we'll have to throw you out."

And Milt would respond with something like, "That reminds me of the time Jack told Rochester to throw out an old loaf of bread and Rochester threw it out the window and it hit a wino on the head and the wino sued Jack."

It was Milt and his then partner John Tackaberry who came up with perhaps the most famous comedic radio line of all time. Jack Benny's character, known for being incredibly cheap, was accosted by a holdup man who demanded, "Your money or your life?" The writers needed a line for Jack, but were stuck. Milt said to his partner, who was lying on the sofa with eyes closed, something like, "C'mon, dammit, there's gotta be a great answer to 'Your money or your life'?" And his partner replied, "I'm thinking, I'm thinking..." They both reacted and realized that was the line!

When Milt finished his book, *The Jack Benny Show — The Life And Times of America's Best-Loved Entertainer*, Milt mentioned Murph and Sean in the front of his book, along with other names, a gesture much appreciated by M&M.

MURPH LIKED *GOOD Times*—a lot. A show featuring a black family was more than groundbreaking, it was pretty much a miracle. Nuclear family sitcoms like *The Life of Riley, Father Knows Best, Make Room for Daddy, Leave it to Beaver, Ozzie & Harriet*, not to mention high concept families like *The Addams Family, The Munsters, The Partridge Family, The Beverly Hillbillies* were ever-present on TV. Black families were nonexistent.

Television is funded by advertising, and advertisers wanted to reach consumers who could afford their products. And the accepted philosophy was that the major consumer base—white people—didn't want to watch black shows.

It was doubly amazing that this wasn't a whitewashed black family, but a black family living in the projects. Neither a white nor blue collar family, but a black collar family where the father, James Evans played by John Amos, struggles to hold down more than one job in order to support his family, which includes his wife Florida (Esther Rolle) and his three children, all of whom have admirable aspirations.

Apparently there was tension among the cast on the show. When Murph, now a writer on *The Jeffersons*, made a visit to the *Good Times* stage to watch an episode, he was disheartened to see that, during cast introductions, the other cast members stood separated from Jimmie Walker. Word was both John Amos and Esther Rolle were upset about the development of Jimmie's character in the show. They thought JJ was too stereotypically buffoonish and blamed it on the writers. Actually, it was director John Rich who suggested JJ's catch phrase "Dy-no-mite!" and instructed Jimmie to say it at least once in every show. As a result, Jimmie became a fan favorite and the show became a hit.

As the oldest kid in his own family, Murph didn't see anything forced or defamatory about JJ acting silly or doing anything he can to get a laugh around his parents or younger siblings. This seemed to Murph like a normal character trait for a teenager regardless of color. Playing the role of the family jester, especially in a family struggling to make ends meet, using humor as a weapon to deal with poverty, seemed to Murph to be a positive step towards keeping up family spirits.

Although Murph certainly understood Amos & Rolle's concerns about black image on TV, JJ's silliness was well-balanced by the seriousness of his two siblings and the cogency and originality of many of the show's storylines.

It appeared to Murph that the dissension emanating from Amos and Rolle, whether they knew it or not, stemmed from simple cases of performance envy—two notable actors being upstaged by a young comedian.

Mr. Amos was not lacking in ego. The license plate on his sports car said HNIC (Head Nigger In Charge). And he was quoted by a writer-producer on *Good Times* as saying about his co-star something like "ain't no sucka gonna believe a man who looks like me gonna be married to no woman who looks like that." This was the same writer, by the way, who claimed you could tell Esther Rolle's age by counting the rings around her neck.

Following season 3, Mr. Amos left the show, according to what Murph heard Norman tell a *Good Times* audience before a fourth season taping, "for reasons known only to John Amos."

How did the show deal with the departure of James Evans? A couple seasons before, Carroll O'Connor was holding out for more money, and *All in the Family* was being forced to shoot without him. Norman asked writer-producers Lou Derman and Bill Davenport to write a script where Archie dies, but instructed them not to tell anyone what they were doing.

They wrote a script where Edith and the kids (Mike and Gloria) are returning from Archie's funeral and the kids are concerned that Edith has not cried since Archie passed. At the end, Edith confesses she hasn't cried because she's afraid if she starts to cry, she won't be able to stop. Then she starts crying.

Carroll O'Connor's agents heard about the script and worked out a quick deal putting their famous client back to work.

Two years later, when John Amos left, Norman used that same script for *Good Times*, with Florida and the kids returning from James's funeral.

Murph was surprised that Norman, rather than have a fatherless black family on TV, didn't simply recast the father role as he did with Lionel. But, even without a father, the show continued to be a favorite, especially with young black kids who appreciated being able to see kids who looked like them on TV. *Good Times* lasted another three seasons even though Esther Rolle left the show after Season 4, with ebullient neighbor Willona (played by actress Ja'net Dubois, who co-wrote and sang *The Jeffersons* theme song) stepping up as guardian. In Season 4 Willona adopted an abused girl named Penny who was played by Janet Jackson.

M&M WERE TAKING story pitches from a number of writers, both young and old, for the coming season. Two of those writers were Michael Baser and Kim Weiskopf. Kim & Michael were a couple years younger than M&M, but basically of the same generation. Kim's father was one of The Bobs, the legendary writing team of Schiller & Weiskopf, currently of *Maude* fame.

The Bobs were the first to educate M&M on what to expect when you become a writing team. One of the Bobs— neither Murph nor Sean remembers which—told them that other people see writing teams as one unit. Schiller, or was it Weiskopf, said when they were working on *I Love Lucy*, Desi Arnaz would pass just one of them in the hall and say, "Hi, Guys." Desi also told the Bobs that when he first heard people mention "Schiller & Weiskopf," he thought they were talking about one writer named Schillern Weiskopf— because he never heard one name without the other.

Murph had already experienced a work colleague asking him "How's Mick?" When Murph responded "I am Mick" the dude then said, "How's the other you?"

While two distinguished men of a certain age like the Bobs, and two Irish-American Boomers like M&M might be relatively easy to confuse, not so with Baser & Weiskopf.

Michael Baser was a tall, lanky New Yorker with long black hair who looked and too often acted like radio shock-jock Howard Stern. Kim, on the other hand, a product of his Jewish father and Japanese mother, made a cameo appearance as a Samurai swordsman in the John Landis film *The Kentucky Fried Movie.*

When Kim and Michael pitched, they began to argue over a story, contradicting each other with comments like, "No, no, get outta here, that's not gonna work!" It was actually funny and they were obviously bright, creative guys; but after they left, Murph said to Sean, "If we give those guys an assignment, they might kill each other."

Word was that Kim's father made it perfectly clear to his son there would be no nepotism in the Weiskopf family. If Kim wanted to follow in his father's footsteps, he would have to do it in his own shoes. But Baser—and that was what most people called Michael; indeed, even Murph, who loved nicknames, agreed there was no better name for Kim's partner than "Baser"—had no such parental directive, so when they bumped into Norman in the hallway, Baser said something like, "Why don't you hire us as writers. Kim's funny and I'll make sure he shows up on time."

So Norman hired Baser & Weiskopf to work on the staff of *A Year at the Top*, a new series in development. The duo shared a trailer brought onto the lot for extra office space. A trailer which on some nights doubled as a bedroom for the two new writers who brought their sleeping bags to work. With "the Baze" and Kim now working on the lot, kismet intervened and M&M and B&W became fast friends, fueled by the fact that Baze made regular visits to M&M's office, often to escape from his partner, whom Baser accused of things like throwing a typewriter at him.

Kim may have inherited his passion from his father. At a Writers Guild strike meeting a while back, the first WGA strike meeting Murph attended, a large group of members were seated theater style while an officer of the Guild addressed them. Infamous funnyman and loudmouth Mel Brooks was present and began walking up and down the side aisle, talking and commenting while the Guild officer was speaking.

Mel's antics, to label them euphemistically, were distracting and annoying, and finally someone in the seated crowd spoke up, yelling "Sit down!" It was Bob Weiskopf. The crowd applauded.

Brooks reacted by employing a German accent, saying "We've got your name!"

Weiskopf responded with, "We've got your name too. From the last strike."

Brooks, referring to his movie *Young Frankenstein*, said, "I directed during the last strike."

To which Weiskopf responded, "You call that directing!?" And the crowd erupted with laughter and applause. Mel then sat down and never uttered another word. The first time anyone has ever seen Mel Brooks speechless.

Another Bob Weiskopf story, which any writer-producer would appreciate, occurred at a meeting of a show's director and writers following an extremely sluggish run-thru. The director, as directors are wont to do, defended the actors, saying they'd been working hard and were tired. To which Bob Weiskopf replied, "They're actors. Tell 'em to act *not* tired!"

Chapter 14

THE JEFFS, SEASON 3

('76)

Lionel and Jenny had been engaged for at least the past two Seasons, so in Season 3 the writing staff, which still consisted of NRW, T&M and M&M, decided it was time for the couple to get married. This Lionel & Jenny arc led to about a third of the 24 stories they needed for the season, including ones where Lionel gets a new job ("The Lie Detector"); Lionel plans to get his own apartment ("Lionel's Pad"); Jenny's getting cold feet, unsure about her true feelings for Lionel ("Jenny's Discovery"); George suggests Lionel have Jenny sign a pre-nup ("The Agreement"); Louise helps solve the problem of where and when to hold the wedding ("The Christmas Wedding"); Louise learns how it feels to be a mother-in-law ("Louise vs. Jenny") and Jenny's scholarship to spend a summer in England causes friction between the newlyweds and among their four parents ("Jenny's Opportunity").

THE FIRST SEASON 3 episode to air was the result of a story pitch to M&M by veteran comedy writers Howard Albrecht & Sol Weinstein. They pitched a story where George's competition was killing him with a new advertising campaign, so George hires an ad agency to fight back. This was 1976, the Bicentennial, 200 years after the American Revolution. The newspapers, magazines and TV were loaded with Bicentennial advertising, promotions and sales.

Murph had read an article about the American Revolution in *TIME* magazine, which mentioned, among other things, that Thomas Jefferson had children by a black mistress named Sally Hemings. It was the first Murph had ever heard of this and was not common knowledge in those days. Murph thought it would be interesting information to deliver to the audience and something the writers could have fun with.

So they worked up a story where the ad man, played by actor David Dukes, tells George about Sally Hemings and builds a Bicentennial promotion around the notion that George is the great, great, great grandson of Thomas Jefferson.

George loves it at first, feeling he's turning the tables on his competition, beating Whitey at his own game. But when the mayor wants George to pose with him at a major event as a representative of the great American Melting Pot; and Lionel, Jenny and Louise begin teasing George that he really could, like Jenny, be a Zebra, George freaks!

"George and the President" became a very funny show chock full of information about Thomas Jefferson, Sally Hemings, Black Patriots and the American Revolution. And we learn that green, the color of money, is George's second favorite color — right behind black. Green is pretty, but black is beautiful!

IT WAS DECIDED in Season 3 to move Florence into the Jefferson house as a full time live-in maid. Marla Gibbs was still employed by United Airlines and wasn't crazy about giving up her UA job, which she would have to do to be available for more episodes of *The Jeffersons*. Tandem offered to pay Marla whatever UA was paying her *plus* her fee for *The Jeffersons* and she acquiesced.

The episode where Florence moves in, titled "Louise Gets Her Way," was written by Tanner & Miller. Florence is evicted from her apartment because her building is being torn down and Louise invites her to move in with the Jeffersons without asking George, who, of course, is furious. But Florence's eavesdropping on a phone in the other room saves George money and he changes his mind.

T&M also wrote "Louise Suspects," an episode where George is planning to expand his business by opening another store, something he's promised his wife he wouldn't do. George is coming home late and acting so suspiciously that Louise accuses him of having an affair with another woman. Rather than coming clean, George, relieved, admits to an affair!

Lloyd & Gordon also penned an episode ("George's Diploma") where George, thinking Lionel is ashamed of him, tries to get his high school diploma by studying for an Equivalency Test.

M&M's Season 3 originals included "Tom the Hero," "George's Guilt" and "The Old Flame." M&M based "Tom the Hero" on a French story Murph read in college about a guy who saves another guy's life, and the guy who saved the other guy's life keeps hanging around the guy he saved, acting like he owns him.

Murph & Sean thought it might be fun to have Tom save George's life, which makes Tom a local hero and annoys

George no end, to the point where George blurts out, "If you ever save my life again, I'll kill you!"

So how can Tom save George's life? Murph remembered reading about a method to help people keep from choking to death, called the Heimlich maneuver. It was developed by a Cincinnati doctor in the early 70s and not widely known at the time. M&M figured using the maneuver in a *Jeffersons* episode would have the added benefit of showing people how to use it and maybe help save lives. At the time, believe it or not, choking to death was something like the fourth or fifth most common cause of accidental death.

So in the first scene George chokes on a piece of popcorn in Charley's Bar and Tom saves him by employing the Heimlich maneuver. George is grateful at first, but soon becomes desperate to find a way to end Tom's gloating and everyone else's hero worshipping.

Florence has heard the news and stands staring at George.

George: "What're you looking at?"

Florence: "I still can't figure it out."

George: "Figure what out?"

Florence: "How a little piece of popcorn got stuck in such a big mouth."

Tom's on the sofa with Helen, gloating about how fast he moved in Charley's Bar. His line below got a huge laugh— probably even bigger than Florence's line about Sammy Davis hugging Nixon.

Tom: "Helen, did you see how fast I moved? Why, I haven't moved that fast since the night you and I drove through Mississippi."

George offers Tom money, but Tom won't take it. Finally, much to George's relief, an opportunity arises for George to return the favor by rescuing Tom (from a bad financial investment Tom is about to make).

M&M WERE KICKING around ideas for another original, thinking about things that George might be experiencing as a successful entrepreneur that he wouldn't be facing
otherwise. The notion of guilt came up—guilt over his
success. Guilt over not staying in touch with his running
buddies from the old neighborhood. He figures they probably think he's a snob. They're probably thinking, 'George
feels he's too good for us now.'

So, in the episode titled "George's Guilt," George decides
to rectify this by inviting the remaining members of his old
gang, the Seven Saints, to his place for a reunion. But when
the gang's bullying leader shows his true colors, George
learns it's better to let sleeping Saints lie.

In "The Old Flame," George's old girlfriend, Harriet
Johnson, is in town and Mother Jefferson invites her to
George's place so she'll see how well George is doing and
regret dumping him. But Harriet, anything but innocent,
wants to be George's kept mistress.

IN THE 1970s, many large companies were considering
mandatory retirement at ages 60 or 65. *The Jeffersons* did an
episode, written by Dixie Brown Grossman, where George
accepts a terrific offer from a conglomerate to purchase his
chain of stores. Everything is hunky-dory (that's *hunky*-dory,
not *honky* dory) until George learns that the conglomerate's
company policy has a mandatory retirement age of 60. That
means if the deal goes through, Ben, George's dear friend
and mentor and manager of his main store, will be forced to
retire because he's 63.

Ben comments that he's alone now, since his wife passed,
and says: "Every morning when I wake up, I thank God for
two things: One, that I wake up. And two, for having a store
to go to. Folks who are able to work, ought to be able to work."

In the first half of the 20th Century, retirement at 60 or 65 may have sounded reasonable. But with many Boomers projected to become septuagenarians, octogenarians, and even nonagenarians, the notion of termination at the age of 60 certainly sounded like premature evacuation.

This episode resonated with viewers, many of whom wrote letters like the following from the headquarters of the Gray Panthers in Philadelphia:

CBS – TV
Producers of "THE Jeffersons"
56TH and Avenue of the Americas
New York, NY

Dear Friends,

We would like to commend you on your October 30th screening of "The Jeffersons" which focused on mandatory retirement.

Forced retirement is a practice which exacts a heavy toll on older workers' lives physically, psychologically, socially, and economically. We receive hundreds of painful letters documenting the severe effects from retired victims themselves. The elimination of mandatory retirement is one of our major priorities.

This segment of "The Jeffersons" very clearly focused on the human element which is often disregarded in this dehumanizing and arbitrarily based practice. It also mildly indicted those corporations and businesses that currently practice forced retirement. Your presentation of this issue in a prime time television show brought it into millions of homes and, in so doing, made a strong contribution to raise public awareness—a crucial element in changing current retirement policy.

Although the credits flashed on too briefly to note the script author, we hope you will convey our message of thanks and support for this effort to all of the key people involved.

Sincerely,
(signed)
Rosalie Schofield
Mandatory Retirement Project
Gray Panther National Office

WHEN MURPH FIRST arrived in California, the only people Murph knew who lived in Los Angeles were the father, mother and younger brother of a high school friend who used to live in Cincinnati. Murph reconnected with the Koesters and his friend's younger brother, Kenny.

Murph learned that Kenny went on an occasional church-led field trip to Mexico to deliver clothes and other items to needy villages; and one of the trip's organizers was Jack Hanrahan, a writer for *Laugh-In*.

It may sound corny, if not ridiculous, but when twenty-two-year-old Murph met Jack Hanrahan—a tall, stocky, imposing dark-haired Irishman—for lunch, it was an epiphanal (yes, that is a word) moment.

Jack, who began his writing career penning greeting cards, had written for the hit series *Get Smart* and worked for Hanna-Barbera Productions where he was co-creator of the popular Saturday morning series *Banana Splits*.

This was the first human being Murph had ever met who actually did what Murph wanted to do—write television comedy.

Murph was inspired. Here was a guy who wore regular clothes, ate regular food, grew up in Ohio (Cleveland) like Murph, was born Irish Catholic like Murph, and laughed at the same things Murph did. In fact, Jack, at age 35, had just won an Emmy for *Laugh-In*. Murph's inner Cassius Clay said, "If this guy can do it, I can do it."

Jack called Murph the following week. He didn't mention the sketch material Murph sent him; but he did invite Murph to visit the *Laugh-In* set, so Murph took that as a positive sign.

Murph was living on Olive Avenue—just a hop, skip, and a sketch from NBC Studios in "Beautiful Downtown Burbank," a tongue-in-cheek description uttered every Monday night on national TV by Dick Martin, co-host of *Laugh-In*, America's Number 1 show.

Murph arrived at NBC and went to the Artists' Entrance, where a studio guard confirmed his name on the invited guest list and waved him by. Jack met Murph on the *Laugh-In* set and showed him around. Goldie Hawn, Lily Tomlin, Henry Gibson and other cast regulars were present in what could pass for street clothes or pajamas, rehearsing.

Murph learned that *Laugh-In*, unlike *Lucy*, did not film in front of an audience. After a brief chat, Jack left to continue working with the writers, leaving Murph to watch rehearsals.

As Murph was leaving the NBC lot, he noticed the guard was seated in his booth, reading; not paying attention to those who were leaving.

Murph had watched enough *Mission Impossible* episodes to realize that if he were to walk in backwards while the guard was reading, he could most likely sneak into the studio. If the guard looked up when Murph was walking backwards, all Murph would have to do is quickly start walking forward and the guard would think he was leaving.

Murph would nervously employ this caperesque (not a word, but should be) method of sneaking into NBC on a number of future occasions. Only once did the guard look up, and Murph started walking forward, waving on the way out as the smiling guard waved back.

At one point, Jack paid Murph to write a treatment for a freelance project he and partner Phil Hahn were doing for Hanna-Barbera. The project never materialized, but Murph was paid $300 for his efforts—his first entertainment-related earnings.

After *Laugh-In*, Jack moved on to write for *The Andy Williams Show*, a variety (music and comedy) show. Like *Laugh-In*, it was a closed set, not taped with a live audience. At Jack's invitation, Murph visited tapings, witnessing music performances by Mama Cass Elliot, Ray Stevens, Bobby Darin and comedy stints by the likes of Phyllis Diller, Jonathan Winters and the Cookie Bear.

In the middle of Bobby Darin's performance, the star abruptly stopped singing and accused the orchestra of missing a note. Band members protested, denying any imperfection. Murph certainly didn't notice anything wrong—the music sounded great to him.

But Darin became vehement and demanded that the tape of the music be played back. During playback, band members and Bobby suddenly reacted to a note or beat undetected by Murph, and one of the band members apologized, "Sorry, Bobby."

Murph was tremendously impressed by Mr. Darin's impeccable ear. And the singer and orchestra began the song again.

Segments with the inimitable Jonathan Winters were often hilarious. In a sketch referred to as "The Attic," an attic set was filled with random props, and JW would walk around the set reacting to and commenting on various items. No script necessary. Producers would then edit the segment for time and would include the funniest gags.

Following the season's last taping in March of 1971, Jack remarked that he was going to recommend Murph for next season's writing staff on *The Andy Williams Show*. "You write stories," he told Murph.

Murph wasn't exactly sure what Jack meant by those three words, but he was stoked, anticipating what could be his first big break. As it turned out, the show was cancelled and Murph would have to wait for another opportunity.

It had been at least a couple years since Murph, now Story Editor on *The Jeffersons*, had heard from Jack. Murph knew that Jack and his wife Rosemarie, who had eight kids together, had split up. He also knew that Jack and Phil Hahn were writing separately now. The last time Murph had seen him, Jack was hanging with singer/actress Mimi Hines at her beach home in Malibu; and Jack was doing some writing with comedian/writer Don Sherman, who was also there.

So when Jack called Murph at *The Jeffersons* and asked if he could come in and pitch, M&M scheduled an appointment for a few days later. When Jack came, he brought a youngish Asian woman with him, the first writer to bring a date to a pitch meeting with M&M. Jack told Murph he'd been staying in the desert for awhile, somewhere near Palm Springs or Idylwild or somewhere like that.

Jack pitched an idea to M&M about marriage counselors and they worked up a story. Murph told Jack they'd run the idea by NRW and get back to him—the usual process. When Murph mentioned Jack's name to Don Nicholl, Don balked. Don knew Jack as a variety show writer, not a half-hour writer. Apparently, Don had worked briefly with Jack on a George Schlatter production called *Turn On*.

Turn On has the dubious distinction of being the shortest run series in TV history—it was cancelled halfway through the first episode. Murph never saw *Turn On* (few people did), but from what he heard, it was a fast-paced mixed media presentation of unrelated things.

Conceptually, it reminded Murph of an idea he had a few years back for a show that would present clips of unrelated things that were interesting, informative, funny, thought-provoking and entertaining. Everything from clips of existing talk shows or scenes from films, to fresh footage of things like asking people on the street their favorite quotes. Murph's title for the show was *TANGENT*.

The title was inspired by a section in *The Catcher in the Rye* where Holden Caulfield is talking about how in speech class when a student would go off on a tangent or veer off topic, the other students were instructed to shout "Digression!" in order to warn the speaker he's off track. Holden says when a speaker is off on a tangent, it's his favorite part.

If you were born after 1985 or so, you probably wonder what the fascination was with Murph's generation and *The Catcher in the Rye*. Murph wondered that himself some-times. If you asked Murph what attracted him to the book, without giving it too much introspection, he'd say it was simply that the story and the writing style were so accessi-ble. In a way, it's more what it wasn't than what it was. It wasn't Shakespeare, it wasn't Fitzgerald, it wasn't Bronte, or Melville, or Dickens, or Orwell, or Tolstoy, or even Hemmingway or Steinbeck.

It was a simple paperback story about an average teenage boy trying to find out who he is and how he fits into the world around him. And it was told in the first person, his own words.

Murph remembers thinking, this is literature? Really? This is assigned reading? Well, if this is assigned reading, it must be good. It must be worthwhile. It must be…literature. As an aspiring writer, Murph said to himself: I like this. I can do this.

Upon reflection, years later, Murph had the following thought and wrote it down:

> *If you can, especially at a young age, discover something, no matter what it is, where you can say to yourself:* **I like that. I can do that**. *—you've found your key to happiness. Use it to unlock your future.*

If you've been shouting "Digression!," Holden would be pleased. And so would Murph.

So back to Jack Hanrahan and Don. Murph reminded Don that Jack had written for *Get Smart* when it was the number one sitcom and explained that Jack helped him when he first came to town.

Don looked at Sean, who said something like, "We'll make sure this is a good script. You can trust three Irishmen."

Don looked at M&M and nodded his approval. "Go well."

Murph was pleased. Payback was a good feeling.

So in Episode 19 of Season 3, titled "The Marriage Counselors," the Willises are extolling the virtues of some Marriage Improvement classes they're taking which they suggest could be beneficial to George and Louise. Louise is interested, but George wants no part of it. He thinks his marriage is perfectly fine and dandy.

In Act 2, when fine becomes strained and dandy disappears, Tom and Helen manage to lead the Jeffersons through some couples exercises including word association and a hilarious bit where George impersonates his wife and Louise impersonates George, complete with the George Jefferson strut.

The now-famous George Jefferson strut, by the way, was something Sherman improvised during the filming of opening titles. Right after the moving truck arrives, George and Weezy are walking to their new building and George swings his arms in a manner common among "the cool dudes" on the streets of Philadelphia, where Sherman grew up.

The series of couples exercises ends when Tom reveals batakas (padded bats) and instructs George and Louise to use them to pummel each other to release aggression. (This bataka scene was incorporated into the opening title sequence which continued to play each week before *The Jeffersons*.)

Murph was a little surprised when Jack wanted his "Written by" credit to read John V. Hanrahan instead of Jack. Using a middle initial or middle name usually indicated a dramatic writer, not a comedy writer.

Comedy writers and performers would customarily use the diminutive—Bernie, Mickey, Eddie, Lenny, Danny, Jerry, Johnny, Freddie, etc. Makes them sound and seem more accessible. Same reason many comics dress casually, or even sloppily, when performing.

The fact that Jack now wanted to list himself as the more formal *John* with a middle initial led Murph to think Jack was maybe looking to expand job opportunities by landing writing assignments in dramatic or hour-long TV. Just a few short years ago Jack and his partner were receiving Emmys for comedy writing. The wheels of the entertainment business are duplicitous—turning both quickly and slowly. A cautionary tale.

OCCASIONALLY A TAG had to be written. A tag is a short scene, usually one or two pages, at the end of the show. Most half-hour scripts are written without a tag, unless the story calls for it. If a show needs a tag, it usually means it came in short. In other words, sometimes, after an episode is edited, it could, for various reasons, be anywhere from 30-90 seconds short of the network's delivery time, which, as mentioned earlier, is usually around 22 minutes.

It takes at least a few days following tape night for a show to be edited and an accurate timing to be determined so a tag can be written. A tag then could be shot at the end of the next tape night after the audience has been released and after all necessary pick-ups for the current show have been completed.

Tags are tricky to write. They have to be timed pretty much exactly and should end with a show-ending joke. M&M had to write a tag for "The Lie Detector" episode this season and were struggling to come up with something that NRW would approve. Bernie stopped in their office to see how Sean and Murph were doing and shared a story about the early days on *All in the Family* when he and Mickey had to write tags for director John Rich.

Bernie said he and Mickey would type up a tag and take it to John Rich on stage where John would read the tag, then tear it up and tell them to keep writing. He and Mickey then started putting dotted lines on the tag pages complete with instructions to "Tear along Dotted Lines."

NORMAN CAME DOWN to Don's office and told Don he had dinner the night before with some dude—Murph assumed it was a white guy—who said to Norman something on the order of, "Oh sure, you'll show a white man with a black woman; but I'll bet you wouldn't show a black man with a white woman."

Murph wished he were there to take the guy's bet. It's not in Norman's genes to turn down a dare. So Norman asked if Don and the writers could do a *Jeffersons* story with a black man and a white woman. That was the genesis of the episode titled "A Case of Black & White," written by NRW & T&M.

George is at work, ready to sign a big cleaning contract with another black businessman who owns a chain of restaurants. Lionel enters, takes George aside, and suggests that they throw a party for the Willises on their upcoming anniversary. George refuses and Lionel leaves upset.

When George returns to Mr. Howard, the restaurant mogul, Howard asks if everything is okay with George's son.

George: "Ah, he married into one of those mixed-up families."

Howard: "What do you mean, 'mixed up'?"

George: "Zebra city. He's white, she's black, the kids are medium rare. That's what happens when you're dumb enough to marry the wrong color."

Then a white woman enters and Howard introduces George to his wife.

George is nailed. Mr. Howard is offended and indicates he's backing out of the contract.

George, desperate: "You've got me all wrong, Frank. I was just making in-law jokes. Everybody makes in-law jokes."

George invites the Howards over to his house tomorrow night to meet his "dear, warm, close in-laws the Willises" who are coming over.

Howard hesitates, but his wife accepts.

As they move to exit, George reacts pleased and says something like: "One thing you're gonna learn about me, Frank: the color of a person's skin don't matter to me. Can't wait 'til tomorrow. Looking forward to seeing you and your white. I mean, wife."

In Act 2, the Willises come over the next evening, but George is being so nice to them they soon realize something's up. When they learn George is just using them as a token couple to help close a business deal, they split.

Now George has to scramble. He gets Florence to pose as Helen, and Ralph as Tom. Things are going well with the Jeffersons, the Howards and the faux Willises, when the real Willises show up, hip to what's going on. Helen introduces herself as Florence, the Jeffersons' maid, and Tom claims to be Ralph, the building's doorman.

It gets pretty silly—but the audience loved it! So did Murph. Especially Florence's seditty (uppity) portrayal of Helen! In fact, years later, looking back on her time at *The Jeffersons*, Marla Gibbs cited this scene as one of her favorites. But Murph couldn't help wondering if this was the show Norman expected to see.

Outside, construction was under way on the Metromedia lot. A large hole was being dug for the foundation of a new structure to hold additional production offices for Norman's shows. Next to the hole a handmade sign had been posted, ostensibly by a Tandem writer, reading: "DIG DEEPER, Norman Lear."

That was Norman's standard note to writers. When Norman was challenged to show a black man with a white woman, was there more to that challenge than meets the eye? Did the challenger really think Norman would balk at showing an interracial marriage of that makeup? And if so, why? Should the writers have dug deeper?

It was established in "Jenny's Grandparents," and re-established in this episode, that Tom and Helen's marriage was not approved by either of their families. Would it have been any different if the marriage was between a black man and a white woman? Better? Worse?

Was there some stereotype or mindset here that could have been exposed as nonsense or irrelevant? Something that could have made the comedy more cogent, more informative? A stronger story than simply "The Importance of Being Willis"? Murph didn't know if NRW had run the script by Norman. His guess was they hadn't.

In retrospect, as much as Murph liked to export relevance and destroy stereotypes, he was still, in his very DNA, about finding the funny. And the number one goal and litmus test of funny is laughter. Were NRW consciously tempering *The Jeffersons* with a perfect balance of cogency & comedy, making sure not to let the cogency overtake the funny, thinking that would be a certain kiss of death for any sitcom? Murph wasn't sure; but if they were, it was working.

Chapter 15

A COUPLE CHRISTMAS STORIES

('76)

M&M pitched a story to NRW for Lionel & Jenny's wedding as a Christmas episode and NRW liked it. So M&M would be writing the Christmas shows for both *All in the Family* and *The Jeffersons* that year.

Titled "The Christmas Wedding," the story was basically that it's Christmas Eve at the Jeffersons' house and George and Tom are at loggerheads over wedding plans.

George wants more of his friends and business associates on the guest list. "I don't want no lily-white wedding."

Tom has asked his nephew, a white minister, to officiate and George objects: "I don't want my son getting married by no honky minister!" When George finds out Tom's nephew is Episcopalian, he really hits the roof!

George: "I follow the Baptist Church!"

Louise: "George, you don't go to church."

George: "I said 'follow,' not 'go to.'"

When Lionel and Jenny try to tell their parents they want a small wedding, George cuts them off: "You two stay out of it. This wedding is none of your business."

Christmas carolers arrive at the front door and all exit to the hall. Ralph and Bentley are there. When M&M learned that Ralph didn't have a last name, they decided to give him one. The white minister, holding a collection container, tells George that Mr. Hart says George is a very generous man.

George: "Who's Mr. Hart?"

Ralph: "That's me, Mr. Jefferson. Ralph Hart."

George: "Oh, Ralph, I didn't know your last name was Hart. I thought it was Handout."

George puts some money in the minister's container and gives Ralph a Christmas tip. Carolers end the song they're singing and begin a new one:

Carolers (singing): "I'M DREAMING OF A **WHITE** CHRISTMAS..."

George reacts, asking the minister to sing something else. The minister protests, saying this is one of their favorites. George makes another donation, and the carolers immediately switch to "SILENT NIGHT..."

When the carolers leave and the others return to the Jefferson living room, Tom and George begin arguing again and George escapes to the bathroom, but Tom follows and they continue to yell at each other as the door closes.

Louise says she has an idea, and huddles the others in the room as we DISSOLVE TO shortly after, when Lionel has returned with the carolers and minister. When George and Tom come out of the bathroom still arguing, the minister attempts to mediate with them and we soon see that Louise has arranged an impromptu wedding with Lionel & Jenny which the minister manages to carry out under Tom's and George's noses.

When George realizes what has happened, he's upset. But when he finds out the minister is a Baptist, he feels a lot better.

ONE REASON NRW embraced M&M's Christmas wedding pitch was because it called for only two sets, both of which were standard *Jefferson* sets—the Living Room and the outer Hallway. Often when you're shooting a wedding, you might think of a church, or a ballroom with a lot of extras, which of course can be expensive. As a writer, you should put on your producer hat and ask yourself, "Do I really need additional sets to tell this story?" If your answer is *no*, you can save your show a significant amount of money and become a budget hero (rather than a budget zero).

On an average-sized multi-camera stage, you can fit three sets. If you examine any multi-camera series, you'll notice most episodes use no more than three sets. And each show will have its standard sets. On *The Jeffersons*, the main set is the Living Room with the Kitchen and outer/elevator Hallway extensions. The pass-through on the Kitchen counter (between Kitchen and Living Room) is great for jokes from Florence when needed.

Other standard, pre-built sets for *The Jeffersons* are the Master Bedroom, the Willis's Bedroom, the Willis Den & Kitchen, Charley's Bar, Jefferson Cleaners Store.

In Murph's freshman English class at St. Xavier High School, taught by Jesuit scholastic Mr. Jerry Lackamp, students had to write a composition each week. Subject matter was open, the only requirement being the writer had to include three items—different each week—named by Mr.

Lackamp. For example a *red wagon*, a *tennis ball* and a *lamp post with a missing light bulb.*

Murph found this exercise to be both fun and challenging. Murph would usually write a story and attempt to include the three required items in a manner that was as creative and clever as possible. For instance, using the items named above, Murph had a character in the story notice that a lamp post had a light bulb manufactured and stamped by the *MISSING Lighting Corporation.*

Murph found a similar challenge in writing a sitcom script, having to tell the story in three (or fewer) sets. When breaking a story, one of the first things Murph would consider is how many sets would be required.

Another requirement for students in Murph's high school English class was that each student had to hand in two drafts of his composition—the first draft in pencil and the second in ink. (Fountain pen, believe it or not!)This practice proved to be excellent training for the primary activity of TV staff writers—rewriting.

On occasion, when the story absolutely requires it, a fourth set or "swing set" can be used where a wall can be swung to fit cameras in and the audience can see inside. Or a small set can be built in the back which the audience will only be able to see on the hanging TV monitors above, but their laughter can still be recorded accordingly.

Some shows will occasionally, when necessary, pre-shoot a scene on a fourth set (during the day) and then show that scene later to the audience in sequence on the monitors and record their laughter. Pre-shooting, of course, is not ideal for an audience show. For one thing, it takes the audience out of the actors' performance in the pre-shot scene. And it risks halting the play's momentum when you have to stop and inform the audience to watch the next scene on the monitor. For those reasons alone, Murph felt pre-shooting should be used only as a last resort.

Murph once attended a multi-cam sitcom filmed on the Warner Brothers lot where the audience was marched outside and onto another stage mid-filming. In that case, the other stage was set up like a Vegas casino.

In Murph's mind, when designing a set for comedy use, a formula to keep in mind is D = C. DOORS equal COMEDY. Especially if you're planning a farce. Stairway to second floor or basement, or window to fire escape is also good. The more entrances and exits available, the more potential for comedy.

WHEN THE TIME came for M&M to meet with Norman to discuss "The Draft Dodger" story, Norman suggested Archie has invited his friend Pinky (Eugene Roche), a widower and Gold Star Father, to Christmas dinner. It was the first time Murph heard the term "Gold Star Father." The Gold Star lapel pin is presented to U.S. parents of a son or daughter killed in military combat.

At first Murph wondered if it would seem too forced, too coincidental, that the same night Meathead's draft dodging friend comes by, so does Archie's Gold Star Father friend. Although Murph certainly could see that the drama would be increased tenfold. A draft dodger and a parent whose son died in Vietnam, both at Archie's house on Christmas Eve...Then Murph thought, 'Geez, why didn't I think of that?!'

Writing about the show here wouldn't do it justice. You have to watch it to see how Carroll O'Connor's performance, and the performances of the whole cast, caused "The Draft Dodger" to be considered by many viewers one of the most impactful *All in the Family* episodes ever, and honored by The Writers Guild as one of the Top 100 shows ever shown on television .

Murph watched the 5:00 taping in the audience sitting next to Nancy O'Connor (Archie's real wife) and, during Archie's climactic confrontation, tears were streaming down her cheeks.

When Archie and Meathead go toe-to-toe about the war in Vietnam, Meathead yells: "Arch, when the hell are you gonna admit the war was wrong?!" And Archie erupts with: "I ain't talkin' about that war. I don't wanna talk about that GODDAM war no more!"

Carroll ad-libbed "God damned," but it flowed naturally in the middle of a powerfully moving scene. And he wanted it to stay. So did Norman and everybody else. Except CBS. The network wanted it changed. They were afraid they'd get an avalanche of mail from religious groups all across the country. According to CBS, the one word that triggers more negative mail to networks and sponsors is the word "God" used in any way other than a sacred sense. (Murph was surprised to learn that John Lennon's song *Imagine*, released in 1971 promoting world peace, was banned from radio play because of the line "Imagine there's no heaven.")

Murph heard Carroll wanted to fight to keep it in and even flew to New York to meet with William Paley, President and founder of CBS. Murph felt confident the good guys could win this battle. After all, if you asked God to damn *war*, who could be offended?

Apparently, a whole lot of people.

CBS refused to budge and sent this Memorandum to Mort Lachman, Executive Producer of AITF, from Jim Baerg at CBS with copies to his CBS colleagues Dick Kirschner and Van Sauter:

RE: ALL IN THE FAMILY "The Draft Dodger"

As last discussed following the taping of this episode on November 19, 1976, we wish to reiterate the fact that Archie's "...that <u>God damned</u> war!" (underlined only) is considered unacceptable for broadcast and again request that it not be present in the episode as delivered to CBS for broadcast. We would ask that his alternate line "...rotten war" be used instead.

Your cooperation is appreciated.

Initialed by JB (Jim Baerg) of CBS

Thus the line was drawn by CBS, and the line was withdrawn by Tandem/TAT. At an upcoming taping of *AITF*, a "wild line" was recorded by Carroll O'Connor saying the words "rotten damn" which were used to replace "God damn." If you look closely at that moment in the scene, you can see Archie's lips form the words "God damn" while the audio says "rotten damn" war. Damn shame. Although even Murph will admit that it doesn't really hurt the scene.

When the show was aired, Murph was surprised. He expected the cogent moments in the episode to influence most viewers toward favoring Meathead's point of view. But letters from viewers, all taking strong positions, were 50-50. An even split between "Right on, Meathead!" and "You tell 'em, Archie!"

Listed below is a sample of each reaction: the exact words of a handwritten letter from a viewer in Connecticut, followed by a brutal review from a newspaper columnist.

December 28, 1976
All In The Family
WCBS
New York, N.Y.

Gentlemen:

*We are rarely moved by any TV program as we were by
All In The Family on Saturday, December 26th. Your
writers deserve the highest praise for their presentation of the arguments and feelings on both sides of the
amnesty controversy.*

*It seems particularly important that they showed Archie
as shaken in his usual prejudices, recognizing for the
first time that he needed to "think about" an idea different from his own.*

*It was a courageous act on your part to try to bring
reason and compassion to this crucial issue. We feel
grateful both to the network and to your sponsors.
Perhaps you will be able to repeat this particular
program soon.*

Sincerely,
Harry & Mollie Klein

Below see the newspaper review (abbreviated):

Christmas for Cowards
By Ken Carolan

*It is not nice to kick in your television set on Christmas
night—but I almost did. ...I called WCBS-TV in New
York instead. ...Why the rage? I had just watched the
most rotten TV show I have ever seen in my life—the
Christmas night version of "All in the Family." I wanted
to let Norman Lear and the liberal lunatics who aired
that piece of raw garbage know what I thought of them.*

*For Christmas night, when the parents of men who
lost their lives in Vietnam were undoubtedly suffering
through a very depressing holiday without their sons,*

some idiot wrote a script in honor of draft dodgers — as a Christmas present to Gold Star Mothers and Fathers no doubt.

They even included a Gold Star Father in the script — a forgiving, understanding type. The actor who played the part is named Ed (sic) Roach (sic) (Eugene Roche) — you know him best as "the professional dish washer" in commercials. I hope in the next commercial somebody shoves his head into the dishwasher and holds it there until the bubbles stop coming up.

In brief, what passed for a plot consisted of having a friend of Archie's son-in-law, Mike, at the Bunker house for dinner. He is a draft dodger who slipped in from Canada for a holiday visit. His father, eminently more sensible than those script writers, wants no part of him — so he ends up with his liberal friend, Mike, the "meathead."

Archie, in the meantime, has also invited his friend "Pinky" to the same dinner. Pinky lost his son, Steve, in Vietnam.

Without going into all the nauseating nonsense, I will simply explain that Archie learns he is sitting at the same table with a "Canadian Coward" about half-way through the meal.

...Draft Dodger then admits what he is and Archie wants to call the F.B.I.--but Edith says she isn't sure she has enough turkey. Granted, funny line. I bet the real Gold Star Mothers and Fathers were really laughing.

Then came the rage, my rage, when Archie asked his friend how he felt about having dinner with the draft dodger.

Gold Star Father: "My son hated the war too, but he did what he had to do—and David (the draft dodger) did what he had to do. I want to have dinner with this boy—and if my son Steve were here, that's what he would want to do."

Then they rose and Gold Star Father shakes hands with draft dodger. "Merry Christmas, sir," says the artful dodger. "Merry Christmas, SON," says the dishwasher-turned-Gold Star Father.

…Who was the imbecile who wrote that script and who was the mental midget who approved it for broadcast? I screamed at no one in particular, "Why? Why? Why was that put on the air—tonight of all nights?"

I could only pray that my friends Al and Mary Korona, certified Gold Star parents, were not watching. Knowing Al, he WOULD have kicked in his TV set—and Mary would have stomped it.

They have told me of the terrible loneliness, the pain, the torture they suffer every holiday. They want to celebrate with their son but all they can do is look at his picture and his medals—and remember—only remember a Christmas past—a Christmas before young Al died a hero.

I don't know what the viewer rating of "All in the Family" is now—but I do know that as of Saturday it is down by one household.

Will I hurt them by tuning them out? Of course not. But I will be able to keep looking Al and Mary Korona in the eye.

Yep, despite the fact that the draft had ended three years earlier, following military withdrawal from Vietnam, amnesty for "draft dodgers" was still a hot-button issue in America. It was an election year, 1976, and Jimmy Carter had just been elected President.

A couple months before, while working on "The Draft Dodger" script, Murph and Sean sent a letter to the President-elect congratulating him on winning the election and expressing their thoughts about amnesty and healing a divided country. Jimmy Carter replied with the following note, on stationery which had two words at the top:

JIMMY CARTER

To Mick Murphy and Sean Malloy:

I appreciate your congratulations and expressions of confidence.

Your thoughts are important to me, and I will carefully consider your suggestions regarding pardons/ amnesty.

I need your help more than ever during the coming years. With the support of friends like you, we will have a good administration!
Sincerely,
Jimmy Carter
JC/sc

ONE DAY AT a Time, starring Bonnie Franklin as a divorced mom raising two teenage daughters was a new CBS series showing promise. Murph happened to be in Norman's office when he got a call from the network about the recently taped episode of *One Day*. The network wanted Norman to shoot a new tag. Apparently, the existing *One Day at a Time* tag featured Ann Romano (main character) and a man in the hallway at the front door returning to her apartment and at Ann's feet was a suitcase. The network person was concerned that viewers would think Ann spent the night with the man.

"They would be right," said Norman.

The person on the other end of the phone told Norman the network did not want to be telling *One Day at a Time* viewers that Ann Romano, an unmarried woman, was engaging in sexual activity. Remember, this was in the 1970s, before cable and during the so-called Family Hour.

They wanted Norman to re-shoot the tag without the suitcase. Norman very calmly, in a manner that very much reminded Murph of Marlon Brando in the *Godfather*, explained to the network person that "people bed each other" all the time. (This was the first time Murph heard "bed" used as a verb and he was both amused and impressed at the usage.)Then Norman explained matter-of-factly that he was not going to re-shoot the tag.

The network person explained that CBS was not going to air that tag. Norman confirmed it was the network's choice. Norman made it clear that his obligation was to deliver a show, and he did. And, continued Norman calmly, if the network doesn't want to show it, they can "put snow on the air" if they want. Not his problem.

Murph couldn't help thinking how another producer—say Gene Plummer, at *That's My Mama*, might handle this situation. (Murph and Sean had watched Producer Plummer rudely berate his assistant in language that would embarrass a Hell's Angel.)

After he hung up, Norman summed up his philosophy regarding dealing with networks on matters of creativity by saying if you give them an inch, they'll take a mile.

Norman then walked Murph to a framed item on the wall. It was a chart from *Daily Variety* which showed how much profit each of the three networks was making. Network Exec Fred Silverman started this game of Demographics and Network Standings, determining who's first, second and third among the competitors—CBS, NBC and ABC—and then proceeded to convince each network that he, Silverman, and only he, could turn a network around from bottom (3rd) to top (1st).

What Norman pointed out to Murph was that financially each network was making a killing. Norman said he had no sympathy for the networks, no matter how much they act like they're operating on a shoestring.

And where money was concerned, Murph's boss made his priorities clear. "They can take away my house and my furniture, but they can't take away the only thing I really care about."

"Your Mercedes?" offered Murph.

Norman chuckled. "My kids and my family."

When Norman walked Murph into the outer office, he turned to Jadi Jo and told her to book a flight to Bora Bora—"but don't tell anyone." It was a clear message to CBS that if they're expecting a new *One Day* tag, they won't be getting it.

Later, Murph thought about what he witnessed and tried to put it into words. What makes Norman Lear Norman Lear, Murph thought, is a nuclear combination of two traits rarely found in the same person: creative genius and business acumen—he's both a brilliant artist and a smart businessman. Norman is a man of opposites, a combination of a lot of things you don't usually find in the same package. Like warmth and ambition. Heart and balls. A realist and an optimist—with an emphasis on optimist.

Norman likes to tell the story about the twin brothers who get a birthday present from their dad and it's delivered in a huge box. So they get a ladder and open the top of the box and all they see is a huge box full of shit. So the one brother says, "Aw, man, all Dad sent us is a box of shit!And the other brother jumps in and starts digging. And the first brother says, "What are you doing?!"And the brother in the box says, "With all this shit, there must be a pony in here somewhere!"Norman's always looking for the pony.

In short, Murph saw Norman Lear as a man on a quest for truth—and he's found his truth in comedy. He's the kind of man who can make you laugh and think. The kind of man you both respect and admire. The kind of man anyone would love to have as a father.

Chapter 16

ARCHIE BUNKER
VS.
GEORGE JEFFERSON

In later years it would annoy Murph no end when he heard or read online a commonly accepted comparison describing George Jefferson as a "black Archie Bunker." Murph felt that character description was not only overly simplified, but inaccurate and unfair. So unfair, in fact, that Murph thought if he ever wrote a book about such things, he would give the subject of Archie vs. George its own chapter.

Let's not describe these two by the color of their skin. That's so American. Sure, you could call each a bigot. But Archie's bigotry is pure prejudice. George's bigotry is a reaction to prejudice. George doesn't hate white people just because of the color of their skin. He hates that they kidnapped, raped, enslaved and lynched his ancestors.

Archie uses slurs to categorize and marginalize others who are not like him—wop, chink, Hebe, spade, fruit.

George uses the word "honky" to describe descendants of the people who enslaved his ancestors and continue to oppress his community in a system stacked in favor of the oppressor. Notice you've never seen George call Harry Bentley a honky. George has no beef with Bentley. Bentley's ancestors didn't own slaves. He's not American. He's just a weird Brit. A looney Limey.

Bentley doesn't even notice color. In an early episode, someone attempting to make sure they're talking about the same person, says something to Bentley like, "Your neighbor, Jefferson. He's black, right?" And Bentley says something quite sincere like, "Is he? I never noticed."

If you're a *Jeffersons* viewer, you might wonder why George is always calling Tom a honky? George is a proud black man. When he calls Tom (or anyone else) a honky, he's bragging. It's a three-pronged brag: He's saying, 'I'm black, I'm successful, and I did it without having to kiss any ofay ass!' With his honky jokes, George is also putting Tom, or anyone else, on notice that his success has come without any benefit of what some now refer to as "white privilege." In other words, as a black man, George's accomplishments are worth at least twice as much as a white man's achievements!

Tom understands where George is coming from and tolerates George's bragging. George knows that Tom, married to a black woman, is not a racist and not the real enemy. But George doesn't want anyone, especially his black brothers—or sisters—to see him hanging around Tom Willis and get the idea that George thinks he's too good to be running with his own people. And to George, making honky and zebra jokes are a way of reminding others that he's his own man—not some Oreo—black on the outside and honky on the inside.

When George makes honky jokes around Tom, he's playing on Tom's white guilt. And, as a black man, he's also exercising the one true freedom he knows he has— free speech. He may not be able to get a cab to Harlem, or join any private club he wants, or live in any building he wants, or work at any job he wants. But, thanks to the First Amendment, George Jefferson can *say* anything he wants!

Archie and George have each had a limited amount of education, but George rose above that.

Archie is a victim, willing to live within the rules and limitations that were thrust upon him. He's content just to be white. George, on the other hand, is a hero, willing to fight a system that continues to be stacked against him and beat Whitey at his own game.

As a buffoon, Archie is both lovable and funny. We can love him and laugh at him because all of us, no matter what our skin color, can recognize some of that buffoonery in ourselves.

George is lovable and funny because he's a fighter. And who doesn't love a fighter, especially when he's fighting against insurmountable odds. He's David fighting a system of Goliaths. George's slingshot is his chain of cleaning stores. He intends to use that chain as a weapon to clear away whatever obstacles may be blocking his path to the American Dream.

Archie, on the other hand, has reached a plateau. He's almost incapable of changing. Archie Bunker is satire personified.

So here, in a nutshell, is how Murph would sum up perhaps the two most iconic figures in American sitcom history:

Archie Bunker – At best, a lovable buffoon. At worst, an ignorant bigot.

George Jefferson – At best, a hero. At worst, a workaholic intent on providing his family with not only the necessities but the finer things in life.

Bernie West, Don Nicholl, Mickey Ross

Office Totem Pole - Don Nicholl, Bea Dallas, Bernie West, Mickey Ross,
George Sunga (associate producer)

Table Reading - Mickey, Don & Bernie

Comedy Duo - Mickey & Bernie (Then & Now)

The Author & Bernie West

The Jeffersons Cast & Crew, 1977
(standing, back row, middle) Writers John Baskin, Roger Shulman,

Mike Milligan (Sean), Jay Moriarty (Murph). (Bernie West is missing.)

The Star & The Author

The Author & The Boss

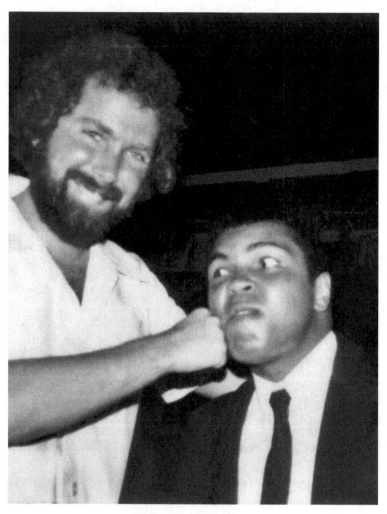

The Author & The Champ

Battle on the $8,000 Bridge - The Author & Michael Moye

Producers & Cast with Billy Dee Williams

Standing 5th & 6th from left, Jack Shea and script supervisor Sylvia O'Gilvie

M&M at Writers Conference in Hawaii

The Jeffersons Cast & Crew - 1979

M&M hanging with George & Weezy

Executive Producers - Milligan & Moriarty (Sean & Murph)

The Author with daughters Colleen & Heather

Chapter 17

GREEN SUIT
(AARON SPELLING)
('76-77)

In those days, television programming was basically divided into two categories, half-hour and hour. Half-hour shows were comedies, hour shows were dramas. A few months back, Sweet Lew got a call from TV producer Doug Cramer who, along with Aaron Spelling, had a deal with ABC to produce a pilot. Cramer and Spelling were noted drama producers, although Doug had been involved as an executive with the *Joe and Sons* series.

Doug wanted to meet with M&M about writing a pilot for an hour series to be produced by Doug and Aaron Spelling. So Lew set up a lunch meeting with Cramer at Ma Maison, a show biz restaurant known for such assignations. Apparently, M&M were permitted by contract to write at least one non-TAT pilot per season.

As the four sat for lunch in what appeared to be a VIP section of this distinctive French restaurant, Doug explained that this pilot project for ABC network was to be a 90-minute TV movie. M&M were somewhat surprised they were being considered for this project since they'd never written a pilot, a movie script or a dramatic episode.

Doug did mention that he and Aaron wanted the show to contain humor. And Murph figured that their *Joe and Sons* episode, which aired as a pilot to stellar reviews, must have had an influence on Doug.

When it came time to order food, pretty much the only word on the menu that Murph recognized was the word "steak." So Murph, last to order, wanting to avoid asking embarrassing questions about items on the menu, ordered "steak tartare, well done."

The waiter chuckled, as if laughing at something Murph intended as a joke, and disappeared with their food orders.

When the food came, Murph, expecting a well done steak, found himself facing a plate which held a mound of raw ground meat topped with a raw egg yolk. Before Murph could say a word, Sean came to the rescue, insisting that he and Murph switch plates. Sean's order of pork chops looked good—at least they were cooked—and Sean insisted he'd rather have the steak tartare which looked "scrumptious." So, unsure what was happening, Murph did not object to a switch.

On the way home, Murph's only defense against Sean's ribbing was that Murph had heard the words "steak tartare" before, but could not imagine why anyone—ever, no matter who you were—would actually order a ground mound of raw meat with a raw egg.

Truth be told, Murph was not a culinary connoisseur. He didn't know what a taco was before moving to California. He never ate salad before he started eating in the commissary at PML. Co-worker Dick Croy talked him into taking a little lettuce, putting a little dressing on it, and tasting it. "It's good for you," Croy said. "Helps clean out your system."

Murph's dad didn't eat salad. Didn't see much point in it. Strictly a meat and potatoes guy. Murph's mom wasn't much of a cook, but she learned to cook what her husband liked. Meatloaf on Mondays; pork chops & apple sauce on Tuesdays; chicken, ham or spaghetti and meatballs on Wednesdays, Thursdays and Saturdays; Mrs. Paul's fish sticks on Fridays; roast beef on Sundays; and mashed potatoes every night. Daily vegetable varied with peas, string beans or corn.

When Murph was about thirteen, his mom took this thing out of the freezer called a "pizza pie" and cooked it for dinner. She said it was something new and it was good for them to try something different for a change. The entire Murphy family agreed it tasted like cardboard with ketchup on top, and Murph's dad 86'd pizza pie from the Murphy menu.

Sean, of course, thought the whole "steak tartare well done" thing was hilarious. And he later made it clear that if Murph ever wrote any sort of memoir, he better include the steak tartare story and mention how Sean subtly saved his guileless partner's ass, or Sean would write his own memoir just so he could mention the horrified look on Murph's face when that lunch plate was delivered.

So a time was set for M&M to meet with Aaron Spelling at his Beverly Hills home. Murph and Sean were told to park in Aaron's driveway, which, as it turned out, was the size of a parking lot. When the duo knocked at the front door, they were greeted by the butler who guided them to the living room where they met Mr. Spelling.

Aaron was a small, slight man with an engaging smile,

described by one adoring actress as Jiminy Cricket. There was an aura of success and self-assurance around the prolific producer, which Murph would tell you was not unlike that surrounding Norman Lear. Indeed, where Lear was the acknowledged king of half-hours, Spelling was fast becoming the king of hours. Most of his shows were airing on the ABC network, causing many in the business to suggest that ABC stood for "Aaron's Broadcasting Company."

While Murph, Sean and Aaron were meeting, the doorbell rang and the butler entered with the new edition of *TIME* magazine. On the cover were Charlie's Angels, the stars of Spelling-Goldberg's newest hit series, featuring Kate Jackson, Farrah Fawcett and Jaclyn Smith as police academy-trained private detectives. Aaron took the magazine, with the cover heading TV's SUPER WOMEN, and looked inside, pleased.

Aaron's wife Candy entered and all four enjoyed the moment of seeing Aaron's show on the cover of *TIME*. Aaron read aloud a quote from partner Leonard Goldberg in the magazine and chuckled, hinting that the partnership would be dissipating soon.

Regarding *Charlie's Angels*, reviewers used labels like "titillating TV," "jiggle TV," "T&A" (tits & ass) to point out that the producers made every effort to put the three stars in revealing costumes such as bikinis, cocktail dresses, etc.

Aaron explained this to Sean & Murph by saying, "I grew up in Texas. My father was a tailor. A guy comes to my father and says 'Make me a green suit,' my father doesn't say 'You know, you'd look much better in brown or blue.' If the man wants a green suit, my father gives him a green suit. If the network wants T&A, I give 'em what they want."

Aaron continued by confiding in M&M that a series of his titled *Family* (also on ABC), about the trials and tribulations of a modern day middle class family, produced in association with Mike Nichols, is the kind of entertainment he really wants to do. Aaron said he'd like to see Sean & Mick write a pilot in the vein of *Family*, only with a little more humor. And he mentioned that the network would like the series to be set at the beach.

M&M left Aaron's house excited about this new challenge. Since the beach setting seemed to be important, they asked Lew to see if he could negotiate two weeks of lodging at a beach location so they could do research. A nice hotel room on the beach in Malibu was arranged, compliments of Spelling Entertainment.

Sean & Mick worked up a concept and pitched it to Aaron. The basic premise was this: Family of five, currently living in Oklahoma. Father, Bud, works in a plant and writes the checks, but doesn't have time for much else. Mother, Ruth, runs the house and raises the kids, but doesn't have time for much else. Family is basically in a rut. Ruth's elderly aunt dies and leaves a Malibu beach house to her niece.

The family decides to take a long overdue vacation, visiting California to sell the beach house. In Malibu, the kids make friends and embrace beach life while Bud and Ruth get to know each other and re-fall in love at the beach. In the end, the revitalized family (including 18-year-old daughter Denise, 14 year-old son Glenn and 10-year-old daughter Kathy) trades Oklahoma life for beach life and Bud decides to follow his dream of owning and operating a gas station/mechanic shop in Malibu.

M&M wrote a brief outline and showed it to Aaron. Aaron gave it a thumbs-up and sent it to the network. In a few days, Sean, Murph and Aaron met with Cliff Weinberg, head of development at ABC. Cliff told the trio he liked the outline but had one note: "Kill the mother."

Murph waited for a laugh from Cliff, but it didn't come. Was he serious? If they lose the mother, there's no romance. If there's no romance, there's no motivation to stay in California. Which changes the whole premise of the show. It's like telling *All in the Family* to lose the bigotry. Or *The Partridge Family* to lose the band. Or *Green Acres* to kill the pig. But wait a minute—Aaron will never fall for this. He wants to do a show about a family at the beach. And what's a traditional family without a mother?

When Aaron didn't respond, Murph asked Cliff, "So you mean it's a show about a single father raising three kids at the beach?" Cliff nodded.

Afterwards, M&M asked Aaron if he were surprised by the network note. Aaron said something like, "Fellas, I've been doing this for a while. I'm never surprised at anything the network says." Two words came to mind for Murph: Green suit.

So M&M got busy writing a six-act 90-minute pilot about a single father of three whose wife was killed by a network executive.

M&M handed in their script, titled *Beachin'*, and waited to hear. The network had double or triple developed for the time slot. That means they ordered two or three pilot scripts and would pick one to shoot and air. The one they picked was titled *The San Pedro Beach Bums*, a show about five guys living on a houseboat in the harbor near San Pedro, California. It was also an Aaron Spelling project.

In William Goldman's book on screenwriting, the author states that in the movie business, "Nobody knows any-thing." In television, as Murph would say, it's the opposite.

"Everybody knows everything." Which, if you think about it, is the same thing. Network and studio executives especially can tell you who watches a TV show and why, and why a show is a hit or a flop. At least after the first season.

Focus groups, the method for testing TV pilots before they air, are famously inaccurate. Two of the lowest-testing pilots of the time were *All in the Family* and *The Mary Tyler Moore Show*, which became two of the tube's biggest hits. (Likewise in the 1990s, two of the lowest-testing pilots were *Seinfeld* and *Friends*, both iconic sitcoms of that decade.)

Murph never saw the *Beach Bums* pilot nor the nine episodes. But he heard that the first episode following the pilot featured all three Charlie's Angels; and another episode had the Beach Bums taking a cruise on *The Love Boat*, also a Spelling show.

You may recall that when Murph first met with Aaron Spelling, he felt a presence that reminded him of Norman Lear. Having worked with Aaron, Murph concluded that, like Norman, Aaron is a nice man. A smart man. A skillful producer. But there's a difference. Where Aaron Spelling, by his own admission, gives people what they want; Norman Lear, with a sense of responsibility, gives people what he thinks they need. The difference is monumental.

Chapter 18

JEFFS PLUS, SEASON 3

('77)

January 28, 1977, seven months after Murph's birthday, Sean joined Murph at age 30. Murph planned to celebrate with a surprise birthday party roast for his writing partner at the Valley Hilton Hotel.

The evening was billed as **Get Even With Sean Night**. Sean, like Murph, only maybe more so (he was younger), enjoyed teasing and playing practical jokes. For example, just a month ago, right before Christmas, they heard "the girls upstairs" going from office to office singing Christmas carols. So they concocted a prank.

When M&M weren't playing Velcro pong darts, or tossing plastic hoops around plastic Moosehead antlers, or yelling "Out Weezy!" and pounding on walls to make others—especially Bernie and Milt—think they were hard at work, they were discovering other items of distraction in their office such as a swivel chair and a pushup section ceiling.

They realized that if you put a belt around your neck, tucked the other end into the ceiling, stood on a swivel chair and swayed back and forth, it would look, since the chair was blocked by the desk, like a dead body hanging from the ceiling.

So Murph approached the carolers upstairs and told them Sean's dog had died and with Christmas coming Sean had been depressed and even threw Murph out of their office about an hour ago and, well, maybe if they came down and sang Christmas carols it might cheer Sean up.

So Murph and the girls stood outside M&M's office and Murph knocked on the door and opened it as the carolers started to sing "Deck the halls with..." and they saw Sean hanging from the ceiling and SCREAMED their lungs out!

If you were to ask Murph to name one instance in the past four years that best defines his partner, Murph would not name the time Sean streaked (in underwear) on a dare from their office to Don's office and back. Nor would he mention the time Sean had everyone in the office dancing around the Christmas tree singing "Grandma Got Run Over By A Reindeer."

What Murph would talk about is the time not long after they met when he and Sean were driving back from working out at the gym and they witnessed a head-on collision across the street. A woman was lying in the street bleeding and Sean stopped the car and ran to help her. He grabbed Murph's workout shirt to wipe the blood from the woman's forehead and held her head up until the paramedics arrived. And then the next day Sean went to visit her in the hospital. Sean Peter Malloy may be a "one man parade," as Murph sometimes calls him, but "Sean's heart and mind are always marching in the right direction."

So on Roast night, a meeting room on the third floor of the Valley Hilton was set up with round dinner tables and a raised dais. A huge poster-sized photo of Sean was placed on an easel near the dais and the room was packed with adult friends and relatives of Sean's.

Judi reserved a room in the hotel and told Sean she was taking him there for his birthday. On the way to their room, she told Sean she wanted to show him some paintings on the third floor. When she opened the door and they entered the meeting room, Sean was met with a booming SURPRISE!

The dais consisted of the Nasty Nine: Sean's high school friends John Harper and Augie Bertino, both of whom travelled from out of town; agent Sweet Lew Weitzman; *Jeffersons* director Jack Shea; writers Michael Baser & Kim Weiskopf; writers John Baskin & Roger Shulman; and Emcee/Host/Partner Michael Francis Murphy. Baskin & Shulman, also represented by Sweet Lew, were Story Editors on *Good Times* who had become cohorts/mentors of M&M. Others in attendance were also invited to get up and speak during the roast.

Jokes included everything from classic roast insults about what an ugly baby Sean was: "When Sean was born, he was so ugly the doctor slapped his mother." To a touching tale from New Yorker Michael Baser who recounted how, since he was spending the recent holidays away from home for the first time, Sean invited him to join Sean's family for Christmas dinner. Baser said he was so moved that he kept his place card from the dinner, then revealed a huge place card which read MURDEROUS JEW.

Murph performed an impression of his partner, wearing a faded maroon paisley button down shirt—secretly acquired from Sean's wife Judi—which Sean "too often" wore to work. Murph's routine ended with him taking scissors and cutting up Sean's "painfully ugly shirt," explaining that the final destruction and burial of the shirt was the main reason Murph organized this roast—which was not totally untrue.

MURPH WAS DRIVING on the Hollywood Freeway on his way to work meditating, with the radio on. He heard something from the radio like: "Comedian Freddie Prinze shot himself in the head and is presumed dead."

Murph could not believe his ears. No way! Is this a joke? Freddie Prinze, star of *Chico and the Man*, committed *suicide*?! The 21 or 22-year-old self-proclaimed "Hungarican" kid who has a hit TV series and a career that's going through the roof!? Makes no sense.

Supposedly, Freddie was seated on the sofa with his agent or manager nearby, reached between the sofa cushions, pulled out a gun and shot himself. Murph heard he left a note that said something like, "I can't go on. There's no hope left. I'll be at peace."

When Murph arrived at work, Sean was at his desk. Sean to Murph: "Guess you heard about Chico." Murph: "Think he just finished watching 'The Invention'?"

And there it was—the first Chico joke. The way comedy writers handle tragedy. It's instinctive. They can't help themselves. Later in the day, sitting on the sofa in their office discussing a script with other writers, Sean said something like, "I can't work like this anymore," reached between the sofa cushions, pulled out a toy gun, pulled the trigger and fell over on the couch. The resulting *nothing is sacred* laughter brought a certain relief from the surrounding pall in the room.

Throughout the day, AITF writer Mel Tolkin was seen roaming aimlessly around the office, stopping only at the water cooler, mumbling words like "Twenty-one-year-old kid..." and shaking his head in disbelief, probably trying hard to think of a joke to ease the tension and dilute the tragic aura of the day.

Murph was introspective by nature, admittedly analytical to a fault. It bothered him that he too could not understand what would motivate Freddie Prinze to kill himself. Prinze had sat in for Carson on *The Tonight Show*, performed at President Carter's Inauguration, had a big Vegas deal in the works. Depression? What was there to be depressed about? His whole life was ahead of him? Drugs? Are drugs really that powerful? Supposedly the star's wife had recently filed for divorce, but they had a baby and... well... Wouldn't that be reason enough to live?

Murph recalled reading a quote a while back that said something like: "There are two great tragedies in life—one is not to get what the heart desires; the other is to get it." Sounds like a line from the writing team of Mark Twain & Socrates.

Murph enjoyed reading the Existentialists in college, writers like Nietzsche, Kierkegaard, Camus, Sartre. With titles like *Being and Nothingness*, *Thus Spake Zarathustra*, *The Myth of Sisyphus*, *Irrational Man*. During that time, between the ages of 19-21, when you examine life and especially death, Murph embraced Existentialist thought: What is is, and that's all we know. Murph, through his own detailed reasoning, came to the simple conclusion that life is a joke. Through no choice of our own, we find ourselves walking on a bridge between life and death; and the bridge leads inevitably to certain death. The only truly logical choice we have is to either jump off the bridge or embrace the journey (the joke) and laugh at it. Having an affinity for comedy, Murph chose the latter.

Given what he understood about Freddie Prinze, Murph would certainly have expected Freddie not to jump. But expectations, though hard to resist, are judgmental. And the two things Murph tried hardest not to be were judgmental and hypocritical.

In Steinbeck's *The Grapes of Wrath*, the book Murph considers The Great American Novel, Tom Joad runs into Preacher Casy, who's given up preaching because he no longer feels he has a right to tell people what's right and what's wrong.

Casy says he just got to thinkin', "The hell with it. There ain't no sin and there ain't no virtue. They's just things people do. And some of those things is nice and some ain't so nice. But that's all any man's got a right to say."

Amen. RIP Chico.

ABC NETWORK, WITH Fred Silverman at the helm, was attempting to develop an American version of a British sitcom titled *Man About the House*. The first pilot script was written by a Broadway playwright and set in New York. The second script was developed by Larry Gelbart, who also developed M*A*S*H, and set in North Hollywood. And the third attempt was being undertaken by Murph's bosses, NRW. The title of the project at this stage was *Three's Company*, now set in Santa Monica at the beach.

Murph knew very little about the project, as he and Sean had been consumed with both *The Jeffersons* and the Spelling pilot. At one point, NRW asked Murph if they could pick his brain about creating board games as they were thinking about making that the main occupation for the male lead in *Three's Company*. Murph hoped they would indeed make the character a board game inventor and maybe use some of Murph's games on the show. Promotion, baby!

On another occasion Murph approached Don's office to ask a *Jeffersons* question, but NRW were busy casting. He found himself standing outside Don's office next to a friendly blonde actress waiting to read. She remarked that Murph's eyes were a "striking" blue just like her boyfriend's. He wished her luck with the pending audition and moved on.

When the *Three's Company* pilot was shot on the lot, Murph went to see it. He noticed the blonde actress he met, Suzanne Somers, was cast as one of the three leads. He was a touch disappointed that the male lead was not a board game creator, but an aspiring chef (as in the original British series).

The premise of the show was two girls and a guy living together—with the twist that, in order to convince their landlord there was no lascivious activity going on, the guy (man about the house) was pretending to be gay. In reality, the character (played by previously unknown actor John Ritter), was quite straight and had a major crush on the Suzanne Somers character, named Chrissy Snow.

It was pure French farce. And although Murph thought the show was silly and frivolous, he was impressed with John Ritter's presence on stage and the actor's skill at physical comedy. As a fan of cowboy movies, Murph was intrigued to learn later that Ritter was the son of famed movie cowboy Tex Ritter.

As it was, *Three's Company*, which first aired in March of 1977, was guaranteed only six episodes. And most mid-season shows at that time were not picked up for another season. But *Three's Company* scored the highest ratings for a mid-season replacement to date and was picked up for next season.

AS STORY EDITORS, M&M were inundated with spec (speculative) scripts from agents hoping to get pitch meetings for their clients. A spec script is just a calling card, a sample of your writing. You never expect to sell a spec script. In fact, you don't send a spec script to the show you're writing.

In other words, if you write a M*A*S*H spec, you don't send it to M*A*S*H. The M*A*S*H writers know their show much better than you do and will tend to be super critical, picking your script apart. But you might send your M*A*S*H script to *The Mary Tyler Moore Show*. They're probably so busy writing their own show that they don't have time to watch other shows, so you have a better chance of them accepting your M*A*S*H characters as accurate.

Also, you never send a spec script of a show that's not on the air. Once a show is cancelled, it's useless as a spec script. So if you were around in 1977, you could toss out your *Brady Bunch* and *Partridge Family* specs.

Story Editors or staff writers will read only scripts from agents registered with the WGA. On a rare occasion someone on a show may read a script submitted by a writer without an agent if it's accompanied by a release form.

When Murph picked up a spec script from the pile in his office, the first thing he would look at is the 'Written by' credit, hoping to find a script with two names. With a writing *team*, Murph thought there was a better chance that at least one of 'em wasn't crazy.

Then he looked at the show (series). If it were a Lear

show or an MTM show, he might read it. If it were a Paramount show—although he liked *Happy Days* and *Laverne and Shirley* and laughed out loud at many of the bits on those shows—he feared the writing, or the writers who chose this show to write as a spec, may be too soft for a Lear show.

Then he checked the last page number. If there were 50-plus pages, he'd put the script down. Too long. Writers or agents should know that. If there were 43-48 pages, he looked to see where the act break came, and if it was around page 20-24, he'd start flipping through the initial pages to see the percentage of dialogue to stage direction.

As mentioned before, comedy is a lot like music. For a sitcom script to "sing," it should have minimal stage direction. A really solid sitcom script should be mostly dialogue and, generally speaking, the shorter the speech, the better. It's a rhythm thing.

Two jokes per page. That's the sitcom rule of thumb. If a script went for three pages without a joke, Murph put it down. Also, the story should start at least by page three or four, and ideally on page one. When Murph read a sitcom script, he looked at two basic things—story and jokes. **Jokes are one thing; story is everything.** Murph thought of jokes as clothespins and story as a clothesline. Without a clothesline, clothespins are useless.

Murph picked up a script written by a team, Larry Balmagia & Dennis Koenig. The show was *Barney Miller*, a sitcom centered in a New York City police station. The show, heavy on character with occasionally pithy humor, had won favor with critics and certain viewers, but Murph was holding off praise until he had seen more.

He liked what he read in this script and handed it to his partner, saying, "Here, read this." Sean read it, laughed in the appropriate places, and said, "Dennis & Larry...Let's meet 'em."

Dennis Koenig & Larry Balmagia were new un-credited writers, but obviously bright guys. M&M saw an opportunity for a practical joke. They decided to stage a fight and secretly record it. Whatever story Dennis & Larry pitched, Murph would love and Sean would hate—or vice versa. The fight would escalate, and then both M&M would leave the room and the two aspiring writers would continue being recorded. Then M&M would give the tape to Dennis & Larry.

Worked like a charm. When the two writers pitched their first story, Sean liked it and Murph kept finding reasons why it wouldn't work. The debate escalated until Murph threw a pencil at Sean and walked out, slamming the door behind him as Sean picked up a circular container of pencils and fired it at the door. Then Sean excused himself and exited the office, leaving the stunned writers seated on the sofa with the hidden cassette tape recorder running.

M&M waited a few minutes and then re-entered the office and told K&B it was all a joke. Larry & Dennis were good sports. The tape was played back and the first thing on tape after M&M left the office was either K or B saying, "I think we just broke up a team." And his partner tried to console him, saying there were other shows to pitch.

M&M offered them the tape, but K&B were unconcerned, although Larry said, "I'm afraid to pitch our next story." When the meeting reconvened, the four writers worked up a story where George Jefferson makes a contribution for the purpose of winning an award, doing the right thing for the wrong reason. Titled "George the Philanthropist," it became one of the last episodes of Season 3.

M&M had hoped to give Larry & Dennis another

assignment for Season 4, but K&B were hired on the staff of *M*A*S*H*. Larry Balmagia, however, stayed in touch with Sean and Murph, and the three soon became pals.

Another spec script M&M responded to was a *Mary Tyler Moore* script written by a young aspiring writer currently working as an accountant. Murph and Sean met with the writer and attempted to work up a Jenny story where the wedding is approaching and she's getting cold feet. Is she really sure Lionel is the one guy with whom she wants to spend the rest of her life?

Jenny could confide in her Mom about the doubts she's having, which are genuine and reasonable. But who or what could turn her around? How do you know if you're really in love with someone? What's the difference between love and convenience...or acceptance...or dependence?

Could there be a moment where... A moment where Jenny...Hey, what if something happened where she thinks she may never see Lionel again? How much would she miss him? Would she be okay living without him? Can you prove a positive with a negative?

Jenny and Helen and Mother Jefferson and Florence could be attending a bridal shower Louise is having for her future daughter-in-law. But if the girls are at the shower, where are the guys? House number: football game. It's Sunday. It's winter and it's snowing. Bentley has access to some Jets tickets—got 'em from somebody at the UN. But he doesn't understand American football—"All stand up, all fall down."—and he offers the tics to Lionel, who talks Tom and George into going. (George certainly doesn't want to stay at the shower!)

They're gonna catch a bus to the stadium. And what if the girls hear, probably at act break, that there's been an accident with a bus on the way to the stadium. Jenny freaks when she realizes Lionel could be on that bus. In Act Two Jenny starts crying, because she's scared and worried about Lionel, but also because she's happy and realizes how much she really loves him. She doesn't want to spend her life without Lionel. They try to find out more about the accident, even try paging the guys at the stadium, but to no avail.

The story was a tough sell to Don. Story about love—sounds pretty abstract. Where's George—our energizer bunny? Do we need to show the guys on a bus or at the stadium? M&M responded: What if the guys miss the bus and instead sit out the snow storm in Charley's Bar—drinking, talking about life, love and marriage?

The recurring role of Charley the bartender was played to comedy perfection by actor Danny Wells, whose first appearance was in the "Louise's Daughter" episode, written by M&M. In accordance with WGA rules, M&M received a token character payment every time Charley appeared on the show; so M&M were always happy to see Charley on the set.

M&M were eventually able to convince Don the story could be fun, had a subject worth talking about and a point worth making. So "Numbers" (Murph's nickname for the young accountant turned writer) had his first assignment, titled "Jenny's Discovery."

Script titles can do more than simply identify the story's theme. Actors, especially the stars, like (make that *love*) to see their character name in the title. Season 3 titles like "Louise Suspects," "George and the President," "Louise Gets Her Way," "George's Diploma," "Louise Forgets," "George's Guilt," "Louise's Friend," "George the Philanthropist," "Louise's Physical"—can tell you (and assure the lead actors) who the stars are.

Occasionally, as a smart writer or producer, you want to throw a bone to a recurring character with a title like "Lionel's Pad," "Florence in Love," "Tom the Hero," "Bentley's Problem," "Jenny's Opportunity."

If you asked Murph to name his top 3 or 4 favorite episodes of Season 3 ('76-77), he would probably put "George and the President" at the top; followed by "The Christmas Wedding," not just because it was an M&M original, but because it was a milestone *Jeffersons* episode with Lionel and Jenny finally tying the knot. "Tom the Hero," another M&M original, would also be near the top.

Thematically, Murph thought "The Lie Detector" and "The Retirement Party" dealt with significant topics and were, for the most part, well-executed. Overall, Season 3 stories were helpful in character development and were peppered with racial awareness jokes; but, with episodes like "Louise Suspects" (George would rather let Louise think he's having an affair than find out he's opening a new store) and "Florence in Love" (George and Louise flip out when Florence allows a male friend to stay overnight), the season's major achievement was keeping the comedy alive.

Additional freelance writers who contributed to Season 3 included Booker Bradshaw & Kurt Taylor, Richard Freiman & Stephen Young, Tedd Anasti & David Talisman, Paul M. Belous & Robert Wolterstorff, Bill Davenport, Bob Baublitz, Brian Levant, John Ashby, Fred S. Fox & Seaman Jacobs.

FUN FACT: During seasons 2 & 3, when approaching a rewrite, M&M would often kick off the process (just to get rolling) with this opening joke:

(George approaches Louise from behind and throws his arms around her:)

George: "How's my foxy brown tomato?"

Louise: "You squeeze any harder, this tomato's gonna turn into ketchup!"

When a draft was passed up to NRW for final polish/rewrite, the ketchup joke would always disappear, replaced by another joke from NRW, which was fine with M&M. But midway through Season 3, NRW kept the ketchup joke and it was shot as the opening of an episode—meaning going forward M&M would have to find a new gimmick for starting a script.

HERE'S A QUESTION Murph heard a lot, but never from a writer:

HOW CAN A WHITE WRITER WRITE FOR A BLACK SHOW?

Murph tried not to be condescending when answering that question. Although sometimes his answers were tongue-in-cheek, like: "I just write lines for Tom Willis. You know, the honky." Or "Sean's mother is black." Murph intended those comments to evoke a chuckle or at least a sly smile; but, believe it or not, each of those answers was too often accepted by civilians (non-writers & non-actors) as a perfectly reasonable explanation.

Toward the end of Season 3, following a Monday run-thru on stage, Murph was asked to speak to a group from the Watts Writers Workshop. He stood on the empty stage facing an African American collection of about 25 or 30 note-takers.

It wasn't long before a young man asked THE QUESTION: "How can a white writer write for a black show?"

Murph's response: Are you a writer?

Young man: I hope to be.

Murph: Do you think you can write for a white show?

As if on cue, and this is 100% true, Sherman appeared crossing the stage and began addressing the young man in the audience who asked THE QUESTION, giving him "what for" as they say in the Midwest. Sherman chastised the dude for asking a question like that and, although Murph doesn't recall exactly what Sherman said in his rant, the words "love," "peace," "color blind," "brothers" and "all one" were definitely included. The subtext was 'Leave the white boy alone, he's my bro and should be your bro too.'

As Sherman crossed the stage and exited, Murph could see the stunned surprise on the faces in the stands.

Murph: You guys just witnessed something nobody else has ever seen on this stage—George Jefferson sticking up for a honky!

Murph was prepared to continue with the controversial topic at hand, but questions quickly turned to other matters and everyone seemed content when they left.

Murph understood the prevalence of THE QUESTION, of course. There's a legitimate question of culture. But in America, he suspected, it's more a question of color. When people learned Murph wrote for *Maude*, no one asked how he could write for a fifty-year-old woman. When people heard Murph wrote for the Joe Vitale character on *Joe and Sons*, no one asked how a skinny Irish kid in his twenties could write for a fat Italian in his fifties. When Murph wrote for *All in the Family*, people didn't ask how a liberal-minded kid could write for a fifty-year-old bigot. But when people heard Murph wrote for George & Weezy, they wanted to know how a white writer could write for black characters.

In a lot of ways, many Americans have been brainwashed to believe that people with different colored skin, especially black vs. white, are totally different species of human beings.

If someone has a genuine concern about whether a particular type of writer can write for, or represent, a particular group of people—for example, if M&M can write for *The Jeffersons*—Murph would suggest the way to explore the validity of that concern is to examine or analyze the product. "The proof of the pudding is in the eating."

Does *The Jeffersons* work as a comedy? How is it received in the black community? Is the enthusiastic reaction from the heavily black live studio audience each week indicative? Are the characters in the show believable? Is the show inspirational? Is it informative? (Entrepreneur Russell Simmons and a host of other black professionals who grew up watching the show have commented that George Jefferson was the first black man they saw write a check.) Does it adhere to and achieve its subtle goal of showing that people of all races and persuasions are equally valuable and deserving of respect as human beings? (Read the extensive research results and letters from African American viewers.) How is it treated and reviewed in the black press? (Read related articles from magazines like *Ebony* and *Jet*. At the time, Murph & Sean were the only white persons besides Carroll O'Connor to have their pictures appear in *Ebony*.) How has it managed to receive so many NAACP Image and family viewing awards? Is there a reason it became the longest-running sitcom of its era and many years later is still the most highly syndicated—both in the U.S. and abroad—of all Norman Lear shows?

In a newspaper interview at the time, Isabel Sanford was asked the following loaded question: "Should the fact that stories on *The Jeffersons* are plotted by all white writers be considered a problem in relating to the black experience?"

Isabel's response: "I've asked about this. They've explained to me that there are certain talents a writer has to have and they haven't found a black writer who has those talents yet."

When Murph read Isabel's quote above, he figured the "they" she refers to must be Norman or NRW or both.

To be clear, from the very beginning, Norman sought black writers for his shows, especially *Sanford and Son*, *Good Times* and *The Jeffersons*. Richard Pryor was one of those who did some writing for *Sanford and Son*. But, as the iconic comedian confirmed when he spoke to a small gathering at Sherwood Oaks Experimental College with Murph in attendance, stand-up and playwriting are two different disciplines.

As Story Editors, M&M heard pitches from an impressive cross-section of the black community, with or without writing samples, searching for story ideas. They met with everyone from cops to ex-cons, including butchers, bakers, candlestick makers and friends of the cast. What were M&M looking for? If Murph were asked to place a classified ad at the time, it may have read something like this:

WRITERS WANTED - TV Comedy series looking for story ideas. Must be situations that are funny and play out with a beginning, middle and end— preferably dealing with the human condition, especially the black experience.

Murph & Sean tried to explain what type of stories the show was looking for and encouraged aspiring writers to call or return when they thought they had something closer to the mark. Murph recalls two gents they met with who were very likable and very funny—they stood up and acted out their pitches—but the stories were much too broad for the show and when it came to putting a scene on paper, it was obvious they were better performers than writers.

In another instance, an agent called on behalf of a client and said this client's favorite show was *The Jeffersons* and he had some ideas he wanted to pitch. So M&M agreed to a meeting, which began with this writer saying he had a great story idea for "Mother Jackson." M&M explained to him that the show was called *The Jeffersons*, not *The Jacksons*, and the meeting went downhill from there.

On occasion, and it was rare, M&M would receive an entire *Jeffersons* spec script from a writer or writers claiming to be "big fans" of the show. Upon reading those specs, M&M would wonder what show these writers were watching!

A common mistake of freelance writers was to a have George yelling at everyone, pretty much presenting him as angry and obnoxious, rather than as simply a determined black businessman out to support his family and share in the American dream. Another common error was including too many fat jokes aimed at both Louise and Tom Willis. It's important to recognize that with weight jokes, there's a thin line (pun intended) between humor and vitriol.

There were very few black writers in the Writers Guild at the time and *The Jeffersons*, along with shows like *Good Times*, *That's My Mama* and *What's Happening!* (the first sitcom centered on black youth, airing in 1976) prompted the WGA to consider the lack of diversity in the Guild which eventually led to the establishment of programs in the Guild and at networks and studios for the purpose of assisting and developing "minority" writers.

As mentioned earlier, M&M continued to meet with and work with black freelance writers on a regular basis.

M&M shared Norman's thinking that an open door policy toward freelance writers helps keep a show open to fresh ideas. Looking back, Murph is confident that if there were an award given for most freelance story pitches taken by staff writers on a Seventies TV Series, *The Jeffersons* would win hands down.

If you happen to be a person who's asked the question about how somebody with white skin could write for somebody with black skin, or vice versa, you may be able to think of other vacuous questions. Like maybe how can a man write for a woman, or vice versa? Or how can a gay man write for a straight man, or vice versa? Or how can you write for a character who is an Army doctor in the Korean War if you've never been in the Army, never been to med school and never been to Korea? Or how can you write for a character who plays a female news producer if you're not female, never worked in a newsroom and have never thrown your hat up in the air? Or how can an actor play a serial killer if he never killed anyone? Or how can an actress play a drug addict if she's never taken drugs?

As an exercise, you might see how many of these questions you can come up with during the day and write them down. And then at night, before you go to bed, take those questions out and read them over. Then, as Murph would suggest, look up the word RESEARCH.

> "Categories like black writer, woman writer and
> Latin American writer aren't marginal anymore. We
> have to acknowledge that the thing we call 'literature'
> is more pluralistic now, just as society ought to be."
>
> ~Toni Morrison

Chapter 19

JEFFS, SEASON 4

('77-78)

With Season 4 approaching, Gordon & Lloyd felt their title on *The Jeffersons* should be Producers; but NRW declined to accommodate. So Tanner & Miller were moved to the *Good Times* staff as Producers; and Roger Shulman & John Baskin (S&B), Writers/Story Editors on *Good Times* for the past three seasons, joined *The Jeffersons* writing staff as Executive Story Editors. M&M maintained the title of Story Editors.

As mentioned before, these titles per se didn't mean much. As far as staff writing hierarchy, the only title that really meant anything was Executive Producer. And *The Jeffersons* already had three of those. So John & Roger, a couple years senior to M&M and respected pals, would replace Gordon & Lloyd; and the writing modus operandi would continue as before, with John & Roger writing/ rewriting half of the season's 24 episodes and M&M penning the other half, and all rewrites passing through NRW for polish.

IN 1977, MUCH to Murph's surprise, in a letter distributed to everyone in the company, Norman Lear announced
his departure. Murph checked the date on the letter to
make sure it wasn't an April Fools' joke. Why would
Norman leave the company he worked so hard to build?

When Murph asked Norman that question, Norman
mentioned that he had recently been invited to appear
on a program with Jack Valenti, President of the Motion
Picture Association of America (a sort of PR lobby for the
major movie studios) and Valenti declined to appear with
Norman because he considered Norman a TV persona, not
a movie figure. Ironic if not foolish, since, as mentioned
before, Norman had an impressive list of feature credits
before founding Tandem/TAT. But now Norman let it be
known he intended to continue his pursuit of writing and
directing features, entering what he called "Act Three" of
his creative life.

As his replacement to take the reins, overseeing both the
creative and business concerns of the company, Norman
anointed Alan Horn, a young Harvard Business School
MBA with a black belt in karate. What at first seemed to be
a questionable choice, especially to creative elements in the
company, turned out to be an inspired pick. Alan proved
to be a quite personable and capable leader, respected by
all. And that black belt didn't hurt.

DURING A VISIT to Cincinnati, Murph asked his brother-in-law, a family man, if he'd been playing the new Ohio
state lottery. Dick said no, he was afraid he might win.
'Afraid to *win*? WTF?'

Dick explained that if he won a lot of money in the
lottery, it might motivate someone to kidnap one of his
kids. Murph responded with a palm-to-forehead hand slap

and, if this exchange were animated, a bubble that said "STORY IDEA" would be shown shooting from Murph's ear or nestled in a light bulb above his head! When you're writing for a show, you're always, consciously or subconsciously, processing input for a story idea.

Now that George Jefferson was rich, kidnapping is something he may have to worry about. So M&M discussed a *Jeffersons* story where Louise gets kidnapped. Doesn't sound too funny, does it? What if, by mistake, the kidnappers get Florence instead of Louise? Starting to sound funnier?

So M&M worked up a *Jeffersons* story where it appears Louise has been kidnapped and is being held for ransom. As they talked out the story, there seemed to be enough material to spread over two episodes. So Murph & Sean considered breaking the story as a two-parter.

That's how two-part episodes are born. Two-parters happen when writers discover that a) the story may take more than 22 minutes to tell, and b) the subject matter is strong enough, or contains enough jeopardy, to hold audience interest over two episodes. The jeopardy in a kidnapping story is obvious, as is the jeopardy in "The Break Up, Pts. I & II," a previously mentioned *Jeffersons* two-parter where it appears not only Lionel and Jenny, but the Jeffersons and the Willises, may be parting ways for good.

Two-parters are usually good things for staff writers, because a two-parter fills up two of the required 24 story spots for the season. However, it's always the story idea that comes first. Writers, as a rule, don't sit down, rub their hands together, and say, "Let's work out a two-parter!"

With the kidnapping story, M&M first had to decide they could walk the line with the bad guys, making them threatening enough, but not too threatening. Kidnappers, but not killers. Bumblers, but not buffoons. And they should be white.

And the writers have to establish how the kidnappers come to know that a) George is wealthy (house number: maybe an article or full page ad in the local paper), and b) an opportunity for a kidnapping caper is at hand (house number: maybe they overhear George bragging in Charley's Bar).

A sitcom two-parter will have four acts, so writers will first want to determine the hard breaks: act break for Part I (establish kidnappers learning of George's wealth); cliff-hanger for end of Part I (George gets call from kidnappers saying they have Louise); act break for Part II (Louise appears, safe, and we learn, unbeknownst to kidnappers, they have the maid instead of the wife); and, of course, the resolution for Part II (the cops are able to locate and rescue Florence). At least one of the cops will be black.

NRW liked the kidnapping 2-parter and suggested John & Roger write one episode and M&M write the other; and the episodes would be shot and aired as the first two episodes of Season 4. Don asked M&M which one they'd prefer to write and they chose Part II. When a sitcom does a 2-parter, Part I is often the set-up, and Part II becomes the punch line or payoff.

When S&B, M&M and NRW got together to discuss more details, you can imagine the quantity of house numbers tossed out concerning things like a) how the kidnappers are motivated to plan their scheme, b) how the writers keep Louise off stage for the second half of Act Two Part I thru most of Act One, Part II, and c) how Florence can communicate a clue on the phone to let George & the others know the kidnappers' location.

If you were to watch a TV episode written by M&M and

ask Murph which lines were his and which were Sean's, he couldn't tell you. Literally. Because he wouldn't know or remember. The source of almost every line, thought and situation is a joint effort, classically untraceable.

It's that way with any true comedy writing team. Murph might explain it like this: Let's say a writing team is looking for one specific word to end a joke and in an effort to find that word one writer says "Green." So the other writer says "Red." Which motivates the first writer to say "White," causing the other to say "Blue." Then his/her partner says, "Red, white and blue." And the other writer says "Flag!" And boom! That's it! That's the one word they've been looking for! Both salute!

Now you could say the writer who said "Flag" came up with the joke. But if it weren't for the writer who said "Green," not to mention all the dialogue in between (and before), they never would have arrived at "Flag." Make sense?

All that being said, if you put Murph's back to the wall and forced him to come up with an example of a joke written by Sean and a joke written by him, Murph would mention the following two jokes because these are really the only examples he could think of. And both lines/jokes, coincidentally, appeared in the kidnapping show.

The first is a joke written by Sean. Murph remembers that Sean typed it and read it to him and Murph laughed. George is at his portable bar and asks Tom if he'd like a drink.

Tom: "Sure, George."

George: "How about a White Mule?"

Tom: "What's a White Mule?"

George: "A Honky Donkey!" (George laughs, proud of his joke.)

Sean asked Murph if he thought it was too silly. Murph said: "I laughed. Let's leave it in and see if it stays." It made it through NRW's pass and to the table. It got a big laugh at the table and made it to the floor and got a big laugh from the audience.

The second joke, written by Murph, is this. George says he'd like to get his hands around the neck of that honky kidnapper. Tom asks how George knows the kidnapper is white. George says: "He had a white accent."

Murph remembers that when he was typing that scene, he was thinking about what knowledge, if any, George could have gleaned from talking to the kidnapper on the phone. Murph remembers thinking that when talking to a strange man on the phone, Murph can often tell if he's talking to a white person or a brother. And he figured it would be the same for George. To George's ear, a brother or sister talking sounds perfectly normal; but a white dude has an accent.

The first joke, Honky Donkey, is what M&M would call a "joke joke"—aka word joke or wordplay. The "white accent" line is a "character joke."

The wordplay punch line, Honky Donkey, is funny because it rhymes. It's a joke that's written backwards— once you come up with "Honky Donkey," you have to write the setup, "white mule." George Jefferson prides himself on his jokes. You might notice George often laughs at his own jokes, which both keeps them from sound-ing mean-spirited and helps insure a laugh (from the audience).

George also does this (laughs at his own jokes) when he trades insults with Florence, in a sense "playing the dozens" (look it up) with Florence as a worthy opponent. The audience especially loves it when Florence is able to get the best of George because, in that relationship, George is the authority figure. (Florence: "Mr. Jefferson, you know how to keep a turkey in suspense?" George: "No, how?" Florence: "I'll let you know next week.")

When Sherman is in character, he's a consummate performer. If George Jefferson tells a joke and it doesn't get the expected response from the audience, he will pat himself on the back as if to say 'Good one, George,' and that will get the laugh! In discussing Sherman's performance, Murph would often compare Sherman to Mick Jagger. At a Stones concert, if the audience doesn't come to Mick, Mick will go out and get 'em. In an early episode when the doorbell rang and Sherman found himself and the door separated by the sofa, George just impulsively walked across the length of the sofa (as if to say 'This is my sofa and I'll walk on it if I want and if gets marked up, I'll just buy a new one!') and answered the door.

Something Norman encouraged and in fact strived for in his shows was what he called a "moment." It was not uncommon for Norman to refer to a particular scene or place in a script and say, "We could have a moment here." A moment could be defined as something that would evoke a heartfelt emotion from the audience, the hopeful result of Norman's directive to dig deeper—what Murph would later refer to in the writing process as "going inward instead of outward."

An example of an attempted "moment" in the kidnapping script appears in Part II when a distressed George confides in Lionel how much Louise means to him and how "All this money wouldn't mean nothing if I didn't have Weezy to share it with."

A "moment" usually involves dialogue, but not always. It could be a slap (when an inebriated Walter slaps Maude), a kiss (when Sammy Davis kisses Archie's cheek), or a hug (when James hugs son JJ, or Meathead hugs Archie, or Louise hugs Florence in "Florence's Problem"). The audience reaction could be a laugh, a tear, a gasp, stunned silence, chills or any combination of the above.

For Murph's money, the best example of digging deeper or going inward in a sitcom is the *All in the Family* scene where Archie and Mike are stuck in the basement of Archie's bar and, under the influence of some available brew, discuss everything from their childhoods to their feelings about each other when they first met. We learn that Archie's family was extremely poor and he was abused verbally and physically by his father, who, interestingly, called Archie "Meathead." Impeccable writing, acting and directing combine to make the interaction in this scene a perfect storm of humor and sensitivity, comedy and cogency.

Many would agree Norman Lear's key contribution to mass entertainment was proving the sitcom format could deal with serious subject matter. Who woulda thought? Raise your hand if you can recall a main character talking about child abuse in *Mayberry RFD*, *Father Knows Best*, *Leave it to Beaver*, *The Brady Bunch*, *The Partridge Family*, *I Dream of Jeanie* or *The Beverly Hillbillies*.

MICHAEL & KIM, aka Baser & Weiskopf, wanted to pitch stories again to M&M. This time their pitching performance was professional and polished. They didn't argue with each other and they pitched three stories, each with a beginning, middle and end.

One of their stories involved a visit from an old Navy buddy of George named Eddie, who, thanks to a sex change operation, is now Edie. Murph recalled reading about Renee Richards, a transsexual tennis player who was formerly a man. And he knew about Christine Jorgenson, a U.S. soldier in World War II who had transgender surgery after the War and was considered a sex change pioneer.

M&M liked the idea and thought it would make a meaningful and funny episode. But when they pitched it to NRW, their bosses turned it down. NRW were exec-producing two shows now, and their availability was spread thin. In the next couple days, M&M took some more pitches and discussed some more story ideas, but they kept coming back to the transsexual idea.

On the way to a run-thru of Part I of the kidnapping episodes, Murph managed to catch up with Don and, while walking sideways alongside Don in the hall, took a last-ditch gambit at selling Don on the transsexual notion. Don mentioned *All in the Family* had already done an episode about a gay man. Murph countered, explaining this was a story about much more—a man who has had a transgender operation to become a woman, something that is now medically possible and has never before been addressed on a sitcom. Murph added he thought it could be a funny and important story.

It seemed to register with Don that a) this was indeed an original notion, b) it could be funny, and c) M&M really wanted to do it. So, in a turnaround that was surprising even to Murph, Don gave his approval.

So M&M worked up a story with Kim & Michael, who wrote a very funny script. Their second draft, titled "Once a Friend," was the best freelance script M&M had received to date, and NRW decided to move it up in the production chain.

When they ran the script by CBS Standards & Practices, aka the censors, the network strongly objected to two jokes. Both were lines from Edie, formerly Eddie. When a befuddled George checks his friend's forearm, asking what happened to Eddie's tattoo, Edie responds, "That was the second thing to go." The other joke they objected to was when George says something like, "Eddie, this is crazy. Can't you go back to the doctor and tell him you want him to put things back the way they were?" And Edie responds, "George, it's not like I went to the barber and asked him to take a little off the sides."

The censors objected to both jokes for the same reason— they said the lines "called up an image of the operation." Well, Murph thought that logic was nuts (no pun int...ok, pun intended), because the whole episode called up an image of the operation. But M&M weren't about to use that argument, because then the network might kill the whole episode.

But despite a little jokectomy from the censor surgeons, Murph felt "Once a Friend" was without a doubt one of the top four episodes of the season, if not the series. The subject matter it addressed was way ahead of its time.

The issue of transgender surgery didn't really make it to the forefront of public awareness until almost forty years later, when former Olympic Gold Medal athlete Bruce Jenner became Caitlyn Jenner. Ironically, when this episode of *The Jeffersons* first aired in 1977, Bruce Jenner, 1976 Olympic Decathlon Champion, was pictured on the cover of the Wheaties box. The box itself, featuring Jenner's picture and The Breakfast of Champions logo, has now become a valuable collector's item.

The significance of the episode resonated with the audience even back then, as evidenced by letters received, including the one below.

Executive Offices, CBS TV
51 West 52 Street
New York, New York
Dear CBS,

I am writing about an episode of "The Jeffersons"
that I saw when it was rerun recently. The show dealt
with transsexualism, and was an accurate depiction
of the condition and those who have it. It presented
a clear look at the transsexual's viewpoint, and was
also a very funny show.

I believe it did a lot of good in increasing public
understanding of the condition. I am sorry I cannot
sign my name to this letter at present since I am
a transsexual who has not "come out" yet, but is
currently under treatment.

Thank you again for a sympathetic, humorous and
completely inoffensive show.

A Transsexual

BEFORE THE JEFFERSONS "finally got a piece of the pie," Louise worked hard. So now George wanted his wife to be able to live a life of leisure. But the writers discussed and decided Louise would want something to do outside the house. Bernie West's wife, Mimi, was a prominent volunteer at the LA Free Clinic, which provided free social & health services. So it was decided that Louise would volunteer at a similar venue in New York.

The writers called it the Neighborhood Help Center. Rather than write an episode where Louise first decides to volunteer at the Help Center, M&M worked up a story and wrote an original script establishing Louise had been working at the Center for over three months and was doing such a good job that the director wants Louise to edit the Help Center Newsletter. But when Helen mentions that she both edited a newsletter while living in Paris and did some writing in college, their friendship is threatened as they find themselves competing for the same job. In the end, they come to their senses, deciding to be co-editors.

NRW, WITH SOME prompting from the network, decided it might be a good idea to add a bit of youth appeal to *The Jeffersons*. So a recurring character was envisioned — a teenager hired by George, at Louise's urging, as part of a work-school program initiated by the Help Center. A talent search was begun and a young actor named Ernest Harden Jr. was chosen to play the role of Marcus.

In the maiden episode, Marcus attempts to steal a suede jacket from the cleaners, and it appears George is going to kick the kid's black ass and fire him. But when Marcus calls George "The Man" and accuses George of not understanding what it's like to have to take something if you want it, George softens and reveals that as a teenager George himself was busted for shoplifting and sent to reform school. "You were sent up?" asks Marcus.

George tells Marcus he met a lot of "hip" dudes up there who thought they were "cool." "And you know where they are now?" he asks Marcus, then answers his own question. "They're either dead or in jail."

"And that's where you're gonna be if you don't wise up," adds Louise.

In the end, not only does George not fire Marcus, he refuses to let him quit; much to the relief of Marcus, Louise, and the network.

When the show was taped, the audience seemed to

embrace Marcus as a new character, and so did the producers, especially Mickey. So more scripts featuring or including Marcus were developed.

In "The Camp Out," an M&M original, city boys George
and Marcus struggle to survive in the woods while sharing
their respective experiences of growing up in Harlem. In
"The Jefferson Curve," Marcus attempts to woo a young
woman by leading her to believe that George and Louise
are his rich parents. And in "The Blackout," when George
and Marcus go to check on the Bronx store, they get
arrested as looters. This episode attempts to deal with the
very real issue of looting in the inner city during a blackout
when George declares he intends to close his Bronx store.

NORMAN SAW A young actor in a bank commercial
and thought a series could be developed around him. The
kid was precocious, black, only eight years old and his
name was Gary Coleman. Norman had signed him to a
deal and asked *The Jeffersons* to put him in an episode and
try him out.

So John & Roger wrote an episode titled "Uncle George
and Aunt Louise." Gary played George's nephew, brother
Henry's son, who comes to stay with the Jeffersons
while his mom and dad attempt to iron out some marital
problems.

Gary was cute and talented; but a bit rambunctious on
the set, a condition to which the adult cast was unaccus-
tomed. Isabel and Sherman, in a very nice but firm manner,
let the producers know they hoped they wouldn't be
working with too many child actors in the future.

Gary, of course, went on to star in *Diff'rent Strokes*,
another of the company's hit sitcoms. Gary and actor Todd
Bridges played young brothers who were adopted by a

rich white former employer (actor Conrad Bain) of the boys' now deceased mother. The series, based on an idea by Jeff Harris and Bernie Kukoff, first aired in 1978 and ran until 1986.

JOHN & ROGER wrote two other originals, "The Visitors" and "984 W. 124th Street, Apt. 5C." In "The Visitors," viewers get to meet Florence's parents who arrive from Vancouver with plans to divorce. And it takes George's candor to set them on the right path.

"984 W. 124th Street, Apt. 5C" was the Christmas episode and Murph's favorite episode of the season. In this episode, Louise discovers George is sending money and Christmas gifts to an address (see title) in Harlem and suspects there may be a woman or a child or both that George hasn't told her about.

When Louise decides to follow her husband to the mystery location, we learn that this is the squalid apartment in which George grew up and experienced many lean and disheartening times, especially at Christmas. He tells Louise he made a promise to himself that if he ever made it big, he'd make sure there was never a bad Christmas in that apartment again.

There's a wonderful scene where George steps inside the apartment for the first time since he was a boy and meets the family currently living there—a man, a woman and their young son. When you can write a story like this exposing George's underside, it's gold. The viewers get to see a whole other side of this often brash character. It humanizes him.

This episode was nominated for the Humanitas Award in the 30-minute category for the TV season ending in 1978. The purpose of the Award is to acknowledge film and TV writing that promotes human dignity and human values in relation to contemporary life. Don't bother reading that sentence again. Even Murph isn't quite sure what it means.

John & Roger were also nominated in 1975, the year the Humanitas Award was first presented, for an episode of *Good Times* titled "The Lunch Money Rip-Off." There were two other shows nominated that year—another episode of *Good Times* ("My Girl Henrietta") and an episode of a short-lived series called *Sunshine*. The Award was scheduled to be announced and presented on NBC's Today Show.

John & Roger were flown to New York along with the writer of each of the other two shows for the presentation. While all four writers were seated offstage, John & Roger noticed there was only one chair next to the presenter, so they knew before it was announced that they'd be walking away empty-handed. The odds were 2-1 that a *Good Times* episode would win, but *Sunshine* got the Award instead. Maybe the two *Good Times* episodes split votes and *Sunshine* slipped in. Or not.

This time John & Roger's competition was an *All in the Family* episode ("The Brother") and a *Barney Miller* submission ("Goodbye, Mr. Fish: Part 2"). *All in the Family* took the prize. But John & Roger and all writers/producers (NRW & M&M) on *The Jeffersons* staff received nice certificates acknowledging the show's nomination.

Another notable thing about the Season 4 Christmas show was Lionel finally got to sing. Damon considered himself a singer more than an actor, and for the past two-and-a-half seasons he'd been begging the producers to let him sing. Of course, in the Christmas episode, it wasn't a solo performance—he was singing *Silent Night* with Jenny, Helen, Tom and Florence. Damon had to be continually reminded that this wasn't a music variety series—"the star is George Jefferson, not George Harrison."

In an episode titled "Lionel Gets the Business," number 17 of the season, Lionel is laid off from his engineering job and George presses hard to get Lionel to go into business with him. But when Lionel starts screwing things up, George has to find a way to fire his son.

On tape day, the cast usually shows up around noon, and begins rehearsing for an afternoon run-thru. But on this particular day, it was around four o'clock and Damon was still nowhere to be found.

Everyone was on pins and needles, especially Don. When Damon finally did appear, it was close to tape time and he was rushed into makeup and wardrobe. From what Murph could gather, Damon offered no real excuse for his absence. So in a case of life imitating art, George fired Lionel on stage and Don pink-slipped Damon off stage, informing the singer's agent there was no longer any need for Damon to show up for work.

Was this a conscious, or maybe subconscious, way for Damon to get out of his contract so he could pursue a singing career full time? If so, Murph hoped Damon enjoyed singing the blues; because he figured in the not too distant future, when Damon is missing those Jefferson paychecks, the "Why-did-I-do-what-I-did?" blues may be the only medicine able to soothe the singer's soul.

SADLY, SEASON 4 also turned out to be Mother Jefferson's final season on *The Jeffersons*. Zara Cully, an accomplished actress and drama teacher, had been ailing during the past year, able to perform only on a random basis. Her presence was sorely missed by her co-workers and an adoring audience. Born in 1892, Zara was in her eighties and had trouble getting around. Don used to say, only half-joking, that he wished they could attach Zara to a wheeled platform and wheel her on and off stage.

Her appearances of late featured Mother Jefferson seated at a table, as in her final episode, titled "The Last Leaf," a show where a superstition about a lost corsage causes Louise to believe her marriage with George is over. Zara died of lung cancer at the age of 86.

MURPH & SEAN wanted to write an episode featuring the Head Honky of the show, Tom Willis. It's been established that Tom's character works for a prominent New York publishing firm. Digging a little deeper, M&M figured Tom's dream, career-wise, may be to start his own publishing company—Willis Publishing or Thomas H. Willis & Co. So what about a story where Tom has a chance to achieve his dream?

Of course, George and Louise would have to be involved somehow. What if Tom needs someone to co-sign for a business loan and he asks George? Would George do it? Let's assume George might, but he gets in a fight with Helen about something else. And now George won't co-sign for Tom's loan unless Helen apologizes to him. And despite Tom's pleading, Helen refuses to apologize to George.

What about Louise? How do M&M keep her alive? What if Louise, after washing some dishes in the sink, realizes her expensive wedding ring is missing and has fallen into the drain. She panics and wants to call maintenance. George says he can solve the problem himself by just removing the trap pipe below the sink and retrieving Louise's ring.

Louise is skeptical about George's plumbing skills; but he assures Weezy it's a piece of cake and she'll have that ring back on her finger in no time. Meanwhile, Tom learns the author he expected to sign with him has signed with another company, dashing Tom's dream of creating his own company. Tom is really bummed, but this leaves room for a nice moment in the Willis den between Tom and daughter Jenny.

Jenny reminds her dad of the time when she was a little girl and Tom found a house they loved but when the owner learned her mom and dad were a mixed couple, the owner refused to sell them the house. But within two years they were able to find a house they liked even better and in a better neighborhood and that worked out for them.

Meanwhile, thanks to a pipe wrench he borrowed from Bentley, George is about to remove the pipe under the sink. Just then Louise discovers her ring has been in her apron pocket all along and she sheepishly mentions to George she isn't a hundred percent sure she dropped her ring in the sink and maybe it isn't in the pipe after all. George, on his back, struggling under the sink, says something like "It better be in here or you're gonna have to put this pipe back together yourself!"

Just as George gets the pipe off, Louise quickly drops the ring down the sink and it falls to George, who responds, victorious! It was a fun and funny ending to the run, and something M&M came up with on the spot. As they were writing this scene, they realized George just finding the ring would play pretty flat, and Louise just finding her ring in her apron would be less than satisfactory. So finding a way for both Louise to find her ring and George to feel like a hero was perfect!

It was a similar situation during M&M's page-one rewrite of the episode that introduced the Marcus character. They knew they wanted Marcus to admit at the end that he took the suede jacket; but when they got to the end of the script, it felt like they needed to go out on something a little more fun or upbeat. So they came up with the 'money bag' switch. George made up two deposit bags, one with money and the other with cut-up newspaper. When George hands Marcus a bank deposit bag as Marcus leaves the store, Louise wonders if George is being too trusting. George boasts that he made up two money bags and gave the bogus bag to Marcus. "Your husband is no dummy!" He proudly takes another money bag from below the counter and opens it to show Louise the...cut-up paper! On Louise's reaction, George runs for the door as we...Fade Out.

MURPH GOT A call from an agent representing a writer who wanted to pitch to *The Jeffersons*. The writer had a few credits, having written for *Get Smart* and a couple other shows, so M&M, without bothering to ask for a writing sample, agreed to meet with him.

M&M worked up a story with the writer and eventually sent him to script. When they received his first draft, the first act was 12 pages and the second act 38 pages. If you've been reading and paying attention, you know both acts are out of whack page-wise, and the writing in general — dialogue, story, etc. — were just as far off. M&M called the writer, thanked him for the script, and let him know they would take it from there.

After a total rewrite, the writer's name remained on the script as the sole writing credit, as was M&M's and the show's custom. When the final script went to the table, a copy was sent to the credited writer and the writer's agent called Murph to say that his client was unhappy with the rewrite. The agent said he wanted to use a pseudonym instead of his real name, and the pseudonym he chose—nothing like his real name—was Danny La Duke. Unsure what to say, Murph told the agent he would talk with his partner and call the agent back.

So the original writer was unhappy with the rewrite and wanted the writing credit to read *Written by Danny La Duke.* M&M thought the writer should be happy that a) he got the assignment in the first place, b) the staff developed the story and re-wrote the script so it was shootable, and c) they were willing to let the writer receive sole credit and thus sole residual payments (with no arbitration).

This would have been an easy script to arbitrate. If they chose, M&M could list the writing credits as *Story by Danny La Duke and Mick Murphy & Sean Malloy, Teleplay by Mick Murphy & Sean Malloy.* Frankly, M&M felt they had turned a sow's ear into a silk purse, and they found the writer's request for a pseudonym to be both insulting & foolish. They discussed the situation over a few laughs with John and Roger and they decided that M&M would register the pseudonym "Manny Others" and list the on-screen writing credit as *Written by Danny La Duke and Manny Others.*

M&M informed the writer's agent they'd be arbitrating for credits to read *Written by Danny La Duke and Manny Others.* It didn't take long for the agent to call back and say his client wished to keep the credit in his name as it was originally. Murph figured the obvious reason for this turn-around was twofold: 1) how it would look to share a credit with Manny Others, and 2) how it would affect residual payments, probably not in that order.

Murph was constantly surprised at how little agents seemed to understand about the amount of staff rewriting that occurs with freelance scripts on almost every success-ful TV series. For example, Murph handled a call from an agent hoping to arrange a pitch meeting for a client who, the agent bragged, had written an episode of *The Jeffersons* (a couple years before) which received an award for social awareness from *Good Housekeeping* or some similar source. Although the freelance writer received sole screen credit on the episode in question, the script was in fact a page one rewrite by M&M.

Murph told the agent what he told all agents in similar situations—that the show wasn't taking pitch meetings at the moment.

THE PHONE IN Murph's office buzzed and he picked it up. It was his assistant, saying Sherman was on the phone. It was early afternoon and no one had seen or heard from Sherman all day. This was highly unusual. The cast was rehearsing without him and the Producers, especially Don, were freaking out.

With no idea why Sherman would be calling *him*, Murph picked up the phone.

"Sherm, where are you? Everybody's looking for you!"

Sherman responded in a low, gravelly voice, spinning a confusing tale about going out last night for some cigarettes and waking up in bed with a transvestite. (True dat.) Sherman asked Murph to inform the others he would be in soon; and Murph assured Sherman he would pass the message to Don.

It was no secret that Sherman was familiar with certain recreational substances. Indeed, each morning on the way to work, Murph would listen to the car radio with more than a smidgen of trepidation, hoping he wouldn't hear that a certain star of a popular TV sitcom was in jail or worse.

Word of Sherman's dalliance that day got back to Norman and by the next taping, Murph heard that renowned black activist Reverend Jesse Jackson, at Norman's behest, would be making a surprise visit to see Sherman after the 8:00 show. Murph liked to sit in the audience during the show, usually in the back row in an aisle seat which was taped off for him. But when Murph got to the audience that night, Jesse Jackson had slipped in unseen through the back entrance and was sitting in Murph's seat.

The show had begun. Murph thought of asking Rev. Jackson to slide over until he spotted an albino-looking gentleman with a bulge underneath his sport-coat (think armed bodyguard) standing behind the famous activist. Murph decided to watch the show from elsewhere.

Ostensibly, Rev. Jackson's mission that night was to talk with Sherman about the perils of drug use. Although Sherman was nowhere to be found after the show, the Reverend's mission may have been accomplished. As far as Murph knows, it was the last time Sherman went AWOL and the last time Jesse Jackson visited the set.

AN EPISODE OF *All in the Family* that had a big impact on Murph was the show where a swastika is mistakenly painted on Archie's front door and he accepts protection from violence offered by a pro-Israeli group like the JDL (Jewish Defense League). In the show's finale, a car bomb goes off in front of Archie's house, killing the Bunkers' "protector" and driving home a message that violence begets violence.

Murph was stunned not only by the way the show ended, but by the fact that a sitcom would actually attempt to tackle subject matter of this gravitas. And he was greatly impressed that the show was able to both make the story believable and deliver an effective message.

Early on at *The Jeffersons,* Murph tried hard to think of subject matter with similar import that might be handled with the same sort of effectiveness as *All in the Family*'s JDL story. The subject of inner-city gangs came to mind; but Murph wasn't sure how or if the troubling topic of gang violence could be worked into the DNA of *The Jeffersons'* sitcom.

In Season 4, a young writing team recently added on staff, Paul Belous & Bob Wolterstorff, mentioned a notion of Jenny working on a thesis for school; and it hit Murph that this could be a road into the topic of inner city gangs.

So Paul and Bob were assigned to pen the final episode of Season 4, titled "Jenny's Thesis." With Marcus's help, Jenny is able to connect with the Black Widows, a Harlem street gang. When Jenny is in Harlem and her parents can't reach her, Tom & George head to Harlem to find her.

They locate the Black Widows' hangout and we meet some of the gang's members, including a 12-year-old named Huey. The Widows currently have a beef with another gang, the Pallbearers, who shot one of the Widows; and the Widows are planning to retaliate. The Widows' leader, Domino, arrives and tears up Jenny's thesis notes. Tom & George manage to leave while they can with Jenny.

Hours later, at the end of the play, Jenny learns a gang fight has taken place and 12-year-old Huey has been killed.

In the tag, Louise laments the situation with gang violence and George says there were gangs when he was a kid and there are gangs now and gang violence is just an unfortunate fact of life. Louise says that's because people are afraid to speak up and get involved when they should. Finally, George picks up the phone and says he's going to do what he should have done a couple hours ago—call the police. When he gets through to the police, he says he has information about some gangs in Harlem. He agrees with Louise that most people are too afraid to get involved—but not George Jefferson. But when the police ask his name on the phone, George quickly replies "John Smith."

Murph figured he would list the street gangs show ("Jenny's Thesis") as one of his top four of the season, mainly because of the topic and the implied message—'violence begets violence.' His favorite, as mentioned earlier, was the Christmas episode ("984 W. 124th St., Apt. 5C"), followed closely by the transsexual show ("Once a Friend") and in third, " Thomas H. Willis & Co.," mostly because it was fun to write, provided strong roles for the supporting cast (Tom, Helen & Jenny) and featured a nice moment between Tom & Jenny, elucidating the courage and bravery required to endure the obstacles of an interracial marriage, especially in those days.

Freelance writers who contributed to Season 4 include Laura Levine, Don Segall, Olga Vallance, Martin Donovan, Patt Shea, Bob DeVinney, Howard Albrecht & Sol Weinstein, Nancy Vince & Ted Dale, Richard Eckhaus, Richard Freiman, Jim Rogers, Andy Guerdat & Steve Kreinberg.

Chapter 20

PILOT PROBLEMS PLUS

('78)

E ven though Norman had withdrawn from the company, bequeathing his huge corner office with a view of the Hollywood Sign to Alan Horn, he couldn't totally divorce himself from the company's creative affairs.

Norman apparently saw Tony Award-winning actress Priscilla Lopez on Broadway and thought she belonged on television. So he developed a series for her, using a pilot written by two credited comedy writers in which Lopez would play a young, liberal-minded nun (Sister Agnes, aka "Aggie") matched with an older ultra-conservative priest (Father Cleary) played by McLean Stevenson, formerly a popular actor on the TV series M*A*S*H. Father Cleary and Aggie would be steeped in a doctrinal battle of old vs. new, while working together at a street mission in Baltimore.

Since Murphy & Malloy were the only Catholic writing team in the company, they weren't surprised to find themselves seated around a conference table with Alan Horn, Al Burton (head of development at TAT), director Jack Shea (also Irish Catholic) and a few other production persons, all listening to Norman Lear on speakerphone, discussing the upcoming pilot for *In the Beginning*.

The show was still in the development stage, and M&M were given the script with sort of an understanding they were being asked to oversee the production. The first thing Murph and Sean did, thinking the title was a bit vague and a bit too Biblical for a Catholic sitcom, was change the show's title to *Amen!* Then they did a rewrite, punching up the dialogue and making some story adjustments.

They delivered the rewrite to Al Burton and the next time M&M saw the script, their jokes had been kept, but their story fixes had been ignored. Following a run-thru on stage, Murph mentioned to McLean Stevenson that he would need to project more since they would be playing to a live audience. Stevenson responded that he didn't care about the studio audience, he was playing to the audience at home, like he did on M*A*S*H. Murph bit his tongue. He decided not to remind McLean that M*A*S*H was a single camera show, quite different from a multi-cam show.

M&M still felt there were big problems with Aggie's actions in Act 2. In real life, Sean's older sister Katie was a nun, and they asked themselves what Katie would do. "Katie would pray," said Sean. So overnight they wrote a scene with Aggie in church talking to God. However, even with a lone wino in the church, M&M had to admit the scene was less than enthralling. But they delivered the rewrite to Al in hopes it would provoke further discussion that might lead to a solution.

But still no discussion or changes appeared imminent, except that the show's title had been changed back to *In the Beginning*. The writers of the original pilot script were not around, and it was unclear exactly who was running the show other than Al Burton. M&M were left to conclude that maybe finding a way to write a cogent comedy in which the main characters are a nun and a priest—at least as long as the priest is McLean (I'm Playing to the People at Home) Stevenson—was like trying to put lipstick on a pig...while the pig was squealing.

So, feeling there was nothing more they could contribute, Murphy & Malloy decided to unceremoniously remove themselves from the project and focus on their regular job of writing *The Jeffersons*. While they were working on a *Jeffersons* rewrite, Jack Shea (set to direct the pilot) appeared in their office and offered some well-intentioned advice to not abandon *In the Beginning*. Murph and Sean appreciated Jack's advice and agreed to give it some serious thought.

If M&M thought they could sit down with Norman and discuss the project in detail, they probably wouldn't hesitate. But it was unclear how involved Norman really wanted to be. NRW had graciously given their blessing for Mick & Sean to work on a second show, as NRW were doing with *Three's Company*, but the trio seemed to understand and appreciate M&M's desire and final decision to stay focused on *The Jeffersons* for now.

In the Beginning aired in the fall of 1978 on CBS. Reviews of the pilot in *TIME* magazine, *TV Guide* and the trades all mentioned two of M&M's jokes: Speaking of liberal-minded Aggie, Father Cleary says: "If she had her way, the Laws of God would be called The Ten Suggestions." And: "She gives new meaning to the term *High* Mass."

In the Beginning taped nine episodes; but *in the end*, only five were aired.

MURPH READ THAT every seven years every cell in the human body changes. So physically, and maybe emotionally, every seven years each of us becomes a whole different person.

Murph and Marianne had been married over seven years now. And for some time, each had felt a distance developing between them; a distance that neither, even if they had wanted to, seemed capable of closing.

They went to see a therapist, a first-ever experience for each of them. The young female psychologist listened and told them it sounded to her like Murph and Marianne were asking for permission to get divorced.

Having grown up Catholic, divorce was not something on their radar. No one in either of their families had been divorced; although Murph's cousin Kiki had married a Protestant dude, but only after he converted.

There was, however, a softer-sounding and somewhat more acceptable alternative to divorce. A relationship state that was growing in popularity, especially among couples who married at a young age. It was known simply as "separation."

When Murph moved back to the Lakeside Apartments in Burbank where he and Marianne lived before the kids, if you asked, he would tell you it was a trial separation.

He wasn't sure what he was doing was the right thing. But when he thought about the image ingrained in his mind—the image of his two daughters looking up at him as he and Marianne were calmly (he thought) discussing some adult matters, asking "How come you and Mommy are always fighting?"—he was pretty sure that, for now anyway, separation wasn't the wrong thing.

Murph was living in an adult apartment, which meant his kids could not swim in the pool. He was making a little money now and he decided the smart thing to do would be to buy a house with a pool. His accountant, Art Caraway, agreed. So Murph contacted a real estate agent and looked at three houses. Each had a pool, but one had a brand new pool with an attached Jacuzzi, a diving board and a pool sweep. It was a ranch-style home on Greenbush Avenue on the border of Van Nuys and Panorama City. It wasn't Beverly Hills or even Encino.

Murph wasn't the kind of person who would make a little money and buy a big expensive house and risk becoming house poor. Nor was he looking to buy a Porsche or a Jaguar or a Mercedes. He was a Toyota guy—ever since Art Caraway drove up in a sleek 1970 Toyota Corolla that cost $2,200 and looked to Murph like a Porsche.

Art had been doing Murph's tax returns since 1969, when they were introduced by Al Robertson, a Lockheed engineer from Scotland who lived in the unit below Murph at Lakeside Apartments. Murph mentioned he needed someone to help with taxes and Al mentioned there was a fellow engineer at Lockheed who was doing some of his colleagues' returns. For the first couple years, Art would make house calls, coming to Murph's house to do Murph's taxes, and then the two would have a beer and BS for a while.

Soon Art, about ten years senior to Murph, decided to follow his dream, leaving the engineering world and starting his own tax and bookkeeping firm. Art and Murph had the same basic philosophy about life and finances, which was 'pay the government what you owe 'em, invest some for the future (real estate became a favorite investment), and spend the rest on things you like to do.'

Although both were driving Toyotas at the time, Art & Murph purchased a stylish white stretch Lincoln limousine and set up a business, renting out the limo only to friends and only when not using it themselves for travel to and from concerts and other events. Both Art and Murph were transplants (Art grew up in a black neighborhood in Texas), both coming to the West Coast following the sun and their independent dreams. Art looked much like Rosey Grier, the famous football player and sometime body-guard for Bobby Kennedy. With political and philosophical beliefs in common, Art and Murph became lifelong friends and business associates.

So Murph made an offer on the Greenbush house. Since he was still married, Murph needed Marianne to sign a quitclaim deed for the house, which she did.

When escrow closed, Murph moved into the house; and what he did next, since you may know Murph better now than he knew himself then, may make more sense to you than it did to Murph either then or later. Murph, guilt-ridden that he was swimming in a new pool while his kids were still running through sprinklers, talked with Marianne and they decided to give their marriage another shot. So the four Murphys moved into the Greenbush house where they lived together for a few months before Murph and Marianne relinquished the impossible dream. Murph then moved out and Marianne and the kids remained in the house.

When family in Ohio learned of the separation, Murph's dad wrote a letter to Murph imploring his son to get back together with Marianne because Murph's mom is really upset. It was out of character for his father, mainly because this was the first letter of import Murph's father ever wrote to him. Throughout Murph's childhood, his dad was the nurturer and his mother was the manipulative disciplinar-ian. But when Murph turned fourteen, he watched his dad turn into a brutish character from a Eugene O'Neill play. Murph's simple assessment of the change was that his Irish father, whose mother died when he was fourteen or fifteen, had no clue how to guide his firstborn from childhood to adulthood.

Unless he was drinking, Michael Francis Murphy Sr. had little to say to his namesake about life. Over the past eight years, for example, when Murph would call home and his father would answer, the conversation would go like this: Sr.: Hello? Jr.: Hi, Dad. It's Mick. Sr.: Oh, hi Mick. (calling) Char! Mick's on the phone.

Murph's mom would pick up a phone and Murph's dad would hang up. Mom: Hi, Mick.

So when Murph first read his dad's letter, Murph relished the opportunity to respond by piling on. One word that came to mind regarding his mother was "codependency," a new hot-button psychology term being kicked around at the time. Murph figured the upshot of his written response would be to inform his father in no uncertain terms that Murph's life as a man is really none of his mother's or father's business.

But then he reasoned if he really believed it was none of his parents' business, why would he bother to engage his father on the subject at all? So after some consideration, Murph took the easiest, and what he hoped was the wisest, action and just did not respond to the letter.

Murph figured, of course, that when friends and family heard of the separation, they would chalk it up as Murph "gone Hollywood." He would be the bad guy and Marianne would be the wronged woman. And he would take the hit, because anything else would just make a bad situation worse, and could have an even more negative effect on the kids. And besides, Murph had to realize that in any relationship between two people, each will hold 50% of the responsibility for its viability.

In the end, Murph chose to look to his Grandma Millie for wisdom, recalling her logically if not grammatically prudent words:"Everybody has to take their own hide to market. "

Many years later, when Murph looked back on this stage of his life, his first decade as an adult, it occurred to him that in both his personal life and work life, his compass was that of most ambitious novices at this stage of the game—he just followed his needs. In his work life, it was effective. He needed to write.

In his personal life, when he married at 22, he needed someone to comfort him, not to mention someone to cook and to clean. If you said Murph married his mother, he'd disagree with you. He'd tell you that's exactly what he wouldn't do. He'd tell you Marianne, brunette with brown eyes, looked nothing like his mother. Murph's mother was blonde and blue-eyed, like most women in his family. Such a relationship would seem incestuous to Murph. But needs are needs, and have nothing to do with appearances.

What were Marianne's needs? Did she need to get out of the house? Did she need adventure? Did she need to comfort or be comforted? Did she need to know someone was willing to support her and provide her with the joys and responsibilities of motherhood? If so, one might suspect Murph filled her needs. But just like cells change every 7-10 years, so do needs. Unfortunately, it's not easy to figure out what those new needs are or how to fill them.

Murph thought of his life as existing in two metaphysical categories: Personal and Work. When he left Ohio eight years ago with his new bride, Murph's personal life was in fine shape; but his work prospects were shaky. Now, at age 30, it was reversed. His work situation was fine and his personal life was dubious.

It occurred to him recently that maybe life is like a teeter totter—both ends can't be up at the same time. Like the poker adage, "Lucky at cards, unlucky at love."

Murph was separated from his family, living alone in a furnished one-bedroom apartment with his typewriter and guitar. He purchased a TV and a couple bean bag chairs for his kids to lounge in when they came to visit and watch television.

It was nighttime at Murph's apartment and he was sitting outside by the pool, under the stars, alone and undisturbed, quietly playing his guitar and softly singing the song that, for some reason, was a soul soother for him—the song he always played when he wanted or needed to relax. It was the first song he learned to play, and the first song, at the age of twenty, he played and sang for Marianne.

Murph bought his first guitar at a pawn shop when he was in college, got a songbook with Dylan lyrics and taught himself to play. Pretty much the only albums he listened to at that time were Dylan albums and *Sgt. Pepper's Lonely Hearts Club Band*. When he thought he was performance ready, he called Marianne—who was unaware Murph had been practicing guitar—picked her up, drove up to a spot in Winton Woods overlooking the lake, sat on a picnic table and played *Don't Think Twice, It's All Right*.

You might wonder why Murph would pick a song like that to play to his fiancée. He's often wondered that himself. After all, not only was this not a love song, it was pretty much the opposite. Lines like "*Goodbye is too good a word, gal, so I'll just say fare thee well.*"This wasn't a song by a guy who was getting married. "*Look out your window and I'll be gone.*" This was a song by a guy who was leaving a girl. *"You're the reason I'm trav'lin' on."* Murph told himself it wasn't about the lyrics; it was about the guitar playing. He figured Marianne would be impressed that he could handle the axe.

But now Murph was starting to wonder. Was this song foreshadowing something he knew was going to happen all along? Was he thinking even then that maybe in eight years or so it would be time to leave? *"We never did do much talking anyway."*

Is that the reason Murph gravitated toward this song and why the lyrics resonated so strongly with him? Nah… that's patently ridiculous.

Murph still remembers the first time he saw Marianne. She was in the sixth grade and he was in the seventh. They were in the same split class, with Sister Mary Pius as teacher. It started with Murph throwing spitballs at this German/Irish girl with the brown eyes and dark hair. Then he was calling her friends to see if she liked him.

Their first date was a hayride when Murph was 15 and Marianne was 14, and they've pretty much been together ever since. Of course, there was a brief period in high school and again in college when they were apart and Murph was dating others. Could one of the others be the person he was subconsciously thinking of when…*"I give her my heart…"* Nah, that couldn't be. None of those lasted long. Nothing serious. No real emotions involved. *"But she wanted my soul."* Marianne was the only one in all that time. *"I ain't saying you treated me unkind."* At 20 years-old, there was simply no other woman in Murph's life. *"You coulda done better, but I don't mind."* Except…*"You just kinda wasted my precious time."* And then it hit him. Murph was singing to his mother. *"But don't think twice, it's all right."*

Wow…No wonder. The mind is a powerful thing.

Murph had a thought and he wrote it down:
Everything means something.

Much later in life, Murph came to realize that **The most important things you can learn in life are the things you learn about yourself.**

MURPH HAD NEVER been to Hawaii, so when M&M were invited to speak at a Hawaii Writers Conference in Honolulu, sponsored by the National League of American Pen Women, Murph jumped at the chance! It was perfect timing, mid-March, hiatus time.

Growing up in LA, Sean had been to Hawaii before; but it would of course be his first visit as a guest speaker. M&M were offered a token honorarium, and they were interviewed by two separate newspapers after arriving in Honolulu.

The first sentence of the first interview article read: "Two of the funniest guys on television aren't even on television." The article went on to list back and forth remarks by Murph and Sean which, when Murph read the article many years later, seemed to be slightly amusing you-had to-be-there remarks to which, if he ever attempted to write a memoir of sorts, he wouldn't want to subject the reader.

There was, however, a paragraph in the interview which may offer a hint into Murph's mind at the time. The interviewer asked about a current common refrain labeling TV as a "wasteland" or the "Boob Tube." Murph's response, according to the interviewer, was:

"In many ways, it's a wasteland. But it's the medium of the future. And the best way to help television to fulfill its potential is to be involved. The people who watch television are the people who need to be provoked. People who read and do stimulating things with their lives don't need to be provoked. You can write treatises and novels to make your point—but on TV there are 100 million watching. In college, I figured I'd be a novelist; but the only people who read are the intellectuals who don't need to be provoked anyway."

So according to self analysis—the only kind of analysis Murph would entertain at the time—young Murph aspired to be a Provoker. A Provoker whose weapon was comedy. A Joker Provoker—should be on Murph's business card. Like Paladin: Have Comedy, Will Travel or Have Joke, Will Poke.

The last two lines of the article, accompanied by photos of the duo, sounded an appropriate summation by Sean: "The bottom line is we like what we're doing. We love it."

Chapter 21

PRODUCERS, SEASON 5

('78 -79)

Before M&M left for Hawaii, Sweet Lew informed Murph that next season NRW wanted to take either John & Roger or M&M to work with them on *Three's Company*, and the other team would stay with *The Jeffersons*. Lew wanted to know how Murph & Sean felt about that. For M&M, it was a no-brainer. Murph told Lew they loved writing for *The Jeffersons* and had no interest in writing for white people who kept tripping over furniture.

"You just said a mouthful," replied Lew.

When they returned from the islands, M&M met with NRW and were told they were being promoted to Producers, along with Jack Shea. This was a big deal, as evidenced by the fact that for the first time in *The Jeffersons* four seasons, NRW were allowing writers besides themselves to share a producer title.

They informed M&M that John & Roger would be joining the staff of *Three's Company*, which would now be taping at CBS Television City instead of here at Metromedia. They made it clear that as Producers, Murph and Sean would have more leeway to assign scripts, hire writing help, do final polishes and share other production responsibilities such as casting, editing, etc. NRW would continue to attend table readings and tapings, at least for the time being, and would make themselves available for any assistance M&M may need, although NRW's main offices would be at CBS.

Don had one special request of M&M. He asked the new Producers to hire a former writing partner of his named Bryan Joseph and keep him on staff for at least the whole season. So Bryan was added to the writing staff as Executive Story Consultant, along with staff writers Bob & Paul (Wolterstorff & Belous). M&M also brought the writer known as "Numbers" on staff for Season 5—Numbers' first full time non-accounting job.

SEASON 4 WAS a season of departures. Two recurring characters were now off the roster, Mother Jefferson and Lionel. NRW decided to bring back the white sheep or the prodigal zebra of the Willis family, Jenny's brother Allan, whom viewers had not seen since Season 1(the first 13 episodes). Murph thought this was an excellent idea. The episode where Jenny's brother returned from Europe was Murph's favorite episode from the first season.

That episode included the classic scene where Allan and George play the dozens; and with all the Willises and the Jeffersons present, Allan says something like, "Tell the truth. Is there anyone here who hasn't wondered, at least once, what it would be like to be white?" And the camera pans slowly to Tom, who sheepishly raises his hand.

Murph thought the actor (Andrew Rubin) who played Allan was perfect for the role. So Murph was surprised to learn that NRW had already instructed Jane Murray, casting director for all TAT shows, to start recasting the role. Murph figured Don and the others had already discussed this and there must be some reason they wanted to recast. Was the original actor hard to work with? Was there something about the performance they didn't like?

Murph wanted to ask those questions. But having just been handed a producer title, he didn't want to start questioning the Executive Producers' decision. When the talent search was narrowed to a few contenders, M&M were able to see the final auditions. Murph agreed that Jay Hammer, an accomplished soap opera actor, was best of the lot; but Murph still felt the original actor was more believable in appearance as the Willises' son and had more comic potential.

As NRW & M&M sat in Mickey & Bernie's office discussing the recasting of the white zebra, Murph waited anxiously for any opening to ask if the original actor was considered. Of the troika, Mickey was the acknowledged virtuoso in matters of acting and directing. Mickey stated he liked Jay Hammer, adding as a plus that the actor had "a swath of the tar brush."

Murph, whose limited acting experience consisted of two high school plays—one, a version of *Pyramus and Thisbe* in which he played a tree; and the other, *No Time For Sergeants,* as a sleeping soldier with one line (upon being awakened in an airplane)—decided he was ill equipped to challenge Mickey's casting instincts.

So now they needed a story to re-introduce the character of Allan. For a working title, M&M settled on "Homecoming" and worked up a story which featured Allan, while involving George's business and Louise and Helen's work at the Help Center, which evolved into enough material for a two-parter.

Allan, who's been living in a commune in New Mexico, comes back east for the funeral of his grandfather and is visiting with his parents, the Willises. The simple story beats are: George needs a warehouse. Tom's father dies and leaves Tom a warehouse. George butters up Tom, hoping to get Tom to lease him the warehouse; then finds out that Tom's father (Allan's grandfather) has left the warehouse to Allan.

Murph's favorite example of how a trained theater actor knows to hold for laughs occurs at the first Act Break of this "Homecoming" episode. George has invited Tom and Helen to dinner, seemingly to console Tom on the loss of his father, but actually to get Tom to lease George his newly acquired warehouse. Tom and Helen are in the kitchen with Louise when George answers the door to Allan, who wants to talk to his father. When George peppers him with half-a-honky insults and refuses to let him in, Allan tells George to tell Tom a lawyer called and said his grandfather's will left everything to Allan. George says okay, then blasts Allan with something like 'Now get your zebra-striped butt outta my pretty black face!' and slams the door.

George turns and starts for the kitchen, then stops, realizing what Allan has said. The script says George whirls around immediately and rushes out the door and across the hallway to stop Allan as the elevator doors close. But when the play is being shot and George stops, the audience erupts at the look on his face and Sherman freezes, waiting out the laugh, and as a second wave of laughter starts he waits that out too, helping it along with a look of puzzled realization. Inside the booth, Murph and the other producers react with glee, Mickey praying "Hold it, Sherm…Hold it…" And Sherman does, knowing where the camera is, waiting till the laughter dies down, then turns and rushes for the door, arriving at the elevator just as the alert stage hands arrange for the elevator doors to close.

Shooting a play in sequence in front of a live audience, stopping only for a costume or scene change, adds major enjoyment and energy for the actors, the audience and, yes, the viewers at home. The audience becomes an integral part of the production, providing a sound track for skilled actors who react with appropriate impromptu choreography. Anyone interested in observing a cast superbly skilled at holding for and reacting to laughs and other audience reactions needs to look no further than an episode of *The Jeffersons*.

Nothing was more annoying for Murph to read in a review of *The Jeffersons* (or any Norman Lear comedy) than the words "laugh track" or "canned laughter." Such a reviewer would have to be blind and deaf to watch an episode of *The Jeffersons* and not know the audience laughter was fresh squeezed. Anyone writing such a review, believed Murph, could not have attended a taping of *The Jeffersons* and could not have made a serious effort to contact anyone in post production.

There was and is, however, a method known as "sweetening" used in editing to help in bridging cuts between scenes, such as merging takes from the first show (Dress) with takes from the second show (Air) to even out audience response.

As evidence of how laughter on *The Jeffersons* is authentic, the unsweetened version of "Florence's Problem" was accidentally aired and no one noticed until later when one of the engineers pointed it out prior to airing the rerun.

There were other sitcoms of course, from other production companies, which did utilize "canned laughter,"

M*A*S*H being one of them. M*A*S*H was a single camera show filmed without an audience; but in all the years it was on, Murph never read a review that mentioned the annoying titters on the M*A*S*H laugh track.

When you're producing a TV series, your responsibilities can range from…well, from casting a nude model (keep reading) to delivering a script to an actor's home. Case in point: Before "Homecoming, Pt I" was taped, revised scripts were received from mimeo late in the evening and had to be delivered to actors' homes that night. Sean noticed that Jay Hammer's address was in Sean's direction so he volunteered to drop it off on his way home, saving the usual runner a trip.

When Sean rang the doorbell, Hammer's mother came to the door, gratefully took the script and asked Sean to wait…which he did. When the actor's mother returned, she handed Sean a quarter and he, of course, smiled, thanked her and left.

On tape night, following the show, Hammer brought his mother into the booth to meet the producer, Sean Malloy, and Jay Hammer's mom almost fainted from embarrassment. All had a good laugh, but Sean told Jay's mom she wasn't getting her quarter back, it was already in the bank.

Homecoming, Parts I and II were commendable episodes; and Jay Hammer as Allan proved to be a solid addition to what in 1978 was arguably the best ensemble cast in television—not to mention the best interracial sitcom ensemble ever.

THE CURRENT WRITING staff under M&M was relatively green. For Bob, Paul and Numbers, it was their first full season on a series. Bryan had experience, but his credits were mainly for variety shows like *The Andy Williams Show* and series like *Adam 12* and *Operation Petticoat*.

So M&M turned to two of their favorite freelancers for support, Nancy Vince & Ted Dale, who had made solid contributions in past seasons. The team's first assignment of Season 5 was a story where Louise takes an art class and, to her surprise and George's outrage, finds herself painting a male nude. Louise tries to convince George that painting a male model is no big deal. But will she feel the same when it's time for George to paint a nude female model? This episode, which could have been called "Good for the Goose?" but was actually titled "Louise's Painting," became the first episode to air in Season 5.

For Jack and M&M, casting the female models appeared a bit of a challenge. Jane Murray sent them three African American females, but the character had no lines so there were no sides to read. "Sides," by the way, is a word used for pages of a script. Why the word "sides" is used instead of simply "pages" is still a mystery to Murph—similar to why a *square* where boxers fight is called a "ring;" why nobody has seen a cob, but everybody sees their webs; and why you can feel *dis*appointed, but not appointed.

An example of when the words *disappointed* and *appointed* (if each could be used to describe a feeling) could be used appropriately would be this casting session of the female models. When the first model, wearing very loose clothing, appeared in front of Jack, Sean and Murph, the three producers struggled with what to say.

Jack made sure she knew she'd be appearing in front of a live audience. Murph asked if she had any scars. And Sean said, "Nice smile."

She left and the next model entered. This second model was also wearing very loose clothes. But before either of the producers could speak, the loose clothing came off and

Model #2 was standing there in her thong bikini. One of the producers said something like, "Whoa…" And Model #2 said, "Jane told us to wear our bikinis." And Murph said, "You mean the first actress was…" And Sean said, "I'll be right back…" and took off running, hoping to catch Model #1.

The guys were *disappointed* that Sean wasn't able to catch the first model; but they were *appointed* that Models 2 & 3 had dressed appropriately for the casting session. Model #1 was likely disappointed she wasn't cast; but Model #3 was quite appointed that she was.

WHEN MURPH & Sean started at *The Jeffersons*, NRW handed them four freelance scripts to tackle. M&M managed to develop stories and rewrite three of the four scripts. The fourth, titled *George's New Stockbroker*, certainly sounds like a script in which a workable story could be found. But alas, after much detailed searching, their efforts had, as Mickey might say, 'come a cropper.'

This seemingly unbreakable script haunted Murph, perfectionist that he was, like an unsolved cold case haunts Sherlock Holmes. Focusing on the script's title, the best Murph could come up with story-wise was that maybe they could do a story about George having a new stockbroker he likes and is doing a good job, but then George finds out there was a brief period in the past where the dude was in a mental hospital. It would be a story about the potential unfair stigma of mental health issues.

In the mid 1970s, when Steve Martin was emerging as one of the top stand-up performers in the country, and people in every workplace, including *The Jeffersons'* office, were attempting Steve Martin impressions, Murph , a wild and crazy guy at heart, had this crazy thought: maybe they could get Steve Martin to play George's new stockbroker.

Martin hadn't done much acting yet, but Murph heard he had appeared on a current sitcom series called *Doc* playing a priest—a curious role for a comedian whose composite description of the world's religions was: "And the fourteen invisible people came down from the sky with the magic rings that only Biff could read." So Murph checked with casting, hoping maybe Martin would be willing to play George's stockbroker, armed with his signature bunny ears, arrow-through-the-head and maybe employing his "happy feet" bit. But the word from his reps was that Steve Martin wasn't interested. Well...EXCUUUUUUSE US!

Now, a couple years later, while Murph was switching channels to see what was on TV, probably on a weekend, because he and Sean were working most weeknights, he saw a ventriloquist and dummy, both black, called Willie Tyler and Lester.

Murph thought 'Great act! Be cool to find a way to use them on *The Jeffersons*.' Then he thought about "George's New Stockbroker." What if George's new stockbroker were an amateur ventriloquist who happened to bring his dummy along on business meetings, etc.? George thinks it's cool, especially since the dummy has a good record of picking stocks. (Hee, hee!) But when George learns this guy was in a mental hospital, he freaks!

Before they started writing a script, of course, M&M wanted to meet with Willie Tyler and make sure he was up for doing the show. So Murph & Sean and Jack (Shea) met with Willie in M&M's office. Willie came in carrying a small suitcase, laid it flat on the floor, and sat on the sofa.

When they started talking, the producers heard muffled noises coming from the suitcase. Jack smiled and asked Willie, "Is there something in that case?" Willie opened the case, removed Lester, and it was a five-way chat—all good! Lester could not only talk, but sing!

At the table reading of the episode, there was a smaller-sized script binder with Lester's name on it. Willie, of course, was a real gentleman throughout the week; but wise-cracking Lester kept everyone in stitches. During the first camera run-thru, that funny ventriloquist thing happened. It wasn't the first time this occurred, and it won't be the last; but the boom operator had to be reminded to keep the overhead mic on Willie, even when Lester was talking.

It was a fun episode and checked a lot of boxes: it was original, funny, cogent (presented a cautionary message about mental health & its stigma) and solved the case of the unproduced script! The original writer received story credit, with a teleplay by Bryan, Murph & Sean.

THERE WAS A running gag on the show about Florence having a big crush on heartthrob Billy Dee Williams. So last season Murph thought it would be cool to get Billy Dee on the show. But everybody he mentioned it to was like "No way Billy Dee's gonna come on the show." Script supervisor Sylvia O'Gilvie supposedly had some connection to Billy Dee, but so far nothing had happened.

The first time Murph saw Billy Dee on screen was back when he was working at PML. One day at work Tom Santley asked Murph if he wanted to go to a screening at Paramount Studios that night. Tom's brother was a PR guy for the studio and they were premiering a new made-for-TV movie.

Murph jumped at the chance. The movie was called *Brian's Song*, the true story of Chicago Bears running back Brian Piccolo, who came down with cancer in the middle of a season. Piccolo's roommate on the Bears, competing for the same position, was Gale Sayers.

With strikingly different personalities—Piccolo an outspoken extrovert and Sayers a quiet introvert; and different racial backgrounds—Piccolo white and Sayers black, they formed an unlikely but riveting friendship. They were in fact the first interracial roommates in the history of the NFL.

Later in the movie, when Sayers receives a team award and is forced to give a speech, he dedicates the award to his cancer-stricken friend in the hospital, saying: "I love Brian Piccolo." If there was a dry eye in the house, Murph couldn't have seen it through his tears. Before the movie aired on ABC, sports announcer Howard Cosell plugged the film on Monday Night Football saying that last night he was privileged to see a movie called *Brian's Song* and "cried unashamedly."

Piccolo and Sayers were played by James Caan and Billy Dee Williams, actors not well known at the time. When the lights went on in the Paramount screening room, Murph spotted James Caan seated in the front row and was ecstatic to see Brian Piccolo still alive!

Murph met Bill Blinn, screenwriter of *Brian's Song*, who also appeared to be knuckling tears. They had a nice chat about the movie and about sentimentality. Murph recalled reading that JD Salinger defined sentimentality as giving more emotion to something than God gave it.

Blinn mentioned that his wife makes fun of him because he cries at everything, even TV's *Gunsmoke*. All in all, it was a watershed night (pun intended) for Murph. He saw one of the most memorable movies of his life. And he met his first real-life screenwriter.

Now that Murph was sporting a "Producer" title, he thought he'd try pushing a little harder to contact Billy Dee.

He talked to Sylvia and to Jane Murray and sure enough, they heard from Billy Dee's people that he'd love to do the show.

Billy Dee was a big star already, and there was concern about how large his entourage would be. But Billy Dee showed up alone wearing jeans, a big belt buckle and a bigger smile. To Florence, Billy Dee was Louis McKay, Billie Holiday's love interest in *Lady Sings the Blues*. And to Murph, Billy Dee was Brian Piccolo's roommate.

When Murph met Billy Dee, Murph's first two words were "Gale Sayers!" Billy responded with that huge smile and Murph begged, "Say it for me, just one time..." Murph expected Billy to ask, "Say what?"But without hesitation, Billy said, "I love Brian Piccolo." Murph was thrilled! Apparently, Murph's request was not an uncommon one.

The *Jeffersons* story was that George is hosting a fund-raising dinner for the Harlem Boys Club at a fancy venue and the expected guest had to cancel. Now George needs a celebrity replacement. He reads in the paper that Billy Dee Williams, who grew up in Harlem, is in town and George tries to get in touch with Billy Dee. But when it looks like he won't be able to get the real Billy Dee, he has Ralph look into hiring a Billy Dee double.

Florence, who initially flipped out when she thought she'd be meeting Billy Dee, learns from Ralph that George is hiring a BDW lookalike; and she's determined not to fall for George's scam. But unknown to Florence, George is able to get the real deal to commit. So while both Louise and Helen dress to the nines in their best blue (supposedly Billy's favorite color) gowns, preparing to meet the matinee idol, Florence remains in curlers, hair net and bathrobe.

It was a fun week with Billy Dee on the set. When they talked, Billy called Mick and Sean by their last names—Murphy and Malloy. M&M had a picture taken with Billy Dee and the cast which is one of Murph's favorite photos! On tape day, following the last camera run-thru before show time, as the writers, producers and cast sat around a table, Jack gave final directing notes to the cast. Sherman, projecting his usual demeanor at this time, was leaning back, eyes only half open, appearing half asleep.

When Jack finished giving very specific notes to Sherman, like "When you open the door, do it with your left hand instead of your right, so camera three can see you better" and "When you tell her to 'Calm down,' yell it, don't be calm yourself," etc. Billy whispered to Murph: "No way he gets those notes." Murph replied, "Just watch. You'll be surprised."

Before the taping, regular cast members were introduced to the audience, but not Billy Dee. Guest cast and day players were always introduced after the show, so as not to tip the story. As he was standing back stage, preparing for his cue to go on, Billy turned to Murph and said, "Murphy, I'm nervous." Murph was surprised. "You kidding me? You're Billy Dee Williams. You're a movie star." And Billy replied: "I never played myself before. Who is this guy?"

Of course, as soon as Billy Dee stuck his head inside the partially open door of the Jeffersons' apartment, the audience reminded Billy Dee who he was! After the show, Billy commented about Sherman's flawless performance: "Murphy, you were right about your man!"

Not long after this episode aired, *Star Wars* sequel *The Empire Strikes Back* was released featuring Billy Dee as Lando Calrissian. Billy said at the time that more people recognized him from his appearance on *The Jeffersons* than from his movies. And *Star Wars* creator George Lucas commented in an early magazine interview that he'd rather have a piece of *The Jeffersons* than Star Wars—which speaks to how dominant TV was as a medium in those days.

DURING THE 1970s, many previously unheard-of surgical advancements were making their way into the medical mainstream, one of the most prominent being the kidney transplant. According to articles in *TIME* and *Newsweek*, an individual diagnosed with terminal kidney disease was now able to seek help by obtaining a healthy kidney from a donor, most likely a relative.

When a freelance writer pitched a notion that George's cousin shows up at the Jeffersons' apartment and asks George for a kidney, Murph sat up straight, sliding closed the lower desk drawer that held his bottle of Maalox. Now *there* was a story that hasn't been done on a sitcom before! A story that could be both hilarious and informative.

M&M kicked it around with the writer for a bit, then sent him off, told him to think about it and call if he came up with any more thoughts, especially an ending. When M&M met with NRW to clear a couple other stories, they also mentioned the notion of George's cousin showing up and wanting a kidney.

Murph & Sean had a beginning—cousin shows up and wants a kidney. Act Break—George gets a test, hoping it won't be a match, but it is! But they had no resolution. How do they find a fun ending for this story?

After a beat, Don says: "What if George gives him the kidney?" Murph: "You mean we leave our main character with only one kidney?" Mickey: "Why not?" Bernie: "Makes him a hero."

Murph couldn't believe the guys who were producing *Three's Company* were telling them to do a show with an actual kidney transplant. If a main character on *Three's*

Company had a kidney removed, Jack would probably trip over it. M&M's first reaction was: It's a ballsy ending. Their second reaction was: Let's do it!

So Murph and Sean beat out a story where George's cousin Dusty shows up and George tells Louise how Dusty was always his favorite cousin, thick as thieves, played stickball every day, etc. Dusty tells George he wants to ask him for something. George says, "Anything I got is yours, Cuz. You need money, you need a job... Just name it."

Dusty tells George he needs a kidney. George is stunned. Dusty asks George to think about it and says something like, "Whatever you decide, George, I can live with. Well, actually I can't. But you'll still be my favorite cousin when I see you in heaven, George." And Dusty exits.

Then George starts telling Louise he and Dusty weren't really close. Louise: "You said you were thick as thieves." George: "Yeah, Dusty was a thief all right. He stole two of my favorite baseball cards." Louise: "And you played stickball every day." George: "Yeah, thanks for reminding me. He hit me in the head with a bat once. Right here. I've still got a scar, see?"

Louise doesn't want George to give a kidney and neither does George. But George decides to see Dusty's doctor and get tested, hoping he won't be a match. Then he won't have to say no to Dusty. But at the act break, George learns he's a perfect match!

In the second act, George decides to give Dusty a kidney and two weeks after the surgery, when he returns home from the hospital with Louise, he receives a hero's welcome from the Willises, Florence, Bentley and Allan.

Murph & Sean were busy with a rewrite, so they went over story notes with Bryan on the kidney episode and asked him to send the freelance writer to story. When the writer, we'll call him Flip, turned in his assignment, it wasn't what they expected. They were expecting to see a seven or eight page story outline in narrative form. What they saw instead was something that looked like a script, but read like—well, to be nice, like it was the first script this "writer" had ever written.

Well, you might ask, hadn't Murph or Sean read some spec material from this writer before they let him pitch? Good question. Means you've been paying attention. The unfortunate answer is: all Murph could recall was that a representative called and mentioned this writer had some connection with UCLA and had some *Jeffersons* ideas he'd like to pitch. Neither Murph nor Sean had much free time at that moment, so rather than spend time reading a spec script, Murph just figured they'd have the writer come in and they'd hear his story pitches.

So now they figured they'd have Flip come back and they'd teach him the ropes and guide him through writing a story outline before sending him to script. But Flip had a different idea. He thought he already wrote a script and should be paid for it now.

Bryan assured his colleagues that he told Flip to write a story outline and not a script. But Flip said he was "sent to script." Murph figured in a best case scenario, there may have been a miscommunication and/or misunderstanding. But now that the process had been explained to Flip, why wouldn't this kid, supposedly an aspiring writer, jump at the chance to meet with professional writers on staff to develop and write a story outline for an idea he pitched?

Maybe he was an aspiring writer until he actually tried writing a script. Or maybe he was an aspiring con man who was showing real promise. If there were anything at all usable in the pages Flip turned in, M&M may have decided to just pay him script money—a few thousand more than story money—and be done with him. But there wasn't.

So they opted to do what they thought was fair—pay him story money and cut him off. And Flip opted to take it to the Writers Guild.

So you might ask, if Flip never sold a script and is not a member of the WGA, what is the Writers Guild gonna do for him? That's an excellent question. And the answer might surprise you. The Writers Guild exists to protect the writer. Any writer. Protect the writer against whom? Against the bad guys who might try to take advantage of the writer—signatories to the Guild like the studios, the networks, bad agents, production companies, producers, executives.

In the case of Flip vs. *The Jeffersons*, Flip was the writer and Murph & Sean as Producers and Bryan as Executive Story Consultant (even though all three were dues-paying members of the Writers Guild and Flip was not) were the bad guys. Murph, Sean and Bryan were accompanied at the Guild hearing by esteemed TAT lawyer Glenn Padnick. If Murph thought Guild representatives would read the "script" handed in by Flip in place of a story outline and let its quality or lack thereof affect their decision, causing them to agree with M&M that Flip was lucky just to get story money, Murph was sadly mistaken. The Guild awarded Flip full script payment.

In the end, Murph & Sean gave Flip sole story credit (they could have shared it), and wrote the teleplay themselves. Did Murph regret losing the Guild decision? Of course. Did he wish he had requested a writing sample from Flip before letting him pitch? Of course not. If he had read a sample, he never would have asked Flip to pitch. And if

Flip hadn't pitched, they wouldn't have been prompted to do the kidney transplant episode titled *What Are Friends For?*

Murph learned an important joke lesson during this show. In a rewrite, Don added a joke. When Dusty explains to George that he has to go to dialysis three times a week, Don had George respond "You have to go to Dallas Texas three times a week?" Murph felt that line was a stretch and was more likely to get a groan than a laugh. When Murph suggested they cut that line, Don offered to "bet a buck" it would get a big laugh. And Murph, always willing to bet on something he thought was a sure thing, took the bet.

On tape night, Murph's finances were down a dollar; and his joke ego dropped more than a notch. In analyzing why the dialysis joke got such a big laugh—which, by the way, funnyman Carl Reiner warns against, stating "Comedy is like walking; if you analyze it, you'll trip."—Murph realized when George says the Dallas, Texas line, it becomes more than just a wordplay joke, it's also a character joke (because of George's lack of medical knowledge), or what could be called a combo joke. Which caused Murph to make this mental note: Combo Jokes equal Big Laughs!

It was a noteworthy episode, both funny and informative—the first and only sitcom episode dealing with a kidney transplant. If you should find yourself on a quiz show and the category is Seventies Sitcoms, and your question is: "On *The Jeffersons*, how many kidneys did George have after the fifth season?"...well, if you haven't seen the episode, you'll be glad you read this book.

Oh, and one more question: Do you think Murph ever invited another un-credited writer to pitch without requesting a sample? Okay, don't rub it in.

THE WRITER KNOWN as Numbers tackled three originals: "George's Dream," Half A Brother," and "Louise's
Sister." In "George's Dream," George, who's been working
night and day, falls asleep in his office and dreams about
the future. Besides the many laughs, it's a cleverly crafted
cautionary tale about the dangers of being a workaholic
and ranks in Murph's top four shows of the season.

When George learns Allan is dating the blue-eyed,
blonde-haired daughter of a board member in "Half A
Brother," George fears it may keep George from being
named to his bank's board. It's a good George/Allan
episode. And "Louise's Sister" is a bit of a tearjerker as
Louise is reunited with a sister she hasn't seen in thirty
years. The role of Maxine, Louise's prodigal sister, is
played by renowned Broadway actress Josephine Premice.

Numbers was a good writer and a nice person and M&M
were glad to have him on staff. However, after months of
writing and rewriting every day, instead of getting more
and more confident, Numbers was feeling the pressure.
He told Murph the recent scenes he was writing were not
very good. Attempting encouragement, Murph shared
his favorite Somerset Maugham quote: "Only a mediocre
writer is always at his best."

Late in the fall, Numbers announced he was quitting and
going back to working as an accountant. On his last day,
Jody Jill and a couple of the writing assistants got a cake
and held a going away party of sorts. Don happened to
appear in the office at the time and was unpleasantly surprised. He looked at Murph and said something like, "He's
quitting and he gets a cake?"

Murph didn't want to be a tattletale; but with the girls
standing in earshot cutting the cake, Murph tossed a glance
to Don that he hoped said 'It wasn't my idea.'

It was of course bad form to quit before the end of the season. No one can deny that. But stress management is an individual skill and must be practiced on an individual basis. Numbers' departure prompted Murph to formulate what he considers to be an adequate sports analogy, comparing a staff writer's season on a TV series to a marathon.

In a marathon run of 26.2 miles, the "Wall" appears around mile 22. The Wall is an invisible barrier that runners will recognize as the point in the endurance contest where a typical participant will face the toughest mental and physical challenge of the race. Your mind and your body are screaming one word: STOP! You feel you've hit a wall! You can go no farther!

By comparison, a writing staff on a TV series begins work around mid-May and ends about nine months later, around the end of February or beginning of March the following year. The Wall for staff writers occurs around mid-November, when writers feel "there are no more stories;" and even if there were, "I can't write them."

Now in his fourth season as a staff writer, Murph developed a "marathon mindset" to help deal with the Wall. The trick, he would tell you, is to follow these instructions:

Don't fear the Wall. Don't fight the Wall. Expect the Wall. *Embrace the Wall. The Wall is my friend.*

When you reach the Wall, celebrate the Wall! You know you're getting closer to the finish. Christmas break is right around the corner. Then you're only two months away from hiatus! Don't try going over the Wall, or around the Wall. Embrace the Wall with arms out and go *through* the Wall as you would a hologram, because the Wall exists only in your mind.

Repeat after me, "The Wall is my friend."

NOTE: The Wall is easier to scale with a partner.

NOT ALL SCRIPTWRITERS wish to work on staff. A daily grind of breaking stories and rewriting yours and others' scripts is not an occupation to which all writers aspire. Freelance writers who are fortunate enough to get an assignment to write an episode for a TV series are required only to write a story outline, a first draft and a second draft. After that, as a screenwriter previously quoted in this book has said, "It's somebody else's problem."

The hard part about being a freelance writer, assuming you care about more than just the money, is seeing your material changed. The hard part about being a staff writer, for a variety of reasons, is having to change and rewrite that material on a daily basis, all the way up to and sometimes including shooting.

If you suspect staff writing demands work ethic to the nth degree, an all-encompassing dedication to a collective goal, not unlike the commitment expected from members of a professional sports team, you would not be wrong. Baser & Weiskopf, while working on *A Year at the Top*, mentioned to M&M that a fellow staff writer we'll call Royce Gilman, after working quite late on an assignment, turned in a script to the Producer that was unfinished, with a note at the bottom that read "This is as far as I got."

To aspiring professionals like Kim, Michael, Sean or Murph, this would be the equivalent of an NFL or NBA player, pick your player or team, saying, "Don't put me in, coach, I'm too tired." To M&M, the names Royce and Gilman became descriptive forms employed in certain instances requiring a modicum of levity, such as when working late to meet a deadline: "Wanna just pull a Gilman?" or "Let's Royce this script!"

Many freelance writers are able to write one or more good scripts a year; but are unable or unwilling to write every day. That's why finding a good partner—which, like finding a good spouse, is easier said than done—can make a lot of sense, especially if you hope to write on staff. When necessary, teams can take turns motivating and inspiring each other.

Writing teams—when you can get them to stop writing and acknowledge you—will tell you different teams operate in different ways. And usually, if both members of a team perform the exact same functions, one of them is unnecessary.

Murph heard of one show where an anonymous writer complained to the producer that Writer A on a team was doing all the work, and Writer B was just goofing around. The anonymous writer suggested the producer just fire Writer B. But the producer explained that if it weren't for Writer B, writer A would never get up in the morning.

AS STORY EDITORS and Producers, M&M had a constant stack of spec scripts in their office, mostly sent by agents. In the fall of 1978, Murph spotted a spec script of a new series titled *Apple Pie*. Murph found this noteworthy for a few reasons. One, for reasons explained in a previous chapter, nobody writes a spec script for a new show. And two, *Apple Pie* was Murph's favorite new show.

Apple Pie was a Depression era sitcom starring Rue McClanahan (who played Maude's best friend Viv) as a woman who created a family for herself by placing classified ads in the newspaper. The thing Murph found attractive and fun was that each member of this family, no matter how wacky his or her dreams might be (there was a tap-dancing daughter and a son who wanted to fly like a bird) was totally supportive of the others' happiness and fulfillment.

It was reminiscent of the Kaufman & Hart play *You Can't Take It With You*, which Murph loved. *Apple Pie* was written by Charlie Hauck, directed by Peter Bonerz and produced by TAT Communications. Eight episodes were taped, but the show was cancelled after only two had aired.

There were two writers' names on the spec script, Jerry Perzigian & Donald L. Seigel. At this point, because *Apple Pie* had already been cancelled, there were probably only three people on earth who would pick up this script and read it, and two of them were Don's & Jerry's mothers.

The story was about a pilot (who turns out to be a young Howard Hughes in the 1930s) crashing his small plane in the *Apple Pie* family's backyard. Murph thought the story was very clever, and the dialogue was funny. He gave the script to Sean, who also liked it, and they scheduled a meeting with Perzigian & Seigel.

The young, un-credited writing team pitched and discussed some stories with Murph & Sean, but the four couldn't land on a specific tale. Following the meeting, and following a hunch, M&M decided to lock up the novice team on a six-week option arrangement, joining Bob & Paul and replacing Numbers as Program Consultants on the crawl.

Jack Shea had pitched a notion about Helen suspecting Tom is fooling around with a younger woman, and M&M decided to assign Don & Jerry to write the script for that story, which became a funny episode titled "The Other Woman."

M&M read a spec script by another novice writing team, Peter Casey & David Lee. It was a *Barney Miller* script and the writing displayed common sense linear logic, the kind

Norman Lear would say "will rewrite well."

Murph and Sean met with the newbies, still in search of their first prime time assignment, and worked up a story titled "Florence Meets Mr. Right." Florence announces her engagement to an attractive, nicely-dressed suitor named Buzz Thatcher, who quotes scripture, thinks modern music is the work of the devil, and says things like "Praise the Lord" and "Lips that touch wine will never touch mine." When Buzz announces he doesn't want his wife to work, George says "You're marrying the right woman." It was a well-written, nicely-paced script featuring a perfect performance by local TV newscaster Larry McCormick as Buzz.

IN THE SUMMER of 1978, the whole town was talking about a young actor/comedian named Robin Williams who was starring in a new sitcom premiering in the fall. It was a spinoff of *Happy Days* in which the actor had appeared as an alien from outer space—Mork from planet Ork. Yes, it was true that viewers of *Happy Days*, an all-white series rooted in the 1950s, would see a dude from outer space appear on the show before they would see a black person.

The series was called *Mork & Mindy*, and two of the writers on the show were former *Jeffersons* scribes Lloyd & Gordon. When Murph finally saw an episode of *Mork & Mindy*, he was duly impressed by the wacky performance of Robin Williams who, much of the time, seemed to be spewing almost stream-of-consciousness ad-libbed dialogue. When asked, however, Gordon told Murph the show's writers wrote all Mork's lines.

Curious to see for himself, Murph attended a filming of the show and it didn't take long to realize he was watching a unique comedy persona who was adept at delivering his own off-the-wall comments while, for the most part, continuing to move the story forward.

As Murph watched the show, Mork's entrance, which followed Mindy opening her front door, was filmed seven times. And each time Mork's entrance, both physically and verbally, was wildly different. So much for the writers writing every line of a *Mork & Mindy* script.

Not long after, Murph was invited to Martin Mull's wedding. Martin appeared on *Mary Hartman, Mary Hartman* as a character named Garth Gimble, a wife beater who dies being impaled on an aluminum Christmas tree. And he played Garth's twin brother Barth in the MH2 spinoff, *Fernwood Tonight*. Both shows were TAT productions. Murph got to know Martin a little and was invited to the wedding.

Murph's party was met at the door of a Malibu beach home by a midget in a tuxedo, and there were three officiants—a rabbi, a priest, and a Protestant minister—who performed the marriage. Among the friends of Martin's who sang at the wedding was Tom Waits. It was the first time Murph heard the iconic singer-songwriter perform and he became an instant Waits fan.

But perhaps the most memorable part of the occasion for Murph was when he found his place card at a round dining table and noticed the card at the seat next to his said ROBIN WILLIAMS. Whoa! Get outta here! Katy bar the door! This is gonna be one wild and crazy meal! A story to be telling for years, thought Murph!

Well, Murph ended up seated with Robin all right. And it was definitely the actor who played Mork from Ork. But today, Mork was no dork. The closest thing to a food fight was when a piece of parsley fell from Murph's plate.

Believe it or not, Robin Williams was one of the nicest, best-behaved, bordering-on-shy gentlemen you'd ever want to meet. If Murph hadn't had a similar experience with Steve Allen a few years back, developing a board game with his favorite TV funnyman, he might have been even more stunned. But as it was, if Murph hadn't yet seen *Mork & Mindy*, he would probably have pegged Robin Williams as a high school friend of Martin Mull's who was now a mid-level supervisor at a department store chain in some place like Grand Rapids, Michigan.

SWEET LEW RECEIVED a call from Don Taffner, one of the gentlemen responsible for bringing the British series *Man About the House*, which became *Three's Company*, to the U.S. Taffner wanted Murph & Sean to write a pilot for another British series he was hoping to develop for ABC. Murph wasn't sure why Mr. Taffner thought of them; but he assumed Taffner may have offered the gig to NRW, now producing *Three's Company* and developing a spinoff of *The Ropers*, and they recommended M&M.

M&M were busy doing *The Jeffersons*, but they agreed to view an episode of the British series Taffner wanted to develop. After viewing, they passed because a) they couldn't see how they could re-work the show into anything they wanted to write at the time, b) their work load at *The Jeffersons* didn't leave much free time, and c) following their *Chico and the Man* experience, they had promised themselves they'd never again write anything just for the money.

How did it feel turning down a pilot assignment? Great! That's when you know you've finally made it as a writer, thought Murph—when you can afford to turn down work. Of course if the series had been developed into a huge hit, M&M may have had different feelings. That never happened, however, and M&M felt justified in their decision.

RATHER THAN A season of three or four standout episodes, Murph felt Season 5 was a season of balance. A collection of comfort comedy laced with poignancy.

The ventriloquist and Billy Dee episodes are memorable on their face. And there's the story where the heat goes out in the Willises' and Bentley's apartments, and they're all forced to spend the night in the Jeffersons' apartment with George, Weezy and Florence. If you like physical comedy, you may get a big kick—as did M&M while writing it—out of the scene where George and Tom are forced to sleep in the same bed in "The Freeze-In," the final episode of Season 5, written by M&M and the team of Jerry & Don (Perzigian & Seigel), who were signed on (their first staff job) for the next season.

In retrospect, Murph feels Season 5 was also a season where the character of George Jefferson begins to make a transition from what some might call a brash loudmouth to a hero. Certainly the episode in Season 4 where we learn George has been helping a family at Christmastime ("984, etc.") reveals the sensitive underside of his character; but when George donates a kidney to his cousin...whoa! How many of us would be willing to do that?

Additional freelance writers contributing to Season 5 were Erwin Washington, Christine Houston, M. Martez Thomas, Bernard Mack, Steven Neigher, Jim Rogers, Fred S. Fox & Seaman Jacobs, Kurt Taylor & John Donley.

In a matter of months—July 9, 1979 to be exact—Barbara Brogliatti, head of public relations for TAT, came down from her executive suite upstairs to hand M&M a framed copy of the Nielsen TV Ratings for the week ending July 8. In the top spot, circled in red, was *The Jeffersons*. The Top Ten shows that week, nine of them sitcoms, were:

1. THE JEFFERSONS

2. ALICE

3. 20/20

4. M*A*S*H

5. CARTER COUNTRY

6. MORK & MINDY

7. ANGIE

8. THREE'S COMPANY

9. BARNEY MILLER

10. WKRP IN CINCINNATI

One Day at a Time was 13th and *All in the Family* 17th. *The Jeffersons* stayed in the top spot throughout the summer and became a regular fixture in the Nielsen Top Ten.

TAT took out a nice two-page spread ad in the trades featuring a realistic photo of Mt. Rushmore with George Jefferson's chiseled face superimposed over the face of Thomas Jefferson. The copy read:

> *In January, 1975, the Jeffersons said goodbye to the Bunkers, moved to a fashionable East Side apartment, their own TV series, and an impressive 45 share.*
>
> *Capitalizing on The Jeffersons' unique ability to attract an audience, CBS used it as their prime time workhorse, moving it ten times over the next five years. With each move, The Jeffersons not only increased the average rating of the time period, but also out-performed its new lead-in and lead-out series.*

*Today, when a single time period change can turn
last year's hit into this year's also ran, The Jeffersons
remains solidly in the Top Ten, enjoying its highest
ratings ever.*

THE JEFFERSONS...

STANDING THE TEST OF TIME PERIODS.

Before Murph framed the ad and hung it on his office
wall, Sherman signed it above his face on Mt. Rushmore.
What Sherm wrote was pure Sherman: "To my bro Mick,
Love has joined us all together. May it last forever. Peace &
Happiness, Sherman H."

A number of articles appeared in the press attempting to
analyze how a show going into its sixth season could be
increasing in popularity instead of decreasing. One explanation offered was the show's new time slot. But Murph
had a preferred answer—the show's new young producers. Who, by the way, heading into Season 6, were named
the new sole Executive Producers.

Chapter 22

EXECUTIVE PRODUCERS, SEASON 6

('79-80)

If you had told Murph a decade ago, when he arrived in LA with nothing but a dream and a new bride, that in ten years he'd be Executive Producing the number one show on television... Yeow! Pretty crazy, huh? Guess Hollywood really is a place where dreams can come true.

The craziest thing was Murph's new parking spot! Since TAT moved to Metromedia, all company employees, top to bottom, parked in the tiered parking garage and walked to their respective offices—except for six reserved spaces located right in front of the main door to the main building. The elite names printed on these spots were Norman Lear, Don Nicholl, Mickey Ross, Bernie West, Alan Horn and Al Burton. With NRW gone from TAT (now at CBS producing *Three's Company* and their new spinoff *The Ropers*), two of those parking spaces were now reserved for Sean Malloy and Mick Murphy. Pretty heady stuff!

M&M embraced their new position with vigor, renting a beach house on Balboa Island and hosting a pre-season party for *The Jeffersons* cast, staff & families. Murph's girls and Sean's boys spent good bonding time with Lenny (Roxie and Sy Kravitz's young son) later to become a rock music icon.

If you asked Murph about the job of Exec Producer or Showrunner on a TV series, in an attempt to find a comparison, he might compare it to that of a symphony conductor. In a TV series, the composition is the script. The instruments are wardrobe, props, art design, lighting, sound, actors, director, etc. The EP or Showrunner must guide and approve all of those. An EP friend of Murph's, describing his job, said, "I make at least a hundred decisions a day. And at least half of them are wrong. But the important thing is to just keep making decisions."

You may wonder where the term "Showrunner" came from and how it came to be used in place of the term "Executive Producer." It resulted from the proliferation of the Executive Producer title. Ordinarily, series Exec Producers came from writers ranks. But eventually, certain star actors/actresses, especially those whose series were named after them or their characters, (and sometimes their agents or managers) began to request or insist on an Executive Producer title. And writer EP's, in order to entice other credited writer-producers, many of them friends, to work on their shows, would offer a title promotion of "co-executive producer" or "executive producer." This resulted in many series having multiple executive producers. So in order for agents, network execs and studio execs to identify the person who actually runs the show, the title "Showrunner"—which is not, at the moment anyway, a screen credit—came into fashion.

WHEN BASER & WEISKOPF started as writers on *Good Times*, they were asked to read script submissions from a college playwriting contest sponsored by Norman Lear. Both Kim and Baser, especially Kim, were impressed with a script penned by a young writer from a community college in North Carolina. So impressed, in fact, they strongly recommended hiring the writer on staff. So Michael Moye became the newest writer on *Good Times*.

Two years later, when *Good Times* was winding down and M&M were named EP's on the thriving *Jeffersons*, Murph made a visit to Michael Moye's office and made a recruiting pitch that would make a college football coach jealous. M&M wanted to enlist Moye's help on *The Jeffersons* before another show scooped him up. So Moye came aboard as Story Editor for Season 6 and became the first African American scribe on *The Jeffersons* staff.

Gone from last season's writing staff were Bryan, Bob & Paul, the latter two focusing on hour series like *Quantum Leap*, *Street Hawk* and *The Incredible Hulk*. Don & Jerry remained on *The Jeffersons* and M&M added Neil Lebowitz, a young writer whose spec they liked.

Alan Horn called and asked M&M to consider using a writer/producer who TAT hired on a development series that had now been cancelled. So Seth Rivers was added as Producer on *The Jeffersons*. Jack Shea, *Jeffersons* director since episode number one, decided it was time to move on; so M&M hired Bob Lally, Jack's AD, as the show's new director.

Shortly after being named EP's, M&M heard from Sherman, who called to say he ran into Mike Evans (original Lionel) at a beach or somewhere. Sherman said he told Mike "we have new Executive Producers" and he should call M&M about maybe returning to the show.

M&M discussed it and concluded Lionel and Jenny having a baby would give a whole new thrust to both the upcoming season and the entire series. They met with Mike and welcomed him back with open arms.

Lionel's return would effect at least eight new stories, including "The Announcement," where we learn Jenny is pregnant; "The Expectant Father," where Lionel is stressed about the obligations of becoming a new father; "The Arrival, Parts I and II," where George agrees to take Jenny to Lamaze class and is shocked when she goes into labor.

In "The Announcement," an original by M&M and first episode of the season, Louise is hurt that the Willises have learned about Jenny's pregnancy before Louise and George. Jenny was hesitant to tell them because of George's propensity for zebra remarks. The show ends with a nice scene on the roof of the building between George and Jenny where George tries to apologize to Jenny for his insensitive behavior and Jenny tells George she thinks he'll make a good grandfather.

In "The Expectant Father," penned by Michael Moye, Lionel is having second thoughts about becoming a father. He pours his heart out to George at Charley's Bar while Charley pours drinks for both. Lionel, bemoaning the fact that he'll never be able to be a kid again, mentions that he always wanted to spray-paint his name on the 145th Street Bridge. George says, "Let's do it."

M&M thought it would be a nice father-son moment in the story and a nice visual if they could actually show Lionel and George on a bridge. But they knew building a bridge on the stage would be expensive. So they went to Alan Horn and pleaded their case. Reluctant at first, Alan finally agreed to approve a bridge—provided M&M could keep costs down in upcoming episodes by sticking mostly to the show's standard sets. So an $8,000 bridge was built; and Murph, Moye and writers on the show had their pictures taken both on, and jumping off, the bridge.

When staging the bridge scene, M&M wanted Lionel to crawl along the rail, struggling to hold on so as not to fall into the Harlem River below. But Mike Evans objected, telling M&M and director Bob Lally if he crawled on all fours, "America will think I want to get (blanked) in the (blank)." Yes, really. "John Wayne wouldn't do that," he said. A similar challenge to the actor's machismo occurred in a later episode when Mike objected to pushing a baby carriage into the Jeffersons' apartment. He said that was a woman's job. Fortunately, in both cases, with Sherman's assistance, Bob and Mike Evans were able to work things out, keeping the actor's sense of self intact.

A COUPLE SEASONS ago, while driving to work, Murph heard something on the radio about a local entrepreneur who had received a Small Businessman's Award. He thought it could be funny if George Jefferson received a Small Businessman's Award then found out "Small" meant 5'6" and under.

But the more Murph thought about it, the more it seemed like just one joke instead of a full story. And he filed it away in his mind. But now, in Season 6, sitting with a few writers trying to think of story ideas and coming up with zip, Murph mentioned the Small Businessman's Award for George and was met with a big laugh and strong interest.

So M&M focused on breaking the story and assigned newbie Neil Lebowitz to write the first draft. Titled "A Short Story," the episode begins with George seeing Tom's picture in the business section of the paper with the announcement that Tom was named a Senior Vice

President of his publishing company.

George's envy is assuaged when he receives a telegram informing him he's been named Midtown Small Businessman of the Year. The telegram, signed by the group's president, says the award will be presented Tuesday night at their annual banquet and someone will be contacting George soon. A proud George invites Tom, Helen and Florence to the banquet so they can bask in his glory.

Florence has made some hors d'oeuvres and George is planning to meet with a couple representatives from the Midtown Small Businessmen's group; but there's an emergency at one of the cleaning stores so George has to split. Louise and Florence are there when two nicely-dressed short men arrive and explain that the Small Businessmen's group is for *Small* Businessmen—five feet six and under.

After the shrimps, er, the short dudes leave, Louise says she's afraid when George finds out the truth about the award, he's gonna hit the ceiling. Florence says, "Not unless he's standing on a ladder." Louise figures she'll wait to tell George when they're alone. But when she attempts to tell him, he's so excited about winning this award that she can't bring herself to spoil his spirit.

At the banquet, George looks around the room suspiciously, saying something like, "Weezy, there's something strange going on here." As Louise starts to respond, George says, "Wait a minute. I know what it is. I've never seen so many tall women in one place before." On a talk show interview years later, Sherman was asked to name a favorite episode and he named this one. Even quoted the above line from the typewriter of M&M.

When Louise finally tells George the truth, he storms out. Louise stops him at the cloak room and tries to calm him down. She says the group's president told her lots of important people won this award. George says, "Like who, the Seven Dwarfs?" In a nice scene, Louise manages to convince George that the true measure of a man is not determined by a tape measure.

George accepts his award in a stirring speech where he shouts "I'm short and I'm proud!" and manages to get the whole room chanting "I'm short!" before a final photo is taken with Louise, the group president and George in the middle.

After the taping, as Murph opened the door to exit the booth, he stood facing Norman, who had apparently been watching on a monitor in the executive offices. Norman had one suggestion: Just as the photo is snapped, have George stand up on his tip-toes (to appear taller). Upon hearing Norman's note, Murph had his usual appropriate thought, which was: 'Why didn't we think of that?'

So they shot a pick-up, which, thanks to Norman, was the perfect ending for this episode.

If you're surprised Norman was even in the building, so was Murph. Murph found himself thinking, 'Could this be a sign Norman misses TV production? Wouldn't it be cool if Norman came around more and helped break stories with us?'

But then he wondered, 'Was Norman watching on the monitor to check up on us? To make sure we could run this show on our own, without NRW?' M&M certainly wanted to prove to Norman, to others and to themselves that they could write and produce *The Jeffersons* on their own.

Still, Murph found himself wishing he could experience working closely with Norman, like in the early days of *All in the Family*. But then a piece of worn but probably worthy wisdom jumped into his head: 'Be careful what you wish for.' Murph remembered John & Roger, as *Good Times* writers, mentioning a time they went into Norman's office intending to quit and came out with a rewrite.

MULTI-CAM SITCOMS WITH a live audience use a "warm-up" person or persons to keep the audience interested, loose and ready to laugh. Many shows hire stand-up comics for that purpose. Since M&M joined *The Jeffersons*, Bernie West had done the warm-up for every episode.

Bernie had a definite comedy persona and look; but he was also an Executive Producer and creator of the show and could pretty much answer any audience questions related to the show, such as questions about the cast or the various episodes. But Bernie was divorced from *The Jeffersons* now and off doing warm-ups for *Three's Company* and *The Ropers*.

And just as with stories, casting, wardrobe, directors, writers, etc., the Exec Producers/Showrunners were also responsible for selecting the warm-up talent. If you were to ask Murph what he would suggest as the key Rules or Requirements for a qualified warm-up candidate, he would — with few exceptions — list the following:

Murph's Rules for Sitcom Warm-ups

1. **Keep the audience involved in the play.** Especially if it's a new show, it's a good idea to screen the pilot or an episode of the show for your audience before the taping/filming. During the taping/filming, keep the audience involved during scene breaks by asking questions about the story, such as "Do you think George will give his cousin a kidney?" "Has anyone here actually donated a kidney? Or know anyone who's had

a kidney transplant?" "How many of us think Florence and Buzz Thatcher will get married and live happily ever after?" "How do you think George will react when he finds out that *Small Businessman* actually means *small* (lowering palm to indicate short) businessman?"

2. **Don't be funnier than the play.** Be cordial and amusing, but don't upstage the star or head-liner—which is the play itself. Recognize that it's about the show, not the warm-up performer. If your audience goes away talking about the warm-up performer and not the play, your play is in trouble.

3. **Create a Family Feel.** Ask the audience where they're from, what they do, whether they've been to a sitcom taping/filming before, whether or not they watch *The Jeffersons*, what their favor-ite episode is, etc., attempting to create a family feel of a group of friends watching a show in someone's living room.

4. **Have complete knowledge of the particular episode and series.** Be able to answer ques-tions about the cast such as, "Did Isabel Sanford play the maid in the movie *Guess Who's Coming to Dinner*?" "Whatever happened to the other actor who played Lionel?" Or the production process—"How long do the actors rehearse for each episode?" Or "How many seasons has *The Jeffersons* been on?"

It's pretty much common knowledge now that among human phobias, public speaking ranks number one. But

Murph always enjoyed speaking to groups, especially when the subject of discussion was something of interest to both Murph and the listeners. So Murph suggested to Sean that he and Sean take turns doing warm-ups for *The Jeffersons*. But Sean was cool with just Murph doing the warm-ups. So beginning with Season 6, Murph acquired an AFTRA card (performing warm-ups for a live audience required membership in the American Federation of Television and Radio Artists and pays at least a scale minimum) and did warm-ups for *The Jeffersons*.

Like Bernie before him, Murph would introduce himself to the audience, welcome them to the Jeffersons' living room, and encourage audiences to laugh when they heard or saw something funny, noting the overhead microphones which were there to record audience laughter.

Immediately following his first warm-up, Murph began hearing compliments on his performance. Apparently word was beginning to spread that Murph's warm-up was something to see. Strangely enough, this freaked Murph out. This is exactly what he didn't want to happen.

Murph would admit, of course, as a comedy person, there was a least a small...okay a medium-sized part of him...that was drawn to becoming, if not the talk of the town, at least the talk of the company when it came to warm-up performances. But if you've read **Murph's Rules for Sitcom Warm-ups** outlined in this chapter, you may understand how Murph thought such an aspiration could be counterproductive. Murph thought of himself—and wanted others to think of him—as a writer-producer and not a warm-up person.

Murph kinda figured if he ever did put together a stand-up act, it would have similarities to George Carlin's act. A focus on early attendance at Catholic school;

exploring idiosyncrasies of language, beginning with silly things like how come you can be overwhelmed, but you can't be whelmed? Progressing to more adult topics such as Carlin's "Seven Words You Can Never Say on Television," which would be over-the-line as material for warming up a live TV audience. So Murph vowed to stay with softer material and keep focused on what he considered to be the number one goal of the warm-up host, which is to keep the audience involved in the show.

Early on, when asking the audience how many were visiting from out of town, Murph tried out a joke he'd heard, mentioning that when he first arrived in Southern California from Ohio, he stopped at a gas station to ask directions to La Jolla (pronouncing Joll as in *jolly*).

The attendant, Murph said, explained to him that it was pronounced "La Hoya." Because of the Spanish influence in Southern California, the J's are pronounced like H's. Like El Cajone (pronounced El Ca*Hone*), Tujunga (pronounced *TaHunga*)... Then the attendant asked Murph how long he was going to be in California and Murph said, "Oh, probably late Hune, early Huly."

The joke got a solid laugh, bigger than Murph expected, so he began using it on a regular basis as his opening joke.

ONE MORNING MURPH arrived at work to find a gold Rolls Royce parked in his spot with a license plate that read CHAMP. Murph asked the receptionist if she knew who was parked in his spot and she said it was Muhammad Ali, who was guest-starring on *Diff'rent Strokes* that week. Murph told her Ali was his idol and she asked if Murph wanted to meet him. She led Murph to the stage and introduced Murph saying, "Champ, this is Mick Murphy, Executive Producer of *The Jeffersons*." Ali looked at Murph with pleasant surprise and announced, "You're not as dumb as you look!"

Senior year in high school Murph had to take an aptitude test where, in addition to answering a lot of multiple choice questions, students were asked to draw a picture of a person—any person. Murph sketched a large black man with the letters CC on his boxing trunks. Then they were instructed to write who the person was and Murph wrote simply "The Greatest."

Murph always wondered how those who graded his test processed his drawing. Did they think this white kid wanted to be black, or a boxer, or both? Actually, between eighth grade and freshman year of high school, at the age of fourteen, Murph attended a two-week summer camp featuring activities from archery to horseback riding, and he won a boxing tournament.

The week Ali was on *Diff'rent Strokes*, Murph's mom was in town. Murph was driving his mom and two daughters to work so they could meet the Champ. He attempted to explain to his daughters the import of the man they were about to see—a man who was not just a World Champion boxer, but a worldwide social force.

Cassius Clay. Olympic Gold Medal winner at 18. World Heavyweight Champion at 22. "I'm the Greatest!" Beat Sonny Liston—"The Big Ugly Bear"—in a major upset. Before the fight, syndicated sportswriter Jim Murray wrote that Liston was an 8-5 favorite against the Marines! "I shocked the world!" "Float like a butterfly, sting like a bee; the fists can't hit what the eyes can't see!" Bundini Brown. "The only heavyweight who could dance like a lightweight." Angelo Dundee. Changed his name to Muhammad Ali, trading his "slave name" for his Muslim name, converting to Islam. "I'm so fast, I can turn out the light and be in bed before it gets dark!" Ali predicted rounds in which he'd win his fights, putting predictions in an envelope for sportscaster Howard Cosell. Ali to Cosell: "I made you famous!" Cosell: "I used to box." Ali: "What, oranges?" Murph loved sports. And the ultimate sport was two athletes battling— mano a mano—no sticks or balls or heavy protective gear. Legendary sports writer Grantland Rice wrote that the most exciting moment in the world of sports is when the announcer steps to the center of the ring and says, "AND NOW, FOR THE HEAVWEIGHT CHAMPIONSHIP OF THE WORLD..." Ali was born and raised in Louisville, Kentucky. About 100 miles down the expressway from Cincinnati. Murph identified with Ali as a homeboy of sorts. Ali refused to fight in the Vietnam War. "I ain't got no quarrel with them Vietcong." As a result, the government took his title away and he couldn't fight for three years. As George Carlin put it, "The government said to Ali, 'If you're not gonna kill 'em, we're not gonna let you beat 'em up.'" Ali returned after three years to win back the title. The Thrilla in Manila. The Rumble in the Jungle. The Ali Shuffle. The Rope-a-Dope. Only boxer to win back the Heavyweight title three times. Murph watched all Ali's fights—at home on TV, in movie theaters on "closed circuit TV," and in the stands with Sean at the first Leon Spinks fight in Las Vegas.

When, on their way to the studio, Murph finished extolling the virtues of the Champ to his daughters, Murph's mom said "Gee, Michael, you'd think we were going to see the Pope." Murph claimed Ali was more famous than the Pope—but he didn't think his mom was buying it.

When they arrived at the studio, snapshot camera in tow, they headed for the stage where *Diff'rent Strokes* had been rehearsing. *Strokes* was the series starring child star Gary Coleman as Arnold. When Murph and the girls walked onto the stage, the Champ was standing there in all his awesomeness. Colleen spotted Gary on the other side of the stage and said, "Heather, there's Arnold!" And the girls took off running to see Gary Coleman.

Ali could not have been more gracious with Murph's family. Upon hearing the girls address Murph's mom as Grandma, Ali said "Grandma? You can't be no Grandma!You're too young!" The Champ sure had a way of charming women, and Murph's mom was definitely charmed. Later she used the words *magnetic* and *enthralling*.

"More enthralling than the Pope?" asked Murph with a wink. His Mom gave Murph a sly smile, but she didn't say "No." Ali posed for pictures with the girls and Grandma; and when Grandma was about to snap a picture of her son and the Champ, Ali turned to Murph, raised a fist and scowled. "Who you calling nigger?" Murph flinched, his mom gasped and Ali laughed!

As a poet and a promoter, Ali was cocky, confident and funny. "If I say a mouse is gonna outrun a horse, don't ask questions, just put your money where your mouse is!"

Murph considers meeting and spending time with the Champ that week, and seeing him on a number of occasions post-Parkinson's, as truly among the highlights of his life.

In time, Ali was recognized as a national treasure. Lit the torch at the opening of the 1996 Olympics in Atlanta. Named Sportsman of the Century by Sports Illustrated. Awarded the Presidential Medal of Freedom, the highest U.S. civilian honor. It seems the former Olympic Champion, once known as the "Louisville Lip," despised at first by many, but celebrated at last by all, was able to accomplish all he set out to achieve. As an athlete and as a man, he became, against all odds, a shining global social force who influenced and inspired many—including Midwest homeboy Michal Francis Murphy.

KICKING AROUND STORY ideas, one notion that came up was Louise spotting a murder through the window of another New York apartment—sort of a *Jeffersons* meets *Rear Window*, a Hitchcock film where Jimmy Stewart, as a character in a wheelchair, thinks he witnesses a murder through his apartment window.

It was a story idea that certainly had what Murph would call the "J word" (Jeopardy); but did it have the "C word" (Comedy)? M&M noticed the air date would be around Halloween, and Halloween means costumes, and in sitcoms costumes equal comedy. TV is a visual medium. You don't want to overdo it, but the right costumes will always get an audience reaction and enhance the laughter and viewer enjoyment. So they decided to make the Rear Window story a Halloween show.

When they stepped it out, with all the regular characters in costumes, they realized there was enough story for a two-parter. In the first act of Part I, it's Halloween and the regular characters are preparing to attend a Costume Party at Charley's Bar.

George is dressed as Charlie Chaplin's Little Tramp character, complete with derby, cane and moustache; while Louise is a glamorous Mae West decked out with diamonds galore, curly blonde wig, decorative boa and appropriately bawdy behavior: "When I'm good, I'm very good. And when I'm bad, I'm even better!"

Florence is Harpo Marx, equipped with honking horn. Bentley—sporting a checkered suit and straw porkpie hat with clashing shirt and tie—claims to be Ducky Dempster, his favorite cockney comedian. And Helen & Tom are Stan

Laurel & Honky Hardy.

Bentley has set up his high-powered telescope on the Jeffersons' balcony so he can observe some astronomical event. Louise happens to look into the telescope and believes she witnesses a murder by a man dressed in a Rabbit costume. End of Act One.

In Act Two, the others feel Louise must be mistaken about seeing a murder. Must have just been some sort of Halloween fun. Louise goes to Charley's Bar for some ice and spots the Killer Rabbit! As she leaves, the Rabbit realizes Louise is a witness and must be erased. End of Part I.

In Part II, Act One, the Killer Rabbit tracks Louise to her apartment and confronts her at gunpoint, threatening to throw her off the balcony so it will look like a suicide at the End of Act One.

In Act Two of Part II, the regulars, one by one, arrive back at the Jeffersons' apartment; and the Killer Rabbit, now hopping mad, is holding them all at gunpoint and attempting to march them all out onto the balcony.

Thanks to an inadvertent action by Bentley (as Ducky Dempster), the gang is finally able to apprehend the Killer Rabbit, played with the proper amount of guile by actor Patrick Collins.

The Halloween episodes, titled *Now You See It, Now You Don't, Parts I & II*, are fun ensemble pieces and, as such, have become fan favorites.

EARLY ON M&M made a note to themselves not to approve a story or script unless they had what Murph would call a PCR—problem, complication and resolution—otherwise known as beginning, middle and end. The only time in Murph's memory they failed to follow that rule was in developing a story notion which became known as "Where's Papa?", which for a time could be called 'Where's the Resolution?'

M&M wanted to give another assignment to Peter Casey & David Lee, freelance authors of "Florence Meets Mr. Right," the episode about how someone who's *too* right can be way wrong. They met with Casey & Lee and discussed stories that might arise from the fact that George, who grew up in a family with little to no money, is now financially successful. They talked about George's father who died poor and they figured he was probably buried in New York's potter's field where indigent or poor people are buried.

What if George decided to dig up his father and bury him in a nice cemetery with a nice tombstone or mausoleum? What's the PCR? Well, the problem or situation is that George Jefferson's father is buried in a potter's field. And the resolution is that George has his father reburied in a respectable cemetery with a stately tombstone.

M&M liked the notion. But the story was kind of flat. What's the complication? Well, what if George can't find his father's grave? Now there's a complication all right!

To set up the problem, aka the situation, George and Louise could be doing some housecleaning, going through an old trunk of Mother Jefferson's stuff and they find a will signed by George's father. In the will, George's father requests that if he should die before Olivia (George's mother), he wants Olivia to make sure she's buried next to him so they can be together forever. So George decides he'll get his father and bury him next to his mother in Shady Hills Cemetery. But when George goes to do this great thing for his father, he can't find his father's grave.

But if they can't find his father's grave, what's the resolution? The four writers had been at it quite a while—hours—and this was the closest they'd come to breaking a story. They had what Murph felt was a good complication. And Murph believed, after all, that the complication is not only the most important part of the story, it *is* the story.

That's what he would tell attendees at the occasional Sherwood Oaks class or seminar where he would speak as a favor for Gary Shusett. (Gary loved being able to mention that Murph & Sean actually met at a Sherwood Oaks class.)

Murph would say, "Without the complication, there is no story." By way of explanation, take the Halloween story. If Louise thinks she sees a murder, but isn't sure where the murder occurred and never sees the killer again, there is no story. But if she sees the killer and he learns Louise is a witness, there's a complication (jeopardy for our main character) and thus a story. An example Murph might mention to a class would be the classic children's story of *Little Red Riding Hood*. If Li'l Red takes a picnic basket through the woods to her Grandma's house, has a nice lunch with Grandma, then returns home, there's a beginning, middle and end—but there's not much of a story.

Without the Big Bad Wolf, there's no complication, no jeopardy, no story. There's a reason Murph's young daughters would say to him, "Tell us the story about the Big Bad Wolf." In the tale of *Little Red Riding Hood*, the Big Bad Wolf is the complication. And the complication *is* the story.

But without a satisfactory resolution, of course, there's not much of a story. For instance, if the Wolf arrives, dresses up like Grandma and eats Little Red Riding Hood—yikes! What kid wants to hear that? So without the hunter, who stops the wolf from eating Grandma and L'il Red—or a similar resolution—there's not much of a story, at least for children or viewers of prime time television.

So in the "Where's Papa?" story, if the problem is George's father is buried in potter's field and George wants to give him a proper burial, and the complication is they can't find his father's grave, what's the resolution?

Time was running out. M&M had to go to a run-thru and they wanted to send Peter & David away with an assignment. So for the first time ever, against their better judgment, without stepping out a beginning, middle and end which they knew would work, M&M sent a writing team off to write a story, hoping they all could figure out a satisfactory ending later.

While working on the "Where's Papa?" story, Peter & David called and pitched a resolution of George and Louise deciding to have a memorial for George's father. That sounded like it might work; maybe with George giving an emotional eulogy for his father and/or creating a plaque to be placed on/or near his mother's tombstone. But a couple drafts later, the four writers agreed the ending felt flat and forced. Maybe they should come up with a different complication. Or maybe just eat the script? What?! Who said that?

They finally decided on a resolution involving hypnotism. Bentley suggests George undergo hypnosis in an attempt to recall where his father was buried. George does this, giving Sherman an opportunity to test his acting chops when the hypnotist takes George back to nine years old at his father's funeral.

George isn't able to recall any information about his father's resting place; but he does recall telling his mother that his father made him promise to take care of her. When the hypnotist leaves, Louise helps George realize that he was able to grant his father's final request, taking care of his mother in ways far beyond what his father—or anyone—could have dreamed.

While it took a lot of push and pull to get this story on the northbound track, Murph was pleased with the outcome. It succeeded in both exploring and expanding George's character and conscience. George's plight in this episode was symbolic of the quest of many young people in the community who found themselves desperate to know more about their missing or absent fathers. And it served as a reminder to work out at least a basic beginning, middle and end before sending out an assignment.

M&M were impressed with how Casey & Lee stayed with the story and, to steal a phrase, helped make lemonade out of lemons. So they hired Peter & David, giving the young writers their first staff job. The two had been working for a company called Movable Feast selling premade lunch sandwiches to office employees.

TOM WILLIS WANTS George Jefferson to teach him how to be black. When Don & Jerry pitched that idea to M&M, all four were laughing. To Murph, this was the quintessential *Jeffersons* story! The honky wants George to teach him how to be black! How did *AITF* miss doing this episode with Archie Bunker?!

If Don and Jerry could make this make sense, even a little bit, it was a sure thing the audience would go with it. So in the setup scene Tom and Helen are socializing with a couple of Helen's friends (both black) from her college days and Tom has a hard time keeping up with the lingo and the references. Among other things, he learns that in street lingo "Hog" means "Cadillac" and "sky" means "hat." Tom feels foolish and left out; and, most importantly, he feels Helen may have been happier if she married someone black.

So Tom shows up at George's apartment with a Black Language Dictionary and asks George to teach him how to be black. George, of course, thinks this is ridiculous; but he finally gives in to Tom's pleading. For the writers, the challenge here is to come up with visual bits—television, after all, is a visual medium. George tells Tom if you want to be black, you gotta be cool. George shows Tom how a white man walks and then how a black man walks.

Tom starts asking a lot of questions and George says something like "That's another thing," and tells Tom white people talk too much. George demonstrates the dialogue between two white men meeting on the street, then two black men meeting. George calls Tom a chump, then chastises Tom for letting him get away with that. "Black people don't let somebody get the best of us," says George. "If somebody sounds on you, you sound back on them one better." At that point, Florence enters from the bedroom area and George says something like, "Here, I'll show you what I mean."

"Florence, your cooking tastes like dog food." Florence responds, "That's because I'm cooking for a Chihuahua," and exits to kitchen. George stretches his arms out toward Florence and looks at Tom as if to say, 'See what I'm talking about.'

When the 'How to be cool' lessons end, George congratulates Tom and says something like, "Give me five, bro." And Tom says, "Sure, George. You have change for a twenty?" and starts removing his wallet as we Fade Out.

In Act II, George, Louise, Helen and Helen's friends are seated in the Jeffersons' living room chatting it up. Tom enters at the front door wearing a sort of Billy Jack hat doing his best cool strut across the room. When a puzzled Helen asks Tom what that is on his head, he says "That's my new sky."

He moves around greeting the others using words like *bro, blood, crib* and *my main man.* When Helen takes him aside and tells him he's acting like a jackass, he says, "Oh yeah, well you cook like a Chihuahua." Tom laughs heartily, crosses to George to exchange hand slaps, then points to George and says, "Your Mama!"

A shocked Helen grabs her husband and hustles him into the kitchen. Tom explains to Helen he feels like he's kept her from being black and he apologizes. In a heartfelt scene, the two lovebirds make up, concluding with the longest, most passionate kiss between a so-called interracial couple ever shown on television.

TWO-THIRDS OF THE way through the season, writer/producer Seth Rivers had not yet written or pitched an original. M&M became aware they were not going to get the support they needed from Seth. When a staff writer or producer is released from a show, it doesn't mean that person is not a good writer. It can simply mean that writer is not right for the show.

Murph would explain to students at Sherwood Oaks that the primary job of a staff writer on a series is to figure out what the Showrunner (Exec Producer) wants and give it to him/her. It's really the same for any job. If you're unable to figure out what your boss wants and deliver it, you're in the wrong job. In the entertainment business, when an actor is released, it could be with a simple phrase like "We've decided to go in a different direction." When a writer is released, only two words are necessary: "Creative differences." Those are the words M&M used to explain the Seth Rivers situation to Alan Horn.

Finding a replacement this deep in the season is hard, because most qualified writer-producers are contractually committed to other series. Murph and Sean were pleased with their current young writing staff of Moye, Lebowitz, Perzigian & Siegel, Casey & Lee. But they felt it would be wise to have at least one veteran around as they approached mile 18 of this season's marathon race. So they contacted erstwhile Executive Story Consultant Bryan Joseph who agreed to return and hang with the gang for the remainder of the season.

Michael Moye wrote four originals for Season 6, including Part II of "The Arrival," a two-parter featuring the birth of Jenny & Lionel's baby. In Part I, we learn Lionel is interviewing for a job in Boston, which would be for more money than he's making now. This would serve as the apparent A story throughout the two-parter.

In Part I, it's established that Jenny is far along with her pregnancy and circumstances occur that find George taking Jenny to her evening Lamaze Class, which is the Act Break. At the end of Part I, Lamaze class is over, everyone else has gone, and George is waiting for Jenny who's in the restroom. When she comes out, Jenny tells George she's in labor and he freaks!

In Part II, George is comforting Jenny in the back of the janitor's van on the way to the hospital. They arrive safely and Jenny is rushed into the delivery room. Up to this point, all members of the cast, including Florence and Bentley, have been involved in both episodes and all show up at the hospital for what turns out to be the birth of Lionel & Jenny's beautiful baby girl!

The name chosen for George and Louise's new granddaughter was Jessica, named after the most recent addition to M&M's extended family, Murph's niece (his sister Lynn's firstborn) baby Jessica.

Chapter 23

"THE FIRST STORE" & MORE

('80)

In the 1970s, categorically speaking, every Catholic family in Ireland had a photo or a bust of John F. Kennedy in their home; just as every black family in America had a picture of Martin Luther King in their home. Early on, Murph had the notion of *The Jeffersons* doing an episode that would somehow acknowledge or discuss the contribution of Martin Luther King to the soul of America in general and the plight of black Americans in particular. But the obvious roadblock was, 'How do you make it funny?'

As much as Murph felt the series called for it, he also felt it might throw an unnecessary pall over the show. Not to mention that he didn't think NRW would go for it.

But now, in Season 6, while Murph and Sean were kicking around ideas for an original, they asked themselves how George Jefferson managed to start Jefferson Cleaners? How indeed was a black man of limited means from Harlem able to open his first cleaning store? Maybe they could do a flashback episode about that—call it "*The First Store.*"

They figured George probably opened his first store about ten years ago—the late 60s. 1968 or '69. It hit Murph that '68 is when Martin Luther King died. Light bulb: What if George were applying for a minority business loan to open his first store the day Martin Luther King was killed? They could do an informative show about George opening his first store and make it a tribute episode to the memory of Martin Luther King.

It seemed like a story idea that came from the cosmos. The timeline was perfect. *The Jeffersons* had never done a flashback episode before, so that would be a nice challenge for cast & crew, hair, makeup, wardrobe, art direction, props and all involved. So M&M began breaking the story and writing the script.

For a real-time opening to this flashback episode, M&M wrote a short pre-taped scene in the current Jefferson kitchen with Louise and George looking at some old photos and reminiscing about the past. Louise says "Remember the day you came home and told me you wanted to open your own cleaning store?" And George says something like, "Yep, that was in, uh, nineteen sixty-eight."

Dissolving to a no-frills apartment in 1960s Harlem, we see Louise dressed in a pedestrian maid's outfit attempting to watch television on an older model TV as the sound continues to drop out. Each time the sound drops, Louise crosses to the TV, hits it with the palm of her hand, and the sound returns. Finally, rather than continue getting up, she grabs a nearby broom, remains seated on the sofa, and reaches to hit the TV with the broom. The TV ANNOUNCER (VO) mentions the Five O'clock news for Thursday, April 4th, the names President Johnson, Senator Robert Kennedy and a reference to upcoming primaries. A picture of MLK is placed inconspicuously on a nearby wall.

George enters at front door and we learn he's planning to meet a banker at their apartment. He's applied for a minority business loan to start his own business. He's been working for Stevens Cleaners for five years and figures he knows everything there is to know about running a cleaning operation. He says he's tired of making somebody else rich and wants a piece of the pie for himself and his family. He tells Louise they're gonna be rich someday and she'll be able to quit working as a maid and hire her own maid.

When the banker arrives, he's white and patronizing; but George manages to bite his tongue and force a smile. Lionel enters at the front door, nursing a bruise on his forehead. Louise asks Lionel what happened and he explains he was at a demonstration and the pigs showed up and started busting heads. When George asks what they were demonstrating about, Lionel says "Police brutality."

Following a brief confrontation between Lionel and the banker, George quickly asks Louise to take Lionel in the kitchen and make sure he's okay. Louise takes Lionel, saying she'll put some ice on his head. George suggests she also put some tape on his mouth.

Louise and Lionel exit while George and the banker continue to talk. The banker says he hopes George's son isn't anti-police and mentions the current unrest in the country with all the protests and marching. He notices the framed picture of Martin Luther King on the Jeffersons' wall and blames MLK for causing most of the unrest. He says he's heard that King is a communist and asks George what he thinks.

George smiles and deftly changes the subject, saying something like "Well, I think we should talk about me and my chances of getting a loan!" The banker is impressed with George's ambition and tells George he wishes all

Negroes were like him. He says he'll be back tomorrow with the loan papers for George to sign.

Excited, George summons Louise and Lionel, tells them he's got the loan, and shows them the key to what he plans to be his first store. It's nearby and he wants to show it to them.

The store is an empty storefront with a dusty counter on one side and a few pieces of worn furniture, including a couple chairs, strewn around. George proudly proclaims this the future site of Handy Dandy Cleaners. Louise isn't crazy about the name. When George asks if she can think of a better name, Louise says "How about Jefferson Cleaners?" George laughs and says something like "C'mon, Weezy, that would never work."

Lionel says he's not sure this whole thing's gonna work. The odds of a black man making it in this system are not good. George says Lionel's starting to sound like those black militants, always yelling "Down with the system! Down with the country! Down with everything!"

Lionel says, "Those brothers are doing a lot more than yelling. They're taking action." George says, "You call it action. I call it violence." Lionel: "Well, call it whatever you want. But all they're saying is the only way to fight white power is with black power." Louise: "They're wrong, Lionel. That's not the only way." George: "Your mother's right. Martin Luther King is fighting back, but he's doing it the right way—nonviolent." Lionel says something like, "What Martin Luther King is doing is fine. But maybe, just maybe, it's time for the marches and sit-ins to end and the fighting to begin." George: "Oh, it's no use talking to you."

George takes Louise and shows her where he plans to stack all his clean laundry and put the cleaning equipment, then guides her to the counter and explains that she'll be first employee of Handy Dandy Cleaners. She won't get a paycheck right away; but one of her perks will be she gets to sleep with the boss. Suddenly, a brick comes flying through the glass window on the entrance door. George rushes to the door and opens it to chaos outside.

He learns from a young black dude running by that "Brother Martin is dead." Louise: "Martin Luther King?" Dude: "That's right. They shot him, and now they're gonna pay!"

George, Louise and Lionel are stunned. George moves inside the store, trying to take it in. In disbelief, George says "They killed him. They really killed him." He turns to a side window and yells "Those bastards!" Then picks up a nearby chair and hurls it through the window!

In Act II, next morning, George is sitting on the sofa, listening to the TV news broadcast as Louise enters. We learn George has been up all night, unable to sleep. Louise makes a call to Mrs. Warren, a white woman for whom Louise works as a maid, to explain she won't be coming to work today. Mrs. Warren objects, explaining she's having guests tonight. George takes the phone and tells Louise's boss it's a day of mourning at their house. When Mrs. Warren continues to object, George tells her to find herself a new maid and hangs up.

When Louise protests that they need that job, George says: "No we don't. From now on you're working for me, President of Handy Dandy Cleaners!"

When Mr. Drew, the banker, stops by with the loan papers for George to sign, George learns he'll have to get a new store in a different neighborhood where people don't "act like animals." George explains people are just upset because of what happened last night. In an exchange where the banker makes more insensitive remarks, George decides he doesn't want to do business with this bank after all. He calls Mr. Drew a "honky" and throws him out!

When Louise enters, George tells Louise he lost the loan but found his dignity. George says the militants are right. The only way to fight white power is with black power. Louise objects. She wants George to go talk to Lionel, who says he's going out to steal a television. George says "Okay, I'll talk to him. I'll tell him to be sure he gets one with remote control."

Louise attempts to stop him, but George insists "The only way we're ever gonna get anything from Whitey is to take it." Louise: "If Lionel goes out there, he'll just be proving what some white people think." George: "I don't care what the honkies think. I'm tired of caring what they think!" Louise: "Okay, George. I guess you're right. In fact, why don't you go out there with Lionel. We could use a stereo too." George: "What?" Louise: (takes picture of MLK off the wall) "And while you're out there, take this thing with you and get rid of it." George: "Weezy, what are you doing?" Louise: "We don't need this picture anymore. The man is dead." George: "What?!" Louise: "Oh, Dr. King is probably looking down on us right now saying, "Get out there and get whatever you can!Burn, baby, burn!" George: "Naw, he'd never say that." Louise: "Then why are you sending Lionel out there?" George: (frustrated & perplexed) "I don't know, Weezy. Dammit, I don't know anything anymore."

Lionel enters, crossing to front door. George: "Lionel, where are you going?" Lionel: "Out. I am going to let this country know that this time they have pushed us too far." George grabs his son's arm, stopping Lionel at the open door. George: "Look, Lionel, Lionel, Lionel, I know how you feel. But violence is not the answer."

Lionel: "Oh yeah, well what is the answer? Non-violence? That's what Martin Luther King thought, and you see where it got him." Lionel breaks free and starts out the door. Louise: (yells) "Lionel!" He stops. Louise (cont'd): "Martin Luther King helped accomplish a lot for our people." Lionel: "Oh, sure, he tried. But what did he really accomplish? Nothing's changed."

George: "You're wrong, Lionel. Lots of things have changed. Maybe not as fast as we'd like, but there have been a lot of changes. (recalls) I remember the first time I found out I was colored..." Lionel: (correcting) "Black." George: "Okay, black. I was sitting on the doorstep with my father, and I hear this siren getting louder and louder and coming closer and closer and closer, right? And all of a sudden this great big red fire truck comes racing around the corner right past our house! And I say to my father, 'Wow, when I grow up, I'm gonna be a fireman.' And my father just looks at me and smiles. And he says, 'Yeah, Georgie, don't you know they don't let Negroes on the fire department?'" Lionel and Louise react as George turns away and continues: "And for a long time after that, I felt like less of a person just because I was col..." (stops, looks at Lionel) "...black. Then Martin Luther King comes along and reminds me that I'm just as good as everybody else. He gave me hope! He gave me the confidence to go out and start my own business! And that's what I'm gonna do!"

George sits on the sofa. Lionel crosses to George and sits next to him, sympathetic. Lionel: "Pop, you see, you're dreaming. Look, we got no car, no TV, Mom's got no job..." George: "No loan." Lionel: (news to him) "No loan?" George: "That's right." Lionel: "Well, then how are you gonna start your business?" George: "I don't know, Lionel. But I'm gonna do it. You can do whatever you want, if you really want to. Right, Weez?"

Louise: "Your father's right, Lionel. We shall overcome."

Louise, at the radio, turns it on.

Radio (NEWS ANNOUNCER VO):"Before his death, Reverend King gave the following speech to striking sanitation workers in Memphis": (tight on radio and picture of MLK, intercut with shots of George, Louise and Lionel gathering at sofa) MLK VO: (actual speech to crowd) "We've got some difficult days ahead. But it doesn't really matter with me now. Because I've been to the mountaintop. I don't mind. Like anybody, I'd like to live a long life. Longevity has its place. But I'm not concerned about that now. I just want to do God's will. And He's allowed me to go up to the mountain...and I've looked over and I have seen...the Promised Land. I may not get there with you. But I want you to know tonight that we as a people will get to the Promised Land. So I'm happy tonight. I'm not worried about anything. I'm not fearing any man. Mine eyes have seen the glory of the coming of the Lord!" Echo out, tighten on shot of George and Louise on sofa, Lionel seated on sofa arm. Go to black for silent, white-on-black credits.

When they finished their draft of the script, M&M read it over and decided the network would probably object to using the word "bastards" at act break. So Sean & Murph attempted to come up with another act break line. A line right before George throws a chair through the window. A line right after he says "They really killed him." A line to replace "Those bastards!"

M&M finally settled on "Damn them!" It felt soft—compared to "Those bastards!" But they figured Sherman could make it work.

A couple days after they sent the script to CBS, Murph

was in his office when a call came from Standards & Practices at the network. They were objecting to the act break line of "Damn them!" The objection was that George was asking God to damn the killers to hell. (Yikes!) Murph told the young woman at CBS that he and Sean had struggled with that line and had a tough time coming up with something appropriate for the moment.

Then, to Murph's surprise—make that amazement!— the young censor said, "What about 'Those bastards'?" Murph was stunned. Did the Censor Gal actually suggest the line "Those bastards"? Murph wanted to make sure he was hearing correctly. So he said, "You mean you think instead of saying 'Damn them!', George should say 'Those bastards!'?"

She said, "Yes."

Attempting to feign disappointment, Murph sighed, "I don't know. Let me talk to my partner and I'll get back to you."

When Murph told Sean, it took Murph about five minutes to convince his partner it wasn't a joke. Murph waited till the end of the day, then called Censor Gal back and tried to sound mildly begrudging as he told her he and Sean discussed the matter and decided to appease the network and change the act break line to "Those bastards!"

At the table reading of "The First Store," all went well. During lunch break, however, Mike Evans showed up in M&M's office. Mike didn't want to play Lionel in the flashback episode. He said he had no problems with the script; but he just wasn't comfortable playing a more militant Lionel. He confided that his mother was white and he felt it would be disrespectful to her. He suggested M&M hire a younger actor to portray Lionel in the flashback episode. When M&M hesitated, Mike offered to pay a sum of

$2,400 in cash to let him sit this one out. How did Mike Evans arrive at that $2,400 figure? Murph had no idea. Did the actor really think M&M might accept a bribe? Maybe Mike felt, with some justification, that all producers—or all white people—were bribable.

M&M very much wanted Mike in the episode. They felt his presence and credibility as Sherman and Isabel's son could not be matched by a replacement. They explained that as an actor, he'd be playing a very important role in this tribute episode. A role portraying the intense feelings of many young people following the tragic event on April 4, 1968.

They encouraged Mike to think about it. Discuss it with the rest of the cast. They assured him that if he still felt there was no way he could play the role, it wouldn't be held against him. At the end of the day, good news. Mike was on board. Apparently Sherman had convinced his young colleague to go for it.

The only other issue which arose during production of "The First Store" was that the network wanted Sean & Murph to write a tag. A tag that would dissolve from the MLK speech back to the dee-luxe apartment in the sky. Pressure from the network continued, even after the show was taped.

Now ordinarily, bookending a flashback show with a present-time opening and a present-time ending, would not only be fine, but expected. But in this case, Murph & Sean felt strongly that going from the MLK mountain-top speech to present-time Jeffersons' apartment for a joke would be a definite moment killer. So they took a page from the NRW/Lear playbook and stood firm. They insisted on ending the show as written, dissolving from the MLK speech to silent credits reversed out of black. Thanks to Norman Lear, M&M learned that every sitcom episode doesn't have to end with a laugh.

Following the broadcast of this episode, a young man sent his thesis to Norman along with this note:

> *By the way, according to my research, "The*
> *Jeffersons" was cited most as the favorite black*
> *comedy in this survey of Atlanta blacks. At the same*
> *time, I take this moment to commend all involved on*
> *the wonderful Martin Luther King story. It was a*
> *beautiful script that in my opinion deserves an Emmy*
> *nomination. Please continue to produce this kind of*
> *quality so much a part of the black experience.*

Many years later (about four decades), Murph noticed an item on the Internet ranking the Top 50 (out of 253) *Jefferson* episodes. Ranked number 1 was "The First Store." Having not seen it in quite a while, Murph watched it again. Coincidentally, it was just days before Martin Luther King Day, established as a national holiday in 1983 and first observed in 1986.

Murph was impressed with how well the episode held up. He saw it as a perfect blend of cogency and comedy. It was powerful and informative. Young people over the years had told him this episode of *The Jeffersons* is how they learned about Martin Luther King. It occurred to Murph that if he and Sean had never written another script, this episode would stand as a fitting summation of their work in television.

Although Murph wasn't aware of any particular awards for which this episode may or may not have been nominated, he couldn't help feeling that everyone involved in this flashback tribute—from cast all the way through wardrobe, props and set design—should be acknowledged for their stellar contributions. He was comforted by the words of Mark Twain, who said "It's better to deserve an award and not get it, than to get an award and not deserve it."

IN ADDITION TO episodes already mentioned, other Season 6 shows generated by the new baby include "Baby Love," "The Shower," "The Longest Day," "The Loan" and "Once Upon a Time."

In "Baby Love," Florence, upset that everyone but her is married and has children ("The only time anyone asked me to pick out china was on a map"), resorts to hiring a video dating service hoping to secure a husband. When Florence admits that she "sorta lied" on her dating resumé, George asks "What did you say, 'You worked for a living'?"

When her quest seems fruitless, Florence confides in Louise that without a child she feels like less of a woman—like a "frame without a picture, a camera without film, a corn cob without niblets." When Louise protests, Florence says Louise doesn't know how it feels to want a child but not be able to have one.

In a touching moment, Louise reveals that before they were married, she and George wanted a big family. But after Lionel was born, Louise found out she couldn't have any more children. She says she was depressed for a while and felt like less of a woman. But then she realized it's not a child that makes her a woman. "It's me that makes me a woman."

In "The Shower," Jenny is upset that Lionel is working instead of attending the baby shower. In a heartfelt "Cat's in the Cradle" (Harry Chapin song) scene, George confesses to Lionel that, instead of working so much, he wishes he had spent more time with his son when Lionel was growing up. And he encourages Lionel not to follow

George's example, but to try spending more time with his new daughter.

In "The Longest Day," when the women head for a fashion show and the men are planning to watch an important football game, George, Tom and Lionel volunteer to watch baby Jessica, saying that watching a baby is a piece of cake. The men begin to learn a lesson long before the third quarter.

Plans for the christening of baby Jessica bookend a fast-paced, laugh-filled teleplay penned by Casey & Lee titled "The Loan." When Lionel and Jenny's loan for a new home is turned down by the bank, George, Louise, Tom and Helen each secretly try to help the kids secure the loan. Lionel is furious when he learns of his parents' involvement, but Louise is able to bring her son to his senses in a nice mother-son moment near the end.

Inflation was a huge topic in the news at the time, and Michael Moye was able to personify this hard-to-grasp economic concept in an episode titled "Once Upon a Time."George fears inflation is killing his bottom line and desperately needs his bank to extend his credit line. While waiting for a call from his banker and watching baby Jessica, George spins a bedtime fairy tale to his granddaughter. Viewers are treated to a visual trip back to the days of the Round Table where George is King, Louise is Queen; Lionel and Jenny are prince and princess; Tom and Helen are Baron Von Day and Lady Von Night, Rulers of the Land of the Zebras; Ralph is a messenger known as Ralph the Greedy; Bentley is the fool or court jester; and a notorious villain named Inflation is out to destroy King George and the Jefferson Empire.

As for Murph's Season 6 favorites, "The First Store" of course is number one and "A Short Story" is number two, with "Brother Tom" third. After that, it was hard for Murph to pick favorites. For consistent comedy, he felt Season 6 was maybe the best *Jeffersons* season yet.

There were laugh-out-loud episodes dealing with Louise's old boyfriend and George's 50th birthday—not to mention "Louise vs. Florence" where those two are at each other's throats while George is trying to entertain and impress a snooty couple from the Black Social Register—all three scripted by Perzigian & Siegel.

Also in the mix was an episode about the Jeffersons' 30th Anniversary where Louise learns about perhaps the most important issue in any relationship—trust. As with Casey & Lee's snappy dialogue in "The Loan," their teleplay for "A Night to Remember" kept the live audience practically rolling in the aisles. Murph felt a special fondness for "One Flew into the Cuckoo's Nest," also a Casey & Lee original where George finds himself mistaken for an inmate while delivering cleaning to a mental institution. There's something funny about George Jefferson in a straightjacket, jumping up and down insisting he's not crazy.

In episodes like "Louise's Setback," "Me and Mr. G" and "Louise vs. Florence" the Neighborhood Help Center continued to serve as a source for stories and provide a viable life purpose for both Louise and Helen.

Season 6 shows were also notable for their touching moments. Moments featuring meaningful character interaction between George and Jenny; George and Lionel; Louise and Lionel; Tom and Jenny; Louise and Florence; George and Tom; Lionel and Jenny; even Bentley and Florence; and of course George and Louise.

With the birth of baby Jessica, this was a pivotal season for the series. And the presence and performance of Mike Evans as Lionel had a lot to do with that. Lionel and Jenny were now parents, and the Jeffersons and Willises were now grandparents. And as such, all were inextricably linked.

George would no longer refer to Jenny, the mother of his granddaughter, as a zebra. And although George, in certain instances and by force of habit (not to disappoint the groundlings), may sometimes toss color-related jokes at the Willises, George will now, by necessity, possess a definite undercurrent of respect for both Tom and Helen who, from this point on, are not just neighbors, not just in-laws, but are mutual grandparents to George and Louise's granddaughter.

Freelance writers who contributed to Season 6 include Mary-David Sheiner & Sheila Judis Weisberg, Susan Straughn Harris, Joanne Pagliaro, Bob Baublitz, Stephen A. Miller, Paul M. Belous & Robert Wolterstorff, Anthony Bonaduce & Celia Bonaduce.

Chapter 24

JEFFS, SEASON 7

('80-81)

A s Season 6 started to wind down, Murph & Sean began to think ahead. They were thinking what pretty much every TV writing staff thinks at the end of every season beyond the third—'There are no more stories for this series.' After struggling to complete the last few episodes of Season 6, were Murph & Sean ready to run another marathon race? There was talk of M&M being offered a development deal, otherwise known as a "sweetheart deal," by more than one studio. Murph & Sean would get paid to think up ideas for new series—a tempting offer for two guys who'd spent the last five years in constant production. They figured they had pretty much proved themselves as staff writers and showrunners.

When their CBS representative learned M&M were having thoughts of moving on, he mentioned one of Murph's favorite words—Hawaii. CBS was considering sending George & Weezy to Hawaii next season. Well, Alo…ha ha ha! That would probably be a four-parter. So there were four, count 'em, *four* episodes already!

Tandem/TAT chimed in with an offer of profit participation, aka a "piece of the show" — for this past season; the upcoming seventh season; and the eighth season, whether M&M remained with the show in Season 8 or not. Plus, M&M's request to list a credit at the end of each episode saying the show was produced "in association with Ragamuffin Productions," à la the former "in association with NRW Productions" credit, was accepted by TAT. (Ragamuffin was the name of M&M's newly-formed production or "loan out" company, the name being a nod to their mothers who would critique their sartorial attire with the declaration, "You look like a little ragamuffin!")

Another reason M&M decided to stay with *The Jeffersons* was because they cared. If and when M&M left, they wanted to be sure to leave the show in good hands. Their hope was that they could find an experienced writing-producing team who understood the import of the series and could be trusted to treat the show with the reverence it deserved.

Michael Moye was talented but had no producing experience. Perzigian & Seigel and Casey & Lee were also strong writers; but, like Michael, they were young with no producing experience. When the show's CBS rep heard M&M were looking for producers, he strongly recommended David Duclon & Ron Leavitt who had been working with Garry Marshall on *Happy Days* and, more recently, *Laverne and Shirley*.

M&M read some material and met with Ron & David. Murph recognized David as one of Garry's original intern writers who had risen up the ranks. Although Garry's current sitcoms were mostly set in the Fifties (*Happy Days, Laverne & Shirley, Mork & Mindy*) and, unlike Norman Lear shows, did not deal with topical issues, Duclon & Leavitt wrote funny. And Murph & Sean knew that funny was the glue that held *The Jeffersons* together.

A recent viewer survey compiled within TAT following the 1979-80 season is printed, word for word, below:

THE JEFFERSONS – Audience Response Report

Our devoted JEFFERSONS' audience watches for a simple, basic reason—they think the show is funny.

No one is trying to relate to any of the characters or solve any of their problems from situations on the program. They just want, and in some cases need, to laugh and they do when they watch the show. There are a number of letters from people who are ill, had injuries or are miserable for various reasons and are home all day. They watch the reruns because it gives them the only laughter and cheering up they can find. They think the situations are funny and the characters are funny. The only specific interchanges mentioned are the ones between George and Florence which they love. Most of the comments are general:

Pure enjoyment, marvelous timing – comical and wholesome – poignant, funny and clean – funniest show – makes me laugh – gives so much pleasure – great comedy show – can't stop laughing – never fails to make me laugh – terrifically funny scripts – real funny – I laughed so much I almost cried – really, really, really enjoy your show – performed continuously with high powered comedy and depth of human frailties – writers and all deserve tribute.

Even though we attracted new viewers when the show was moved to its current Sunday night slot, we seem to have many who have been with us from

*the beginning. They have watched George and Louise
since ALL IN THE FAMILY days and have been
fans for years. Some say they watch every day but
Saturday. They feel the show is the high Norman
Lear quality and has retained it over the years.*

*The majority of the audience seems oblivious to the
fact that there are Black and White characters. Those
who did notice liked the interracial couple shown as
a normal, average family without exploitation. They
liked that there is a group of both Black and White
people with talent who can joke about color differences without being offensive. They feel we portray
adult Blacks with some class and dignity and the
younger Blacks with purpose as they would be in real
life. One said it was the only black show his family
watched.*

*One point of interest is the popularity of the theme
song "Movin' On Up." We get many more requests
for the words to it than any of our other themes. They
seem to be genuinely fond of the song and one even
admitted to being "hopelessly smitten" with it.*

A FEW DAYS after M&M hired Ron & Dave as producers, Murph was walking past his assistant's desk
toward his office. The phone on her desk rang and it was
Alan Horn. Standing at her desk, Murph took the phone
and spoke with Alan, who expressed his concern that, as
Laverne & Shirley writers, Duclon & Leavitt may not be
"the right guys" for *The Jeffersons*.

Murph told Alan that Ron & Dave wrote funny stuff, had
some producing experience, and assured Alan that he and
Sean would be overseeing and doing the final rewrite on
every script. Alan seemed appeased.

With their new producers now in place, Murph and Sean could focus on the Hawaii episodes. They figured they, along with Michael, would write the four episodes. When they went to Hawaii to shoot the episodes, they would take Michael, whose new title was Executive Story Consultant, with them. Ron and Dave would stay here and oversee the rest of the writing staff, which consisted of Perzigian & Siegel and Casey & Lee, all four now promoted to Story Editors. M&M would approve all writing assignments and give notes on all stories and drafts, either in person or on the phone when in Hawaii.

Regarding cast, M&M figured they could take George, Louise, Florence and the Willises to Hawaii. They considered the other regulars—Lionel, Jenny and baby Jessica plus Bentley and even Ralph—but that seemed to stretch credibility and logistics too far.

Before starting to write the Hawaii episodes, M&M planned to go to the islands for research and to check out possible shooting locations. But before leaving, they wanted to get some other Season 7 stories in the pipeline.

Not long ago Murph was teaching (pro bono) an eight-week comedy writing class at Sherwood Oaks. When class ended one night, Murph noticed a young student named Bob Bendetson exit the classroom and cross to another young man who was seated in the hall. The other young man began copying notes from Bob's notebook. Curious, Murph moved to them and Bob introduced Murph to his brother, Howard. Cost for the class was thirty-five dollars per student and the Bendetson Brothers could afford only enough for one of them to take it. So Bob was taking the class and sharing his notes afterward with Howard.

Murph was duly impressed when he learned that the brothers kept a master file of original jokes for most sitcoms currently on TV. The brothers seemed talented and committed, a promising combination. And Murph invited both to attend class from then on at no extra cost.

Not long after, Murph invited the Bendetsons to pitch stories to him and Sean at *The Jeffersons*, figuring it would be a good experience for the brothers. The meeting ended as pitch meetings usually do, with M&M and B&B unable to land on anything solid. But the unusual thing about this meeting—in fact, as far as Murph knew, it never happened before—the brothers arrived for the meeting on a bus. They didn't own a car. Bob & Howard weren't able to score a writing assignment; but they did receive a confidence boost. Murph & Sean assured them they were talented and would eventually be driving their own car.

That was last season. Now, at the start of Season 7, Murph invited the Bendetson Boys to pitch to M&M and Ron & Dave. Following the initial pitches, Ron asked the brothers why Bob did all the talking and Howard remained silent. "Because he shakes when he pitches," Bob answered.

This time the writers were able to come up with a story: George and Tom get into an argument about who's in better shape, so they decide to run in the New York Marathon to see who lasts the longest. The men start exercising, but soon realize they're in no condition to be racing. Both Helen and Louise, however, begin defending their husbands' respective athletic prowess and, at the women's insistence, the competition is back on in this show titled "Marathon Men," the first *Jeffersons* episode to air in Season 7.

So the Bendetson Brothers had their first official assignment. Sweet Lew became their agent and commented that B&B were now on their way to becoming the next M&M.

TO THE SURPRISE of most people he worked with, mainly because he never announced his illness or showed it, Don Nicholl passed in the summer of 1980, a victim of cancer. Don left no children, but his wife Gee established the Don Nicholl Fellowship, which has become one of the best known and most sought after fellowship programs for aspiring screenwriters.

In the summer of '77, Murph had learned that "Don is sick and in the hospital but he's going to be okay." Murph went to visit Don at Cedars-Sinai hospital and was encouraged to see that Don was in good spirits and appeared to be his usual ebullient self. Murph and Don had a nice chat away from the office. Murph was temporarily taken aback when Don asked Murph what he wanted to do going forward.

Having just turned 31, Murph was perfectly content doing exactly what he was doing. But when pressed by Don, Murph found himself saying he'd like to be a producer, like Don. Murph was well aware of, and amused by the Bobs' (Schiller & Weiskopf's) definition of a producer as "a writer gone bad." But, in those days at least, being a producer usually meant having more control of your material. And what writer doesn't want that?

Don responded with a knowing smile. A smile that said a lot of things. And one of those things was, "No worries, I'll be fine." Murph believed it; and he thinks Don did too. In a very short time, Don, the N in NRW, was back at work writing and producing both *The Jeffersons* and *Three's Company* until his untimely death at the age of 54.

Chapter 25

THE JEFFERSONS GO TO HAWAII

('80)

So M&M and their line producer flew to Hawaii to scout locations. At first they thought they might want to do some shooting on outer islands, like Maui or the Big Island. But they soon realized that shooting on Oahu made more sense.

At that time all flights from the mainland went through Honolulu on the island of Oahu. Maui had some great scenery, with iconic towns like Lahaina and Paia, but not many hotels. The resorts and golf courses along Kaanapali were just being developed, and Wailea was still virgin territory. Plus, any shooting on the outer islands would require having to barge camera equipment and supplies from Oahu, creating a definite logistics hurdle.

George Jefferson didn't play golf; and it made sense that the Jeffersons would spend their Hawaiian vacation in Honolulu on or near Waikiki. So Sean & Murph focused on Oahu for locations.

Discussing the story for a four-part episode, the first question they had to answer was how to get George Jefferson to Hawaii. In other words, "Why would George Jefferson, an established workaholic entrepreneur, take a Hawaiian vacation?" For an answer, they settled on George has high blood pressure and his doctor orders or recommends a trip to Hawaii.

Another question was "Why would George take Florence with them?" Hmm...well, what if Louise bought Florence a ticket as a surprise gift before she knew she and George would be going?

And then there was the problem of how to get the Willises to Hawaii at the same time. What if Tom and Helen are already there on vacation? Maybe they're scheduled to be returning home, but they decide to stay longer because they're having such a relaxing time in Hawaii.

And Florence...well, Florence should have a story of her own. So...what if Florence, on vacation, has romance on her mind and is hoping to meet a beau? And her horoscope is encouraging.

Murph and Sean made notes of things the *Jeffersons* characters could see and do as tourists in Hawaii. Things that might be employed in the scripts. Like riding in pedicabs, shopping at Honolulu's International Market Place, tossing a Frisbee on the beach, snorkeling, sailing, sunbathing, bikini ogling, leis, flower-in-hair custom, shaka sign (hang loose), swimming pool, mai tais, poolside bar, Hawaiian words like puka, wahine, mauka, makai, shaka, haole, mahalo, da kine.

Murph & Sean noticed the ubiquitous coin-operated blood pressure stations where George could continue checking his blood pressure, seeing it drop successfully every day he stayed in Hawaii. On Waikiki Beach, M&M

spotted a magnificent sand castle constructed by a local dude. They got the young artist's contact info, hoping they could use his talents somewhere in one of the episodes. They also checked out a popular Polynesian Show, realizing it would make an entertaining visual and figuring *The Jeffersons* characters would definitely want to attend such a show.

Murph and Sean began writing in their room overlooking world famous Waikiki Beach; but they found the view too distracting and had to close the drapes. They checked a lot of locations, but decided the sprawling Hilton Hawaiian Village resort along Waikiki, if they could arrange it, would be the perfect place for most of the shoot.

The threat of a possible actors' strike had been looming and, to the surprise of M&M and others, the strike became a reality mid-summer of 1980 while M&M were still on Oahu. Murph was surprised because, although the Writers Guild, always eager to take on a challenge or a cause, will strike at the drop of a pen, the actors and directors guilds are usually quick to settle.

M&M decided Sean would return to the Mainland and oversee story development and writing for other *Jeffersons* episodes, while Murph would remain in Honolulu and meet with management at the Hilton and the local CBS affiliate, KGMB, which, as it turned out, was very helpful in assisting with technical operations on the ground for *The Jeffersons* upcoming shoot.

You might think a hotel would be happy to have a TV series shoot on their property, but that's not always the case, especially at a high-end hotel or resort. Many. such establishments feel shooting a film or TV show on their premises runs the risk of interfering with the vacations of their other guests. So when he had lunch with the general manager of the Hilton, Murph was quite pleased to learn that the fellow was a *Jeffersons* fan and was willing to host the cast and crew and permit the show to shoot on the premises.

Coincidentally, at that time *The Jeffersons* was also the number one show in Hawaii. Which gave M&M all the more reason to want to do more with these episodes than just show the *Jeffersons* characters having fun on a vacation. M&M were hoping to dig deeper and land on a story point that would, at least on some level, resonate with the kamaaina (local residents) and explore the unique culture of the islands.

To that end, Murph visited the Bishop Museum Library where he spent most of a day perusing books on Hawaiian history and culture. A hefty, bearded local dude, not much older than Murph, approached the library table where Murph was seated, curious to learn why this haole (Hawaiian for honky) was wading through the scholarly selection of books about Hawaiian culture assembled on Murph's table.

Murph explained he was doing research for some *Jeffersons* shows. The two soon became brahs (Hawaiian for buddies or pals) although in later years Murph forgot his name, so we'll just call him Alika (Hawaiian for guardian).

Alika noticed Murph was reading about luaus, and Murph mentioned he was thinking maybe they could have the *Jeffersons* characters attending a traditional Hawaiian luau. Alika mentioned he was going to a local luau that weekend and offered Murph a chance to tag along.

So Murph met Alika at the luau and Alika described what they were about to witness. Alika said there would be lots of beer, plenty of pupus (Hawaiian for snacks or hors d'oeuvres), more beer, pig wrapped and roasted in taro leaves and voluminous side dishes like lomi-lomi salmon, poi (mashed taro root usually eaten with your fingers, with a taste rarely appreciated by haole tourists).

Alika explained that as the sun goes down there would be music and dancing with an abundance of Aloha spirit and celebration of Ohana (family). Husbands and wives would dance together and, said Alika, eventually husbands would start dancing with other men's wives and vice versa, and ka lili (quick-tempered jealousy) would rear its ugly head, causing hoo wahawaha (a brawl) to break out. It all went down exactly as Alika predicted. When an attractive wahine (woman), the wife of some moke, asked Murph to dance, he figured it was time to thank Alika and his hosts and head back to his hotel before this pig roast became a haole roast.

Murph fully intended to invite Alika to the set when they started shooting in Hawaii; but by that time he had misplaced Alika's contact info and didn't recall the exact location of the house in Waianae where the luau was held.

It looked like the actors strike wasn't going to end any time soon, so Murph decided to fly his kids over to join him in Hawaii for a week. Colleen was almost 11 and Heather was 9. Marianne put the girls on a plane and Murph met them at the airport in Honolulu. They stayed in the Rainbow Tower at the Hilton Hawaiian Village, which is where the cast and crew of *The Jeffersons* would be staying during the filming.

Murph and Marianne had been living apart now for three years and neither had filed for divorce. The biggest concern in Murph's personal life was that Marianne might move back to Ohio with the kids. Marianne and the kids were living in the Greenbush house while Murph continued paying the mortgage plus support. Murph would tell you, both back then and later in life, he considered his greatest accomplishment, both personal and professional, was being able to keep his daughters living close by as they grew up.

In Hawaii Murph and the girls swam in the ocean and the pool, went snorkeling at Hanauma Bay, visited the Polynesian Cultural Center, shopped till Murph dropped at the International Market Place and chose oysters for personalized pearl necklaces.

A highlight for the girls occurred in the hotel gift shop when they met Murray Langston, aka "The Unknown Comic." Murray found fame performing on TV wearing a bag over his head with holes for eyes and mouth. When Murph introduced his daughters to "The Unknown Comic," the girls were dubious. Murray was dressed in everyday attire, and they thought their dad might be kidding about Murray's identity. But when Murray pulled a paper bag from his back pocket and placed it over his head, the girls were star struck: "He *is* The Unknown Comic!"

WITH NEGOTIATIONS IN the actors strike coming to a standstill, it appeared it was going to be a long strike. The good news for M&M was that it gave them more time to develop both story and scripts for the Hawaii episodes.

Murph had noticed, while talking to Hawaii residents and reading local newspapers, that locals were being forced off their land by developers intent on building oceanfront condominiums and hotels. This was a heated issue on the islands and M&M decided it could be the cultural connective they were seeking to develop in the four-part Hawaii story.

Most of **Part I** takes place in New York. Louise receives a postcard from Tom & Helen in Hawaii. Florence laments that her vacation starts this weekend and the only place she can afford to go is the Zoo. Louise and Florence talk about Hawaii and agree it would be an amazing place to visit. We learn that Blue Sky Cleaners has been trying to buy out Jefferson Cleaners, but George is not interested.

Louise informs George it's been five years since they've taken a vacation and tries to talk him into going to Hawaii. But he begs off, saying he's too busy right now. She persists, but George pooh poohs the idea, saying if Hawaii were so great, why would God separate it from the rest of the country? George tells Louise he has to leave for a meeting and exits.

The next scene is a shot of Tom & Helen on a beach in Hawaii. We learn they're planning to return home this weekend, but Tom wants to stay longer. For one reason, Tom is hoping he can talk Helen into going sailing with him.

Cut to George in his doctor's office. We learn George has been experiencing headaches, fatigue and occasional dizziness—symptoms of high blood pressure. The Doc explains that as a 50-year-old black male in a high-powered job, George is a prime candidate for a heart attack or a stroke.

George learns (as do viewers) that black males have the highest incidence of high blood pressure and everyone should have his/her blood pressure checked at least once a year. Most people, says the Doc, don't even realize they have high blood pressure until it's too late.

This is what might be called a "teachable moment" or an "information opportunity," not uncommon in a Lear show. Similar to the "Florence's Problem" episode where Tom Willis mentions facts about suicidal behavior or "Tom the

Hero," where millions of viewers were informed about the Heimlich maneuver.

This 'intent to inform' is one thing that sets Lear shows apart from product developed by other sitcom shops at the time—like the *Mary Tyler Moore* and *Bob Newhart* shows from MTM, or *Happy Days* and *Laverne & Shirley* from Paramount. Although *The Bob Newhart Show*—first sitcom to feature a psychologist as the main character—was witty and entertaining, Murph always felt the show passed up a good opportunity to expose and explore current theories relating to the mind and human behavior.

When the doctor advises George to take some time off work, George mentions Louise was bugging him this morning to take her to Hawaii. Doc says that's a great idea and suggests George go on vacation to Hawaii. George says Louise doesn't know about this doctor visit and asks Doc not to mention anything to Louise about his blood pressure.

When George arrives home later with surprise Hawaii tickets for himself and Louise, he learns that Weezy has already surprised Florence with a ticket to Hawaii. In the following scene, Lionel & Jenny are saying goodbye to Louise, George and Florence as Ralph helps with luggage. As they head for the elevator, George comments that the best part about Hawaii will be "No Willises!"

In the final scene of Part I, which takes place near the Hawaii pool, Tom has just convinced Helen to stay another week. Fade Out. End of Part I.

At the end of Parts I, II and III, the words **To Be Continued...** will appear on the screen. And the beginning of Parts II, III and IV of the Hawaii episodes will start with a recap: "Last week on *The Jeffersons*..." or "Previously on *The Jeffersons*..."

In **Part II**, the Jeffersons and the Willises are surprised to see each other in Hawaii, but they soon join forces. We see a musically scored montage which includes: the Gang of Five riding in pedicabs along Kuhio Avenue and shopping at the International Market Place; George attempting to snorkel; and George continuing to slip away to a coin-operated blood pressure machine where he checks his blood pressure—which improves each day. While she and George are sunning on the beach, Louise mentions that George seems like a new person in Hawaii, much more relaxed—he even seems to enjoy being with the Willises. George agrees, saying Tom is much easier to take now that he has a tan.

Florence's horoscope has predicted a love connection, so her heart is jumping. She's learned the Hawaiian custom of putting a flower in her hair. Left side means: spoken for. Right side means: available. She's wearing a flower on her right side. Walking along the beach with her beach chair, Florence accidentally trips in a hole on the sand.

A nice-looking dark-skinned local man named Leon helps her up and explains that she stepped in his puka. Alarmed, Florence checks her foot; but Leon explains puka means "hole." Leon is working to build an elaborate sand castle and Florence offers to help.

Meanwhile, a Frisbee lands on George's towel and he gets involved in tossing a Frisbee with some men on the beach. Intercut a musical montage of Leon and Florence constructing their sand castle with scenes of George and his new friends sailing Frisbees on the beach.

When the montage ends, we learn Leon is in charge of security at the hotel and he offers to escort Florence to the Polynesian Show tonight. They make plans to meet at 7 p.m. and, as Leon moves off, Florence gleefully switches the flower in her hair from right to left side.

We learn that one of George's Frisbee friends, Bill Wilson, who looks to be around George's age, moved here from Chicago over twenty years ago on his fiftieth birthday. George is amazed at how young and healthy Bill looks for his age! Bill credits that to the islands. He explains that his doctor in Chicago told him if he didn't learn to relax, he'd be dead in a year. So he sold his business and moved to Hawaii. George's interest is piqued. Bill explains he doesn't have to work because his money works for him. And he extols the investment wisdom of his financial counselor, Ken Sanders, who takes care of everything for Bill. Ken has a great nose for business deals, says Bill. George asks if Bill thinks Ken could do some sniffing around for him.

Bill says he's meeting Ken in the bar at the hotel tonight and offers to introduce George. George jumps at the chance—then remembers his plans to go to the Polynesian Show tonight. But he tells Bill he'll figure something out and they agree to meet at 8:00 p.m.

George heads for a nearby beach bar where he uses the house phone to call his accountant. He instructs his accountant to find out how much Blue Sky Cleaners would pay for Jefferson Cleaners. When he sees Louise approaching, George quickly hangs up.

In a sweet moment, Louise tells George how much she appreciates him bringing them to Hawaii. It's such a beautiful place. George agrees, saying he feels like he jumped inside a post card. Louise says she could stay here forever. George says he was thinking the same thing. Fade Out. End of Part II.

Part III opens with the gang (Jeffersons, Willises, Florence & Leon) arriving at the Polynesian Show. The Show features Tahitian & Samoan male & female dancers, complete with a fire-eater and island drums. Dancers choose partners from the audience and Helen, Louise, Florence, Tom and George all get turns on stage.

Following his dancing on stage, George checks his watch and tells Louise he has to use the restroom. He exits and re-enters at the hotel bar, joining Bill Wilson and Ken Sanders. George learns about a major real estate deal Sanders is putting together called Paradise Acres—300 condominium units on prime oceanfront land. A sure-fire money maker! George is intrigued and says he'd like to check it out. Sanders says he's going up to survey the land tomorrow afternoon and asks if George would like to go with him. George indicates he would and takes Sanders' business card.

When George arrives back at the Polynesian event, the show is just letting out. George gives Louise some excuse for why he missed the rest of the show. We learn that Leon and Florence have gone for a walk on the beach, and George suggests he and Louise do the same.

As they walk along the beach, George begins talking with Louise about how nice it would be to retire in Hawaii. They agree Lionel and Jenny may even consider living here; but Louise says she would really miss Helen and Tom. Tom & Helen come walking up and Tom, who's been bugging George to go sailing, tells George he just found a place on the beach where they could rent a sailboat.

Helen tells Tom to quit bugging everybody about going sailing, nobody wants to go. George does a sudden turn-around, telling Tom he'd love to go sailing with him tomorrow morning. (Thinking maybe he can talk Tom into moving to Hawaii too.)

Next Morning: George makes a call to Sanders from a pay phone and suggests Sanders meet him at the hotel at

one o'clock on his way to survey the Paradise Acres land
site.

Tom and George rent a fourteen-foot sailboat and head
out together, just the two of them. Tom claims as a teenager
he spent every summer weekend sailing with his uncle on
Lake Placid and George brags about his time in the Navy.

Louise and Helen are having breakfast by the pool when
Florence comes up and reveals that her horoscope says
something like 'Expect an important question from a recent
romantic interest.' Louise & Helen caution Florence not to
get too carried away with expectations. Florence says Leon
is coming soon to teach her how to surf. She's convinced
Leon is about to pop the question, and she's not sure how
to answer.

Meanwhile, George and Tom have drifted beyond the
breakwater and have lost sight of the shore. They begin to
panic and aren't sure which direction to head.

At the pool, Leon arrives and tells Florence they'll have
to cancel surfing lessons today because there's a storm
brewing and the water will be too rough. Helen is concerned about the men being out on a sailboat. But Louise
figures Tom and George are probably docked at some bar
right now swapping sea tales over drinks. Cut to a shot of
Tom & George's empty sail boat floating on the seas. Fade
Out. End of Part III.

Part IV opens with Tom & George's empty sailboat floating on the ocean.

Tom & George, wearing life jackets, manage to make it to
shore on what first appears to be a deserted island. After a
bit of a hike along a secluded beach, they come across some
local inhabitants fishing with nets from the shore. They
find out that Honolulu is on the other side of the island, so
they're still on Oahu. Andrew, one of the fishermen, says

they can call their wives from his house.

Back at the hotel pool, Louise gets paged and takes a call from George; while Florence learns Leon was not about to propose like she told Louise and Helen. She tells Leon she's so embarrassed. As she moves away, Helen approaches and asks Florence how things went. Leon overhears and steps in, telling Helen that Florence let him down easy — helping Florence save face.

Louise approaches with directions from George. She tells them Tom & George are okay; but their boat capsized and they're at a house on the other side of the island. Leon volunteers to take them there in his jeep.

Back at Andrew's house, we learn a) Andrew has called a doctor to check out Tom and George, and b) Andrew & family are planning a luau tonight to celebrate his nineteen-year-old son Robert's birthday. Andrew invites Tom, George and family to stay for the luau — food, music, dancing. George mentions he had something scheduled for one o'clock today, but since he missed that, he's free. Tom and George both agree the luau sounds like fun.

We also learn Andrew's family may have to move from their home soon. They own their house, but not the land; which is a common state of affairs in Hawaii. Their land will be part of a large condominium complex called Paradise Acres. This resonates with George, not in a good way.

Eventually, friends & families start arriving for the luau, and Leon's jeep pulls up with Helen, Louise and Florence. Helen and Louise are reunited with their husbands. Then, sure enough, Ken Sanders and a surveyor approach from the beach area. George sees Sanders and tries to hide in Leon's jeep, but Sanders spots him. A confrontation occurs between Sanders and the locals, and George the hero steps in to side with Andrew and Robert and kick the "damn haole" (Sanders) off the property.

George finally tells Louise the truth about his high blood pressure and why he was thinking of moving to Hawaii. The doctor (a haole friend of Andrew's who was coming to the luau anyway) informs George and Louise that it's not where you live that determines your blood pressure, but whether or not you can learn to relax and manage stress. George is convinced and relieved to know he can keep living in the Big Apple.

THE 1980 ACTORS strike lasted a record 94 days. It was October when Murph found himself climbing the spiral staircase to the First Class Lounge above the first class seats in a 747 headed for Honolulu. With him were Sean, Bob Lally and a handful of colleagues embarking on a mission. A mission to shoot what would amount to a two-hour movie—not on a stage, or even on a set, but on "location." Gazing down at the clear blue liquid surrounding the island of Oahu as their plane approached the harbor was perhaps the most Godlike Murph had ever felt.

They spent days mapping out locations around the resort, acquiring the necessary permits, scheduling delivery of the necessary equipment and meeting with local union reps. M&M had heard rumors about local Teamsters holding producers by the ankles over a towering balcony while negotiating to hire more drivers, but they considered such stories amusing and apocryphal. When the local teamsters, who seemed like nice enough mokes (macho Hawaiians), told them they needed to hire more drivers, M&M, in budget-minded mode, explained most of the shoot would be at the resort and they wouldn't need more drivers.

When it came time to pick up Sherman at the airport, M&M greeted him at the gate. Following the obligatory alohas and brah hugs, they said, "Okay, Sherm. Let's go get your luggage." Sherman's response: "What luggage?" Turns out Sherman—dressed in his usual white T-shirt, worn jeans & sneakers—was travelling light. Not even a toothbrush. Thank goodness Betsey Potter, the show's wardrobe guru, was on the island.

M&M's newly hired assistant, Maggie, arrived and checked into the Rainbow Tower where most of the show's cast and staff were staying. In the middle of the night, Sean received a call from a distraught Maggie, who claimed she awoke to see a ghost—a large, muscular Hawaiian warrior standing in her room. She was terrified and couldn't sleep. So Sean, unsure what to do, spent a good part of the night sitting as a ghost-guard in Maggie's room so Maggie could go back to sleep.

Next day, Sean was exhausted. Sean & Murph explored options: 1) Get another room for Maggie? The hotel was full. 2) One of them switch rooms with Maggie? Room with the ghost of a Hawaiian warrior? Not in their contract! 3) Send Maggie to another hotel? What if the ghost follows her there? 4) Send Maggie home. They needed an assistant. 5) Call Ghostbusters?

Sean finally came up with the solution: Bring Maggie's boyfriend over here to stay with her. So Ragamuffin paid to fly Maggie's boyfriend to Hawaii. As Murph would say to aspiring writers at Sherwood Oaks, **"There's more to writing than writing."**

All things considered, it appeared everything was proceeding smoothly until the first day of production. The crew arrived early in the morning, ready to hula (rock and roll), only to find they had no power—a result of water in the generator. How did that happen?!

Murph remembered the Teamsters wanted them to hire more drivers. Sean recalled the stories about holding ankles while hanging dudes over balconies. So M&M contacted da kine moke (boss man) and hired more drivers—and they never had a power problem again.

When they started shooting, there was one big thing missing: The Audience. The cast was used to working off, and playing to, the energy of the audience. With no audience, there would be no laughs. And with no laughs, the Hawaii shows would not have the sound and feel of the usual *Jeffersons* episodes.

Of course they could sweeten the sound track in post production, but there's a technical issue involved. Laughter has to build and trail off. You can't just take a recorded video and drop laughs in and out willy-nilly. Laughter has to have room to start and trail off. If you try laying in a quick HA! here and there, it will sound forced and false. M&M considered the possibility of setting up some chairs for tourists as the crew moved from location to location, but decided that wouldn't be practical.

So Murph decided he would lie in the sand or stand nearby during the shooting and provide the laughter. The actors, of course, were instructed to listen for and leave room for Murph's laughs, so in post the full sound of sweetened laughter could be laid in.

You might ask, "Why Murph? Why not get some anonymous tourist or someone in the crew to provide the initial laughter?" The twofold answer is: 1) Writers are usually the ones who know best where to expect the laughs, and 2) Although audiences will sometimes laugh in unexpected places, Murph was used to watching the tapings seated in the audience, and felt he had a good sense of how a typical audience might react.

Water in the generator and a missing audience were not the only alterations M&M and crew had to deal with while shooting on location. The resort grounds were covered with palm trees, and the sound of an actor's dialogue was no match for a gardener with a chainsaw trimming trees. It took a six-pack of Longboard Lager to lure a Hawaiian Chainsaw Tree Trimmer from his perch atop a palm.

Another sound issue was not so simple to fix. As mentioned earlier, M&M had spotted a sprawling sand castle on the beach and met the young artist. They hired him to construct a sand castle for the scene where Florence and Leon meet. After the first take, Murph went into the sound truck to watch a playback of the scene. There was a distinct noise on the track.

"What's that noise?" asked Murph. Georja Skinner, the sound engineer, replied "That's the ocean." Murph was surprised. "You mean we're married to the ocean?" asked Murph. "Yep," answered Bob Lally. "Unless we move that big-ass sand castle up the beach somewhere." So the group decided they could embrace the natural sound of the ocean and live with it.

Another scene where nature intervened was when a big white gooey bird bomb launched from above landed on Sherman's shirt. Everyone wanted to laugh, but it was more of an "Oh, nooo..." laugh. They had to stop tape and figure out what to do. It was a solid blue top (shirt) that Sherman had been wearing over his bathing suit in a related sequence. Wardrobe had no duplicate, so Sherman's shirt had to be washed and dried before shooting could resume.

In between scenes, Sherman would turn up his boom box and play something he called "rap." "Cool, huh?" Sherm asked Murph. Murph wasn't even sure if it was music. Sherman was nothing if not a cat whose beat box boomed to the rhythm of a different rapper. But in the coming years, as rap became not only popular but mainstream, Murph realized that musically speaking, Sherman was way ahead of his time.

Looking back, one of the best decisions M&M made in Hawaii was putting an assistant stage manager—we'll call him Fritz—in charge of Sherman. Fritz was told to stay with Sherman and know exactly where he is at all times. Sherman is at heart a trusting soul whose direction can shift with the wind, especially away from home.

Without going into unnecessary detail, at one point Sherman and some newfound friends (young locals) embarked on a tour of a lush mauka (mountainside) ranch where illicit crops were grown and processed. Think Maui Wowie and Oahu Yahoo. Thanks to Fritz, Sherm's mountain high (pun intended) trip ended without incident.

Early next morning Isabel called M&M and alerted them to the fact that a cap fell off one of her teeth. So they couldn't start shooting until they found a dentist who could take care of Isabel's tooth.

Later that day, having avoided a dental disaster, a logistics conflict arose when *The Jeffersons* cast & crew showed up on the same day and at the same site as *Magnum PI*'s cast and crew. *Magnum PI* was a popular series that took place in Hawaii and starred Tom Selleck as a private detective. The funny thing was, one series had a permit for the previous day, and the other had a permit for the following day. But neither had a permit for the day they were there.

Each show tried to chase the other away. Magnum's helicopter was there; and when *The Jeffersons* started to shoot, the helicopter began whirling, drowning out *The Jeffersons'* sound. And when Magnum started to shoot, *The Jeffersons* trucks shifted into reverse, creating a loud ringing noise.

The shows finally decided to call a truce and buddy up, each taking turns shooting. Roger Mosley, a brother who played the helicopter pilot on Magnum, was a friendly and super cool guy. And if you asked Murph to name the best-looking man he ever met, without skipping a beat, he'd say "Tom Selleck." This Magnum star was hands down the best thing that ever happened to a Hawaiian shirt! If you were straight, you'd start to wish you weren't. And if you were gay, you couldn't help wishing you could share a home with this former Marlboro Man for the rest of your life. At least until he started bugging you every day about getting a reverse mortgage.

M&M checked out the Polynesian Shows in Honolulu and determined that the show at the landmark Ala Moana Hotel was the best. So a date was set and it was arranged for *The Jeffersons* to shoot the Polynesian Show with the cast attending in character. With cameras and cables in place and crew ready to hula, M&M got a call from Alan Horn on the mainland who apparently got a call from the Musicians Union in Honolulu saying the Musicians were going on strike and *The Jeffersons* had to shut down tonight's shoot.

Say what? Musicians Union? What did that have to do with a Polynesian Show? Was the fire dancer going to play the harmonica while swallowing fire? Or were they adding a horn section to the fertility dance? It was baffling to Murph, but it seemed somehow the Ala Moana Hotel had an entertainment contract with the local Musicians Union. And the bottom line was, in spite of all the effort and preparation by *The Jeffersons* crew and staff, there would be no shooting taking place tonight.

Murph was starting to think this shooting on location

stuff was not all it's cracked up to be. He was beginning to miss the sound stage and dread the edit bay. Editing a sitcom taped on a sound stage was a relatively simple undertaking. Scenes were shot in sequence and you could pretty much decide on preferred takes before leaving the booth. The AD (Assistant Director) would put together a first cut; the Director would view it, making his or her adjustments; then the Executive Producers would view and approve the final cut.

Editing what was in essence a two-hour movie shot out of sequence on location was going to be a different animal. Like putting together a jigsaw puzzle. And right now, with no Polynesian Show, *The Jeffersons* Hawaii jigsaw puzzle was missing a big set-piece. As for solving that problem, M&M were told the best they could hope for was that the Musicians strike would be settled soon and they could reschedule the shoot.

Eventually, M&M and everyone with the show would be leaving Honolulu and heading to the other end of the island. The final set-piece of Part IV (a luau) was scheduled to be shot at a local house near the North Shore. The North Shore hotel where they would be staying was smaller, not a huge resort like Hawaiian Village. But M&M learned the hotel had a nice-sized showroom they could rent for a private show.

They then contacted a local outfit that could provide a private Polynesian Show, complete with drums, dancers and fire-eater. They reserved the showroom and the dancers separately; and told only Bob Lally what they were up to, hoping to keep their plan on the down low—and away from the Musicians Union—as long as they could.

Meanwhile they continued shooting in Honolulu, including the bit where George attempts snorkeling and the scene where Tom and George rent a sailboat. The script called for George, in a silent montage bit, wearing fins and a snorkel mask, to flop through the sand and into the ocean up to his knees, then bend down and put his mask in the water looking for fish. After Sherman announced he couldn't swim, he gamely marched into the water—but stopped at about his ankles, which may be even funnier—before bending down to look for fish.

When it came time to shoot Tom and George on a small sailboat, Sherm's fear of the water became even more of an obstacle. M&M had to assure Sherman that a) he wouldn't be more than ten feet from the shore; b) they wouldn't be in water over his head; and c) Murph and the stage manager, both of whom could swim, would be in the water at each end of the boat.

So in that Part III scene where Tom and George are in the sailboat on the ocean, Murph is just off camera on one side, rocking the boat so the water looks rough—serving as rocker, laugher and lifeguard.

When they moved to North Shore, somewhat isolated from Honolulu, Murph had been keeping his fingers crossed that their nemesis, the diabolical Musicians Union, was unaware of their plan to record the *Jeffersons* cast at a private Polynesian Show. The cast rehearsed in the showroom, and in the lobby leading to the showroom, in the afternoon. And under the cover of night, "extras"—also referred to as "atmosphere"—were ushered into the showroom dressed as tourists coming to be entertained.

Standing underneath his Panama hat in a Hawaiian shirt, doing his first warm-up since arriving on the island, Murph explained to persons in the showroom seats that they were about to be in a TV episode titled "The Jeffersons Go to Hawaii." The whole time Murph was talking, he kept a concerned eye on the showroom door, wondering what he would do if a dozen Musicians wielding picket signs came bursting in!

Fortunately, that never happened. When that night's shooting was finished, they had everything they needed for the Polynesian Show set-piece. A few days later, as they were close to finishing the final scenes at the luau location, M&M received a call from Alan Horn informing them that the issue with the Musicians Union had been worked out and they were free to reschedule shooting a Polynesian Show at the Ala Moana. Murph was more than pleased to inform Alan they had already taken care of that. The Polynesian Show scenes were "in the can."

Indeed, Murph was feeling pretty cocky. Maybe like when Tom Sawyer was able to show Aunt Polly that painted fence. To use a sports analogy—pretty common for a former high school sports writer, who pretty much looked at life as a sporting event or a poker game—Murph felt he and Sean, playing for Team Jefferson, were finally able to score a Win in the Union League. Team Jefferson was walloped by the actors union; rendered powerless by the Teamsters; behind at half time vs. the Musicians Union—but came back in the second half to orchestrate an unexpected upset W!

Notable in the final luau scene was the casting of Andy Bumatai. Andy was and is da kine comedian in Hawaii. Murph and Sean saw Andy in concert, met him and cast him as Robert, the son of Andrew and the young man whose birthday it was at the luau.

Pidgin is the name given to a language spoken at home and with friends by a lot of young locals in Hawaii. It's sort of a shorthand combination of English and other languages spoken on the islands. Andy was fluent in pidgin, and when shooting the luau scene, rather than give Andy specific dialogue to memorize, M&M explained to Andy the key points they wanted him to communicate, and asked him to communicate them in pidgin. A little touch of authenticity.

Speaking of authentic, there was a real pig in the imu (luau pit). All the drinks and food shown in the scene were also real. And when the luau scene ended, the wrap party began. That's right, the wrap party for *The Jeffersons Go to Hawaii* cast, crew and staff was held right there in the oceanfront yard of the house where the luau scene was shot.

Murph was sad to leave Hawaii, but thrilled to be back on the sound stage in Hollywood where there were no pooping birds, noisy chainsaws, Hawaiian ghosts or tenacious Teamsters to deal with. A tag was shot in the Jefferson living room, as George, Louise & Florence return with their luggage, helped by Lionel & Jenny who picked them up at the airport. Louise has brought back souvenir gifts; and we learn if it's true that, as George now claims, Hawaii has taught him how to relax.

When the Hawaii shows first aired, they aired in four weeks, one part per week. In syndication, they occasionally aired in two parts, as one hour each. And other times all four parts would be combined and aired as a two-hour movie titled *The Jeffersons Go To Hawaii*.

The Hawaii episodes were well received by viewers. Below is a letter to the show typewritten on personal stationery, from JUDY K. TANQUYE of KAILUA, HAWAII 96734.

25 November, 1980
Dear Sirs:

I am writing to express my enjoyment of the recent episodes of "The Jeffersons" which were filmed in Hawaii. As a resident who has seen motion picture production companies romp through Hawaii creating shows with weak plots while exploiting the lush tropical scenery, I feel your series here was the first exception to that pattern. Maybe not the very first — but the first in a very long, long while.

I feel you are to be congratulated for showing that your writers had their pulse to the actual island heartbeat when developing their scripts; i.e., the story of long time residents being threatened by condominium developments on the shorelines. Your treatment clearly depicted the problems here while keeping in the familiar Jeffersons' humor and style.

Also the usage of the Hawaii Production Center was a wise one which showed on the screen. And another big mahalo for utilizing the local talent and entertainers in your episodes. Not only were they employed but their roles were significant ones (a lot of lines and portrayed human characteristics — not the one dimensional types I have almost come to expect).

I could tell the cast enjoyed working here and judging from other newspaper articles I have read, the islands may have taken to the Jeffersons cast also. (Professionals without chips on their shoulders.)

Finally, the scenes were great. They were typical scenes yet not exploitative — they showed the tourist experiences while providing a painless mini-lesson in understanding some of the Hawaiian ways here.

I don't want to get carried away so I shall conclude here. It was a most enjoyable series. I have enjoyed Marla Gibbs (her characterizations get better all the time), the woman who portrays Helen is a gem, Louise continues to grow in her role, and Sherman Helmsley (sic) sometimes looks like he's playing himself.

A few years back your story editors spoke at a National PenWomen workshop about their experiences as comedy writers which was very informative also.

Yours truly,

Judy K. Tanquye (signed)

Chapter 26

DOORKNOBS, DIAMONDS & THE KLAN

('80-81)

Murph's favorite *Jeffersons* title and one of his favorite *Jeffersons* episodes is the Season 7 episode titled "And the Doorknobs Shined Like Diamonds," written by Michael Moye. The story is based on personal experience and the script is pure Moye.

Louise learns the building she grew up in is scheduled to be torn down and she returns to her Harlem apartment to revive old memories, both bitter and sweet. In flashbacks, a much younger Louise is played with haunting perfection by younger actresses at different stages of her life.

The script digs deeper and viewers learn details about Louise's relationship with her mother and older sister Maxine. Louise mentions that as a young girl, she used to gaze at the glass doorknob in her room and imagine it was a diamond and someday she would sell that diamond and she could buy anything she wanted. Upon leaving her old

run-down apartment, Louise removes the shiny doorknob
and takes it with her.

To Murph's way of thinking, based on this script and
other writing on the show, Michael Moye can make a pens-
down claim to be the single best writer to serve on the
Jeffersons staff.

Below is a letter addressed to M&M as Executive
Producers of the above show:

> *First of all, let me thank you for taking the time to
> read and respond to this letter.*
>
> *Ever since its inception several years ago, I have been
> an unwavering fan of your program, 'The Jeffersons'.
> It is an extremely well-produced, well-directed and
> well-written show. The chemistry of each character
> is such that when all are put together, they yield a
> product unparalleled in quality and show-stopping
> humor. Allow me to say that in producing 'The
> Jeffersons', you have done an excellent job. Which
> brings me to the reason for my writing to you.*
>
> *This past Sunday evening, Feb. 1, at 8:30 PM
> (C.S.T.), I viewed what I consider to be one of the
> finest of 'The Jeffersons' episodes to date; i.e. when
> Louise revisits her childhood home the day before it
> is to be torn down. This episode was superb, and it
> particularly succeeded in making George appear to be
> a more humane person than he is apt, at times, to be.
> It also brought home to many of us, through Louise's
> accurate portrayal, what it feels like to lose the home
> where you grew up. Believe me, I know—I've lost my
> childhood home, too, as I'm sure many other people
> have.*

That is why I have taken it upon myself to write to you. I am inquiring, with hopes you might comply, into the possibility of having a copy of the script sent to me at the above address. I am a communications major at the University of Missouri at St. Louis, and would consider it an invaluable opportunity to see first-hand how all the facets of this episode were put together to make one unforgettable show. Again, congratulations.

Thank you, once more, for your time and patience.

Sincerely,
(signed)
Melanie J. Roble

IN AN AMERICAN TV series where the primary characters are African American, the themes of race and racism are, unfortunately or not, essential. In the first six seasons, the series tried not to shy away from issues of race, especially as they applied to relations between blacks and whites.

There was, however, one subject M&M had discussed more than once as intriguing fodder for a show; but they couldn't quite figure how to do it. George and the KKK seemed like a strong, volatile mix of comedy and cogency—but how do you make it funny? And how do you even get into it?

Would George have to be visiting some state south of the Mason-Dixon Line where he and Weezy come into contact with a gaggle of hooded crackers? Seems way too forced. Would the Jeffersons discover a burning cross on their balcony? On the twelfth floor?

What if George discovered a white hooded Klan outfit

someone had left at one of his stores to be cleaned? Would George burn it? Stomp on it and pour ink on it? Or maybe try to find out whose it is? Could it belong to one of his employees? Could it be someone's Halloween outfit? Even so, the question remains—how do you make it funny? By now, M&M had pretty much concluded that the KKK was the third rail of comedy.

So in the seventh season M&M were kicking around story ideas with Casey & Lee and David mentioned something about a B story involving a CPR class. He mentioned reading a story where somebody for some reason refused to perform CPR on one of those CPR dolls because they didn't know whose lips had touched it before.

Boom! The engine started churning in M&M's wheelhouse. Could this be the KKK story? Would George put his lips on a CPR doll lipped by a KKK member? Or vice versa? Would this be too much of a reach for a *Jeffersons* episode?

Murph recalled reading about Klan groups popping up in Northern states where you might least expect them. But in New York City? In an upscale building? A supposedly educated, nicely-dressed white supremacist whose demagoguery could maybe someday attract enough followers that he could run for and, who knows, maybe even get elected President? Did we say President? Well that, of course, could never happen.

But white supremacy is a cancer that could pop up anywhere and needs to be addressed as the evil it is. The writers discussed whether to use the "n" word, or a similar word like 'spade'; and they discussed whether to actually say Ku Klux Klan or just say 'white supremacy.' They decided not to soft pedal it. Klansmen would use the "n" word, so let's play it real. And they decided to go with the full KKK.

It took a while, but the writers eventually worked out some story beats that sounded pretty solid, as follows:

The show opens with Louise and Florence heading to a CPR class being held for tenants in the building. George isn't going because he already knows CPR. He sponsored a class for his employees. Florence says that was a nice thing to do. George says it was especially nice since it lowered his group insurance rate.

Louise and Florence exit crossing with Bentley who enters to annoy George with something. George is working on some business accounting and as he attempts to throw Bentley out, Tom arrives with news that his apartment has just been robbed. The three guys discuss their concern about security in the building and Tom pledges to organize a tenants' watch in the building.

At the CPR class, Louise and Florence are chosen to demonstrate CPR on the doll. The instructor works with them, as Louise blows air into the doll's mouth, while Florence pumps the doll's chest. This is a teachable moment where viewers can learn important information about CPR while Louise and Florence get laughs.

When Louise and Florence are finished, the instructor selects a man and his teenage son to be next, but the man declines, saying something like "We don't touch anything that's been touched by a nigger." Florence reacts, livid and attacks the man as his son and others attempt to keep them apart. The instructor demands an apology from the man, but the man refuses. His son, indicating Florence and Louise, says something like "Klansmen don't apologize to their kind."

In the elevator, Tom coincidentally runs into the KKK man and his son and learns they're planning a meeting tonight. "Something has to be done about the low-life in this building," says Mr. K3. Tom agrees, saying his apartment was robbed. Tom is invited to the meeting at 7 p.m. in the tenants' meeting room and says he'll bring his friend, George, who thinks just like they do.

In Act 2 George is resting on the sofa when Louise and Florence enter. Florence is still furious, asking where the baseball bat is. Louise tells George they were called "nigger" by Klansmen in the building. George gets furious like Florence. Louise tries to calm both of them down with quotes from the Bible about loving thy neighbor. George tells Louise about his mama's cousin Elvin who was falsely accused of raping a girl in the South and was killed by the Klan. George says there are only two ways to handle the Klan, then delivers two quick air punches. Tom arrives to tell George about the 7 p.m. tenants' meeting.

Later, Tom and Bentley enter the meeting as it's about to start. Mr. K3 introduces Tom and Bentley to his right hand man, a Klan guy named Stanley. Tom explains George has an issue to handle in one of his cleaning stores but should be here soon. At the podium, Mr. K3 tells the room full of white men (and Mr. K3's son) that he's sick and tired of undesirables in the building and Tom and Bentley agree with "Hear, hear!," etc.

George enters upbeat, greeting others and taking a seat next to Tom, thinking this meeting is simply about building security. George tells Mr. K3 and Stanley that he's with them 100%! Mr. K3 and Stanley react, baffled! When George learns it's a Klan meeting, he erupts in anger. And when Mr. K3 says something to George like "You're the scum we're trying to get rid of, boy!" George goes at him and has to be held back by Bentley and Willis.

Mr. K3 goes into a rant about the virtue of white supremacy, getting so emotional that he has an apparent heart attack and ends up on the floor. His son announces that his dad has a bad heart and tries to revive him. Frantic, the son asks if anyone knows what to do. Does anyone know CPR? No one responds—including George. (Expect big laughs for George's obvious inaction.)

Finally George goes into action, pushing others out of the way, rolling Mr. K3 over and performing CPR to revive him—mouth to mouth resuscitation plus pumping his chest! "Breathe, you bastard!"

TIME DISSOLVE: Paramedics are there and Mr.K3 is on a gurney. When his son explains to his dad that Mr. Jefferson saved his life, Mr. K3 reacts and says to his son, "You should've let me die."

Mr. K3 is rolled out on the gurney and George, Tom and Bentley leave. Stanley tries to keep the meeting going, but the others file out. Stanley sits next to Mr. K3's son and tells him they need to keep the "white race" together. He hands the flyers to Mr. K3's son and the boy gets up, crosses to the door, tears the flyers in half and tosses them in the trash.

The episode, titled "Sorry, Wrong Meeting," was one of Murph's absolute favorites, right up there with the MLK tribute episode, "The First Store."

Viewer response to this KKK episode was recorded in the following Audience Response Report sent to M&M in March of 1981:

SORRY, WRONG MEETING: There were a few unfavorable letters. They thought the show caused undue hard feelings among many, didn't find anything funny about the man having a heart attack, etc. On the other hand, we had comments like:

*Not since the early days of ALL IN THE FAMILY
has the racist problem been handled so delightfully
and thoughtfully. We sincerely commend you for
the program about the KKK. We need more to speak
out against this disgraceful organization. This show
should be shown often. The producers and directors
should be commended on the excellent show.*

Prior to airing, TAT took out-full page ads in *Variety* heralding both "And the Doorknobs Shined Like Diamonds" and "Sorry, Wrong Meeting." It was nice gesture, and indicated a new corporate respect for *The Jeffersons* as the current top-rated and longest-running TAT series.

Chapter 27

SPINOFF

('80-81)

A buzz had been building for a while now, both in the company and at CBS, regarding a spinoff starring Florence. M&M had mixed feelings about that. As did cast members, including Marla herself. A considerable concern was, "How would this affect *The Jeffersons*?"

For many viewers, the exchanges on the show between George and Florence were some of their favorite parts. After each taping, many in the audience would line up at the rail hoping for autographs or just to meet cast members—and the line to meet Florence was usually the longest. In many ways, Florence was the star of *The Jeffersons*. Why would she want to leave a show where a) she was already a star, and b) she loved working with her co-stars?

Whenever the subject of spinning off the Florence character came up, Murph & Sean were noncommittal. Push came to shove one day when Alan Horn took M&M to lunch at Alan's favorite place of business, the Palm Restaurant. For the past few years now, Alan had done an exemplary job with perhaps the toughest assignment in the entertainment business—replacing Norman Lear.

Alan was young, bright, personable and a raconteur of sorts. He once told Murph & Sean about a Thanksgiving trip to Hawaii with his then-girlfriend (later his wife, Cindy). Cindy had to fly back home to be with her family for the actual holiday, so Alan found himself alone on Thanksgiving, ordering room service for dinner. He ordered turkey for two, embarrassed that he was there by himself. When the food arrived, before opening the door for the room-service dude, Alan turned on the shower and pretended his wife was in the bathroom. How can you not love a guy who would tell a story like that on himself?

Alan brought up the topic of a Florence spinoff, explaining the network was dead set on doing it. When M&M hesitated to commit, Alan said something like, "I don't get it. It's like you guys ran the race, but you don't wanna pick up the trophy. If you don't want to do it, I'll give it to Mort Lachman."

Mort, you may recall, was currently Exec Producer of *All in the Family*. M&M, of course, felt protective of *The Jeffersons*. Too protective to let Mort or any other writer with no real experience with the show write and produce the spinoff.

Alan also told the duo that Marla was hesitant about M&M writing the spinoff. "She's concerned you guys are too green." Murph was disappointed to hear that. Maybe even hurt. But he wasn't surprised. He was pretty sure 'too green' meant 'too white.'

Unlike other members of the cast, Marla seemed to nurture what even Murph might describe as a healthy distrust of white people. Murph figured Marla was probably asked some version of THE QUESTION from family, friends and strangers on a regular basis—"How can white writers write for a black show?"

In interviews, Marla would respond to this question by implying that she, especially, gave constant feedback to the show's writers and was heavily involved in both story and dialogue. Murph felt empathetic to the degree that if he were in her shoes—in other words, if he were a black actor on a TV series with white writers—he might very likely adopt the same defensive attitude Marla employed in response to this racially sensitive issue.

However, since Murph was stuck in his own size 10 ½ white writer's shoes, he tended to take exception. Marla liked to say she based the character of Florence on her aunt and grandma in Detroit. Which, of course, is a common and useful method for an actor to use. And granted, as a performer, Marla had developed a killer delivery and a strong identifiable character for Florence. But Murph couldn't recall a joke, a story, or even a line that either Marla or her aunt or her grandma ever pitched to *The Jeffersons*.

You may remember that M&M wrote the first episode featuring Florence as a central character ("Florence's Problem"), and they received a nice Kwanzaa thank you note from Marla. That was six years ago. Murph & Sean were now 34 and had served as sole Exec Producers/ Showrunners for the last two seasons. Hardly green.

Motivated by Alan, especially his line about running the race and not picking up the trophy, M&M left the restaurant committed to develop a spinoff series for Florence. M&M decided there were two things they should try to do in the spinoff. One was keep Florence's ability to crack wise with an authority figure—a worthy opponent like George. And two, in keeping with the movin' on up theme of *The Jeffersons*, have Florence make an upward move as opposed to a lateral move. In other words, give Florence a better job with more money, which would also explain why she would leave her job as the Jeffersons' maid.

But she's been a maid for a while, so what sort of skills is she going to have in order to land a better job? Eventually, M&M settled on the idea that an eccentric hotel owner, call him Mr. Claymore, would offer Florence a job as Executive Housekeeper. Claymore visits George at the Jeffersons' apartment and admires how Florence handles George with her witty comebacks. He thinks Florence could be the perfect person to handle the demanding hotel manager who was too overbearing for a number of head housekeepers who have quit.

Claymore offers Florence a salary of twenty-six grand a year. George wants Florence to take the job because he wants the hotel's cleaning contact. Florence decides she wants the challenge—and, of course, the money.

Logistically, it was decided they would introduce the Florence spinoff in a two-part pilot episode ("pilosode") titled "Florence's New Job."

Florence is offered the job at the act break of Part I and accepts at the end of Part I.

Part II opens with Florence's first day on the job. She meets her co-workers at the St. Frederick Hotel, including her irksome boss, hotel manager Lyle Block. George arrives at Florence's office with a gift—a decorative nameplate for her desk. He's hoping to seal a deal for the Hotel's cleaning contract. In the second act of Part II, Florence has to face the issue of firing an employee who's become a friend and telling George he won't be getting the Hotel's cleaning contract.

WHEN SCRIPTS FOR the pilosode were finished, there was a rush to cast other recurring parts. Casting in general is a highly underrated and misunderstood skill. A skill attempted by many and mastered by few. In fact, Murph came to realize that **casting professionals are probably the most unsung and under-acknowledged creative force in the entertainment industry**. Casting lead roles is an extremely tricky craft, requiring a real feel for chemistry and, in this case, comedy.

The tough part to cast was the role of Lyle Block, Florence's new boss. The network and various agents were tossing out a number of names, including Bill Cosby. M&M liked Cosby, but didn't think he was right for this role. The network and TAT's development head Al Burton suggested Larry Linville, who played Major Frank Burns on *M*A*S*H*. Linville left *M*A*S*H* after five years to pursue other roles, but was now looking to get back in a TV series

When Murph met Linville, he asked the actor what it was like working on *M*A*S*H*. The man who played Major Burns mentioned they had to be there very early in the morning and work till late at night. Larry said all he remembered was "going to work in the dark and coming home in the dark."

So Linville was cast as Lyle Block; and Liz Torres, who had been a recurring character on *All in the Family*, was chosen for the role of Elena, Florence's assistant with a desk outside Florence's office. Patrick Collins, who played the Killer Rabbit in the previous season's Halloween episode, was cast as Earl, the wacky house detective. Distinguished actor John Anderson was cast as Mr. Claymore, the hotel owner.

MURPH REMEMBERED READING an interview with Bill Persky and Sam Denoff, key writers on *The Dick Van Dyke Show*, where Persky said the longest any sitcom should run is seven years. The Dick Van Dyke Show lasted five years, but they did 30-plus episodes a season for a total of 158 shows, about the same number of *Jeffersons* shows M&M had worked on so far.

Murph had also heard that seven seasons was the perfect number for sitcom episodes to make a nice syndication package. Indeed, Norman left *All in the Family* after seven seasons, even though *AITF* ran for two more.

Murph figured that *The Jeffersons* would maybe last one more season, Season 8, and M&M would already be sharing in the profits of that season, whether they stayed with the show or not. They also felt they had contributed about as much as they could to the show creatively; and it was probably time for some fresh blood to take over. Although they hadn't yet mentioned to the writing staff that they might be leaving, Murph & Sean had been getting Ron & David more and more involved in production & post production matters such as casting and editing, hoping to prepare Duclon & Leavitt for a smooth transition to EP positions on *The Jeffersons*.

M&M had met with Bob Daly and Harvey Shephard, President and Vice President at CBS, and were guaranteed a pilot deal at the network. Both 20th Century Fox and Warner Brothers had offered development deals to M&M for the next two years, where they would be making the same amount of money they were making now to write and produce *The Jeffersons*—and all they'd have to do is think up ideas for new series.

Although the Fox deal offered slightly more money, M&M were leaning toward Warners since Burbank Studios was much closer to each of their homes. Sean was living in Toluca Lake now and had been coaching his sons' baseball teams in the Toluca Lake Little League. The League was short on coaches, so Sean got Murph to coach a team last season. Murph's daughters would go with their dad to watch, and when they saw a girl on another team, they decided they wanted to play. So having family time to coach their kids' Little League teams was another big perk of taking a development deal.

It was spring and production for The Jeffersons was just winding down. In addition to episodes already mentioned, Season 7 featured a Christmas show titled "All I Want For Christmas" where George plays Santa Claus for a group of orphans. His promise to get each kid what they want for Christmas backfires when one boy insists George get him parents.

Other shows include "Not So Dearly Beloved," where George is asked to give a eulogy for a former employee everybody hated; another episode where we learn the truth about Louise's father; and an episode where, against Lionel and Jenny's wishes, George and Louise enter their granddaughter in a baby calendar contest and return with the Wong—er, wrong (Asian) baby.

Freelance writers not yet mentioned who contributed to Season 7 include Stephanie Haden, Marshall Goldberg, David Silverman & Steve Sustarsic, Lesa Kite & Cindy Begal, Fred S. Fox & Seaman Jacobs, Ted Dale & Nancy Vince.

Chapter 28

CHECKING IN

('81)

It was an inopportune, if not insane, time to order four episodes of a new series. But that's what happened. CBS liked the two-part pilosode enough to order four episodes of the Florence spinoff and they wanted them right away.

Because of the 1980 actors strike, Season 7 premiered later than usual in the fall, so *The Jeffersons* was still in production in mid-spring of 1981, with another strike looming on the horizon, this time a Writers Guild strike.

M&M talked with Al Burton, explaining they would need more time to break stories and prepare scripts for a new series, and there may be a writers' strike soon, and...

But Al didn't want to hear it. As the company's Development Guru, Al's POV was 'When you're lucky enough to have a network order something, you deliver it.' Sounded sort of familiar. Murph could picture Al in a green suit.

M&M named the Florence spinoff *Checking In*. You know, like checking into a hotel. They called Jack Shea and

Jack agreed to direct the four episodes. They brought the Bendetson Brothers in as writers. B&B's first staff gig.

Sure enough, negotiations between the Writers Guild and Management regarding pay TV and home video came to a standstill and a potential strike was only five days away. If a strike happened, according to WGA rules, Murph and Sean would be able to show up on the set to produce, but not write. It's kind of like being sent into battle on the front line, but you can't bring your rifle.

Murph & Sean considered taking a stand to try to get production postponed; but they knew if they did that, the company would just get somebody else to produce the episodes.

M&M thought maybe they should plead their case to Norman about getting the network to hold off and give them time to develop the new series. But then they reasoned either a) Norman must know what's going on and Al Burton and Alan Horn have his blessing; or b) Norman doesn't know what's going on and doesn't want to know. Murph figured the only thing they could do at this point was somehow try to get four scripts together in five days.

Bob & Howard wrote one script and were working on another with writers Lesa Kite & Cindy Begal. M&M decided they'd have Michael Moye write one script and ask the Bobs, Schiller & Weiskopf, to write the other. With top caliber writers like that, maybe there was at least a chance they'd have a couple shootable scripts by the strike deadline.

M&M talked out a couple story ideas; then Sean continued working on *Jeffersons* business, while Murph met first with Moye and then with the Bobs, giving quick story notes and telling them, basically, to shoot their best shot and deliver a script in four days.

When the strike hit, the writing stopped. When Murph found himself sitting around the table with Sean and Jack and Marla and the cast on the first day of production, ready to read the first script, Murph was still holding out hope that Al Burton or someone from the network would come to their senses and step forward to postpone the shoot until after the strike. But no such luck.

Marla was smart and not too worried. When she signed on to do *Checking In*, she made sure her contract said that if this spinoff didn't go, she could return to *The Jeffersons*.

Although Murph and Sean were planning to go into Development at Warners, they figured they would stay with *Checking In* if it were picked up, at least at the beginning.

For Murph, it was an unusual week, to say the least. Imagine going to a reading and attending run-thrus and observing a play you know could use a lot of help, but you can't do any writing. All you can do is pray.

There was a joke in the script that Marla refused to say; but by Guild rules, M&M weren't allowed to replace it. They could only cut it.

On tape night, Marla locked herself in with her hairdresser. Apparently either Sean or Murph or Al had mentioned to the hairdresser that for the time being, Marla's hairstyle should be similar to how Florence would usually wear it. Murph's understanding was that Marla had something much fancier in mind, so she defiantly locked the producers out. Murph was sure he and Sean would have understood if Marla really wanted her hair styled a certain way. But Marla wasn't taking any chances.

Murph realized that he and Sean should have sat down with Marla before this and made sure they were all on the same page. Maybe the reason they didn't was because they were concerned the results wouldn't be what they hoped.

Without Isabel or Sherman or the others to keep Marla's activist instincts in check, it was becoming clear that, unlike *The Jeffersons*, this set was not going to be all kumbaya. It was pretty clear to Murph that Marla felt she was black and she wanted to do a black show with black people in charge and Marla at the top. And who could blame her for that? It was as if she were saying, "I like you guys. But don't think for one minute I don't know you guys are white."

It seemed to Murph the best thing they could hope for now was that somehow these four episodes would get aired and the series would get picked up and then all parties involved would have time to smooth things out and develop a healthy work environment and a quality series.

The next day, however, Murph was feeling guilty about going to work during a Writers strike. He was technically sticking with the rules—no writing—but he knew if he heard that another writer-producer were doing what he was doing, well… Well, he wasn't sure whether or not he would approve.

Murph called Sean and told his partner how he felt. Sean understood. So Murph skipped the next reading and the whole week. Sean didn't. Murph wasn't sure how this was going to end up. Part of Murph wished Sean had made the same decision he had. And another part, maybe a larger part, was glad Sean would be on set to oversee this whole crazy thing.

So Murph took the week off and took Colleen and Heather to Palm Springs where they swam, rode horses and spent some much needed quality time together.

The following week Sweet Lew called Murph to let him know TAT was not going to pay him for the show he missed. Murph talked to Sean. The second show went without incident and Sean was going to continue going in. Murph had second thoughts now and realized he wasn't going to accomplish anything by not going in. All he was doing was depriving himself and his kids of money he might need (and felt he already earned) during the strike. Plus he now felt bad about abandoning his partner. So Murph showed up for the final two shows.

The four *Checking In* episodes aired as the writers strike continued. (The strike continued for three months, at that time the longest WGA strike in history.) The first episode received around a 34 or 35 share in the ratings. The next episode dropped a point or two, as did the one after that. When the show was cancelled, the rating was still a 30-plus share, what would be a knockout rating in latter-day TV viewing.

Chapter 29

CHECKING OUT

('81)

With *Checking In* a footnote in sitcom history, the cast of *The Jeffersons*, including Marla, were happy to see Florence back on the show. As were the fans. And the writers. And, believe it or not, Murph & Sean. It was hard to imagine *The Jeffersons* without Florence. The way her return was explained on the show was the St. Frederick Hotel burned down.

When M&M sat down with Duclon & Leavitt to talk about the future, Ron & Dave said they would be leaving. Before they could say any more, Murph & Sean began a sales pitch explaining they were leaving for Development and they were going to recommend Ron & Dave to be Executive Producers of *The Jeffersons*. They reminded Ron & Dave it was an established show, the cast is great, you'd supervise all the writing, the network leaves you alone and the company execs don't bother you. It was such a good sales pitch that Murph & Sean had second thoughts about leaving.

But with Duclon & Leavitt, Michael Moye, Casey & Lee and Perzigian & Seigel overseeing *The Jeffersons*, M&M were confident the show was in good hands. In fact, *The Jeffersons* continued for another four seasons, making it, at eleven years and at that time, the longest-running sitcom in television history.*

Another bit of history—a cherry on top of the sundae, if you will—occurred following Season 7, when Isabel Sanford became the first—and to date the only—black woman to win an Emmy for Best Actress in a Comedy Series.

WHEN MURPH AND Sean first agreed to embrace the ampersand and become an official writing team in the eyes of God, Guild and Hollywood, Murph made a point to let his partner know he wasn't looking for a friend. But after eight years of familiarity, that thing Mark Twain says "breeds contempt—and children," Murph felt he and his partner had formed an unwavering friendship. So much so that a few years down the road when Murph remarried, he asked his partner to be his Best Man. And it wasn't just because he knew Sean would write a good toast.

But that's another book.

---

*FLASH FORWARD *Jefferson* Writers in following years: David Duclon, Ron Leavitt & Michael Moye developed the series *Silver Spoons*. Duclon created the TV series *Punky Brewster*. Leavitt & Moye became a team and created not only a series but a network, *Married With Children*, which was the first hit of the fourth network (FOX). Peter Casey & David Lee wrote and produced *Cheers*, created *Wings* and created *Frasier*, which won a record five Emmys in a row for Best Comedy Series.

EPILOGUE

To show you how naïve Murph was back then, when he and Sean left *The Jeffersons* after the seventh season, Murph felt the country was well on its way to racial harmony. Finally, people of color were visible on TV. In the '80s, the # 1 show was a sitcom called *The Cosby Show* which featured an upscale black family, with the father a doctor and the mother a lawyer. Martin Luther King and eventually Malcolm X could be celebrated for the truth tellers they were. And in the first decade of the 21st Century (2008), lo and behold, a black man (Barack Obama) was elected President! It appeared to many that MLK's dream was coming true. We were all about to overcome.

But in the years approaching 2020, America had to be reminded that "Black Lives Matter." WTF? Really? Racial profiling? Why is America still so intent on defining and judging individuals by the color of their skin? Will this ever change?

Murph recalled a line from *The Jeffersons* 1980 Audience Report: *The majority of the audience seems oblivious to the fact that there are Black and White characters.* To Murph, this was a hopeful revelation. It said something about the power of television. Viewers watching people of mixed color on TV tend not to notice color.

It reminded Murph of sports. Most would agree that the integration of sports has played a major role in improving racial harmony—helping the masses see beyond color. As a rule, when we're watching our favorite teams, the only colors we see are the jerseys.

The very next line in the 1980 Audience Report read: *Those who did notice (color) liked the interracial couple shown as a normal, average family without exploitation.* This tells us that even people (at least these *Jefferson* viewers) who *do* notice color difference are not offended by interracial marriage, but embrace it as normal and acceptable. President Obama, in fact, elected to two terms, was a zebra (white mother).

And the next thing the Report says is: *They liked that there is a group of both Black and White people with talent who can joke about color differences without being offensive.* Comedy and satire—they like both.

So it might be fair to believe, or at least hope, that a combination of mixed casting, mixed marriage and the willingness to laugh both *at* and *with* each other could eventually bring about an end to judging any of us based on the color of our skin. An encouraging example of mixed casting would be the musical *Hamilton,* which purports to be about Alexander Hamilton but is really the story of America and assimilation. Although many historical white characters are portrayed by actors of color in this play, the audience is no less enthralled.

But of these potential cures, the strongest would seem to be mixed marriage. Murph remembers reading that if marriage between black and white persons should continue at the current rate, there will be no discernible difference in genetic makeup between Blacks and Whites in America by the year 2050. That may sound overly optimistic, even to Murph—but what if it's off by ten, or twenty or even 30 years?

The funny thing is, most marriages in America now are mixed marriages. And most of us are mutts, a mix of all sorts of nationalities and DNA. Although Murph likes to think of himself as Irish (his paternal grandparents were both from Ireland), on his mother's side he's a mix of German, French, British and who knows what else?

In the Irish movie *The Commitments*, a character justifies attempting to organize a soul band by claiming that the "Irish are the niggers of Europe." Murph always found truth and admiration in that assessment. The Irish were screwed over by the British for centuries. But while the language and culture was different, there was one thing that favored assimilation—skin color.

If Irish skin were a different color—say, green—Green people would likely still find themselves ostracized in both the UK and in America. You could tell an Irish person from a block away by his green skin and pre-judge him accordingly. You would probably still find signs like NO IRISH NEED APPLY, banning Green people from most businesses—except bars, of course.

The Irish, like most immigrants to America after the original settlers, were discriminated against. Of course, the Europeans didn't arrive here on slave ships. Slavery no doubt is the scourge of America. The mortal sin for which there seems to be no easy absolution. Still, as Reverend King said, "We may have all come on different ships, but we're in the same boat now." And he added, "Only in the darkness can you see the stars."

This may be where comedy comes in. Being a comedy person, Murph would suggest an adage of his own about the power of humor: "If we can laugh at it, we can deal with it." And he might end this book with a comforting thought from one of his favorite philosophers:

> *"Continue to allow humor to lighten the burden of your tender heart."*
>
> ~*Maya Angelou*

MORE MURPH?
If you'd like to follow more of Murph's writing adventures in Hollywood, you can show interest by contacting the author or the publisher at <u>antlerpublishing@gmail.com</u>.

The Author & his Muse

INDEX

CPSIA information can be obtained
at www.ICGtesting.com
Printed in the USA
LVHW021457301219
642078LV00013B/1103